WHO IS TO JUDGE?

WHO IS TO JUDGE?

THE PERENNIAL DEBATE OVER WHETHER TO ELECT OR APPOINT AMERICA'S JUDGES

CHARLES GARDNER GEYH

UNIVERSITY PRESS

Oxford University Press is a department of the University of Oxford. It furthers
the University's objective of excellence in research, scholarship, and education
by publishing worldwide. Oxford is a registered trade mark of Oxford University
Press in the UK and certain other countries.

Published in the United States of America by Oxford University Press
198 Madison Avenue, New York, NY 10016, United States of America.

© Oxford University Press 2019

All rights reserved. No part of this publication may be reproduced, stored in
a retrieval system, or transmitted, in any form or by any means, without the
prior permission in writing of Oxford University Press, or as expressly permitted
by law, by license, or under terms agreed with the appropriate reproduction
rights organization. Inquiries concerning reproduction outside the scope of the
above should be sent to the Rights Department, Oxford University Press, at the
address above.

You must not circulate this work in any other form
and you must impose this same condition on any acquirer.

Library of Congress Cataloging-in-Publication Data
Names: Geyh, Charles Gardner, author.
Title: Who is to judge? : the perennial debate over whether to elect or
appoint America's judges / Charles Gardner Geyh.
Description: New York, NY : Oxford University Press, 2019.
Identifiers: LCCN 2018031973 | ISBN 9780190887148 (hc : alk. paper)
Subjects: LCSH: Judges—Selection and appointment—United States.
Classification: LCC KF8776 .G49 2019 | DDC 347.73/14—dc23
LC record available at https://lccn.loc.gov/2018031973

To Shirley Abrahamson, Margaret Marshall, Mark Martin, Tom Phillips, Loretta Rush, and Randy Shepard: Wonderful Chief Justices—appointed and elected alike—with whom it has been my privilege to work on matters related to law, the legal system, and the administration of justice.

CONTENTS

Preface ix
Acknowledgments xi

1
INTRODUCTION 1

2
A SHORT AND POINTED HISTORY OF JUDICIAL SELECTION 24

3
THE NEW JUDICIAL SELECTION LANDSCAPE 44

4
THE ARGUMENTS 77

5
WHY EVERYONE IS WRONG 99

6
MANAGING THE SELECTION DEBATE 125

7
THE FUTURE OF JUDICIAL SELECTION 159

Notes 173
Index 193

PREFACE

In 2003, I was invited to participate in a law review symposium on state judicial selection. It was my first word on the subject. I decided against mincing words in favor of a polemic, entitled "Why Judicial Elections Stink." In the years since, political science papers, articles, and books aplenty have referenced that screed. One leading scholar has characterized it as a "classic" in the field, and another has paraphrased the title for an article of her own. Fifteen years after its publication, my antipathy toward contested elections lingers for reasons that justify the default position I advocate in favor of appointive systems here. But I have come to view the stridency of my earlier work as unwarranted, wrongheaded, and emblematic of a larger problem that this book seeks to rectify. There is a saying in some academic circles that "it is better to be interesting than right." "Why Judicial Elections Stink" was about as interesting as I get, but it was not right. With all due deference to those who think otherwise, I have concluded that being engagingly pugnacious but wrong is no virtue, particularly in polarized political times. Hence, this book.

The original working title of the book was "Lies, Damn Lies, and Judicial Elections." This paraphrase of Mark Twain's famous wisecrack, referring to "lies, damn lies and statistics," struck me as a provocative and attention-grabbing way to highlight a phenomenon the book sought to explore—that the interminable, intractable, dichotomous feud over how best to pick judges is fueled by fact-fudging. Both sides overstate their claims. Neither side cedes points that it should. We have massaged the truth to fit the conclusions that we think are right. Hence, the working title.

Then the 2016 presidential race roared to full throttle. New turns of phrase entered the vocabulary: "fake news" and "alternative facts." Bald-faced bullshit flooded the marketplace of ideas from both ends of the polarized political spectrum for the purpose of distracting, deceiving, confusing, and overwhelming the public. Truth was obscured and sucked from the room, creating a vacuum for power-hungry opportunists to fill.

The "lies" I was writing about bore no resemblance to this. To the contrary, the judicial selection debate is dominated by honorable and engaged lawyers, judges, social scientists, historians, law professors, policy analysts, and others, who are committed to understanding how judicial selection works and determining what is the best means of selection. Our enthusiasm may get the better of us from time to time, and our biases may sometimes cloud our vision, but our work has produced an enviable wealth of data and analysis that has informed public discussion and motivated me to write this book.

The "lies" and "damn lies" at issue here are not in the nature of fake news or alternative facts. They are discardable byproducts of truth-seeking done right. This kind of debate, among forthright, well-informed participants, is an antidote to the scurrilous, subterranean misdirection of those who exploit information shortfalls to their advantage. Ultimately, my editor took me aside to gently but firmly suggest that under the circumstances my proposed title was kind of lousy, and I grudgingly conceded the point.

If it were possible to dedicate a preface, I would dedicate this one to Chris Bonneau, Jim Gibson, and Melinda Gann Hall: three pioneers in judicial selection research who have redefined the field. I take issue with some of their conclusions, as they do mine. But their ambition—like mine—is to get it right, and to that end they have been stunningly generous with their time, reading my drafts and fielding questions for the benefit of someone intent on testing their conclusions. I have learned much from them and their example—so much that our differences, while still extant, are far less significant than they were a decade ago.

ACKNOWLEDGMENTS

This book has undergone a fifteen-year gestation, in what can only be described as a complicated pregnancy. In 2001, I was asked to serve as Reporter to the American Bar Association Commission on Public Financing of Judicial Campaigns, which issued its report in 2002. That experience served as my introduction to judicial elections, and I remain indebted to Chairman Dudley Oldham for the experience. Between 2002 and 2003, I served as Reporter to the ABA Commission on the 21st Century Judiciary, and drafted its report, "Justice in Jeopardy," which focused in no small part on issues of judicial selection. The collaboration with friend, mentor, Commission Chairman, and inspiration to the legal profession, Ned Madeira, transformed my career—I remain in his debt to this day.

My early education on judicial selection left me deeply skeptical of judicial elections—a skepticism manifested in my early writing. Antipathy gradually yielded to ambivalence during my tour of duty as co-reporter to yet another ABA Commission—the Joint Commission to Evaluate the Model Code of Judicial Conduct, which proposed amendments to the Model Code that were adopted by the ABA in 2007. I want to thank Commission Chairman Mark Harrison for his patience, wisdom, and insight into the ethical implications of running for judge throughout an intense but enlightening, three-year process.

As informative as my ABA Commission forays proved to be, they created a kind of echo chamber for the judges, lawyers, and law professors involved that reinforced our preexisting views of judicial elections—views that tended to run a tight gamut from fiery hatred to episodic irritation. At the same time, a new generation of political scientists was hard at work generating a body of data on judicial elections that challenged the legal community's traditional critique. I grudged my way to the conclusion that if the scholarly mission was a search for truth rather than fig leaves, simply dismissing, deriding, or ignoring information that inconvenienced my views was probably poor form. And so I went back to school. I would like to thank political scientists Chris Bonneau, Melinda Gann Hall, Bert Kritzer, Malia Reddick, and Steve Wasby, for reading and commenting on drafts, and Keith Bybee, Jim Gibson, Greg Goelzhauser, Matt Streb, Benjamin Woodson, and Jeff Yates, for their insights and assistance at critical stages of the project.

Meanwhile, back in the legal community, Alicia Bannon at the Brennan Center offered numerous, thoughtful comments and suggestions on 3—many thanks. Thanks likewise to my law school colleague, Victor Quintanillia, for his insights into the implications of psychological science for judicial selection research, and to my friend, former law school classmate, and retired Federal Judicial Center Director of Publications and Media, Syl Sobel, for his comments on the introduction. Finally, I'm indebted to the Indiana University Maurer School of Law Center on Law, Society and Culture, for the chance to workshop some of the ideas developed here; to the DePaul University College of Law for the opportunity to submit a paper germane to this book for its annual Clifford Symposium; and to the *DePaul Law Review*, for publishing that paper, "Judicial Selection and the Search for Middle Ground," which has been incorporated into this work, in modified form.

Around the time that I was mustering the courage to begin work on this project, something wonderful happened: I was awarded a stunningly generous Andrew Carnegie fellowship to write this book, on the strength of a nomination from Indiana University President Michael McRobbie. Boundless thanks to the Carnegie Corporation for financing my leave during the 2016–2017 academic year, which made this book possible. The folks at Carnegie have asked me to say that "This book was made possible (in part) by a grant from the Carnegie Corporation of New York;" and they know me well enough to request that I add: "The statements made and views expressed are solely the responsibility of the author." Thanks likewise to President McRobbie, Provost Lauren Robel, law school dean Austen Parrish, law school executive associate Dean Donna Nagy, and law school budget director Mary Edwards, for their roles in making my fellowship and leave a reality.

This book has been many years in the making, but was ultimately written during a highly compressed and productive year and a half, thanks in no small part to extraordinary research assistance. Dan Matheny did the initial spadework. He assembled binders of materials that served as the foundation for my analysis, and offered thoughtful insights that structured my thinking in important ways. Katie Thrapp, who did the heavy lifting as a research assistant on my last book, collaborated with me to co-author a entitled "The Changing Legal Landscape of Judicial Elections," for Chris Bonneau and Melinda Gann Hall's edited volume, *Judicial Elections in the 21st Century*, which served as a running start for this project. Priya Purohit went above and beyond the call during my fellowship year: She edited each for substance and style, hunted down source materials, completed numerous research assignments, and assisted in the development of my arguments across innumerable conversations. Without her, this would have been a different book. Pooja Sanjay was instrumental in assembling information for the tables. And Emily Guillaume, Kevin Jones, and David Saylor brought the project to conclusion, by checking the notes and editing the manuscript for form and style.

Finally, and as always, I would like to extend heartfelt thanks to Rita Eads, my secretary and administrative assistant. Rita maintained the files, perfected and proofread them for form and typographical errors, organized materials gathered by my research assistants, and managed my external communications.

INTRODUCTION

This is a book about how Americans pick their judges. More specifically it is a book about how we pick our state judges, who manage 95 percent of the nation's caseload. How judges should be selected is best explored, not as an abstract thought experiment, but in the context of the political rough and tumble of the real world, where different answers portend different consequences for judges, litigants, the general public, and the rule of law. To illustrate the point, I begin with a tale of two judiciaries that includes the U.S. Supreme Court as a point of comparison to and departure from the state systems that will be the focus of this book.

When historians retell the story of the nation's struggle over same-sex marriage, two cases decided by the U.S. Supreme Court in 2013 and 2015 will feature prominently in the tale's action-packed climax. In *United States v. Windsor*, decided in 2013, the Supreme Court invalidated the Defense of Marriage Act (DOMA), which Congress had enacted in 1996.[1] The DOMA defined marriage, for purposes of determining a spouse's eligibility to receive federal benefits, as the union of a man and a woman. In states that recognized same-sex marriage, the Court concluded, DOMA violated the Fifth Amendment right of legally married same-sex couples to due process and equal protection of the law by denying homosexual spouses access to federal benefits enjoyed by their heterosexual counterparts. But in another case decided the same day as *Windsor*, the Supreme Court declined, on procedural grounds, to address whether state laws that prohibited same-sex marriage were constitutional.[2] It would take another two years for this second shoe to drop, in *Obergefell v. Hodges*.[3]

In *Obergefell*, the Supreme Court heard a cluster of cases that had worked their way up through the lower courts, in which same-sex couples challenged the constitutionality of so-called mini-DOMAs—state laws that limited marriage rights to opposite-sex couples. A sharply divided Supreme Court invalidated those laws, on the grounds that they violated the rights of gay men and women to due process and equal protection of the law, guaranteed by the Fourteenth Amendment to the U.S. Constitution. Writing with obvious emotion on behalf of the five to four majority, Justice Anthony Kennedy concluded:

> No union is more profound than marriage, for it embodies the highest ideals of love, fidelity, devotion, sacrifice, and family. In forming a marital union, two people become something greater than once they were. As some of the petitioners in these cases demonstrate, marriage embodies a love that may endure even past death. It would misunderstand these men and women to say they disrespect the idea of marriage. Their plea is that they do respect it, respect it so deeply that they seek to find its fulfillment for themselves. Their hope is not to be condemned to live in loneliness, excluded from one of civilization's oldest institutions. They ask for equal dignity in the eyes of the law. The Constitution grants them that right.[4]

Writing with comparable passion in dissent, Chief Justice John Roberts argued that by stepping in to invalidate state laws across the country, the majority had, in effect, hijacked the democratic process: "It can be tempting for judges to confuse our own preferences with the requirements of the law," he explained, "but as this Court has been reminded throughout our history, the Constitution is made for people of fundamentally differing views." [5] Accordingly:

> [C]ourts are not concerned with the wisdom or policy of legislation . . . The majority today neglects that restrained conception of the judicial role. It seizes for itself a question the Constitution leaves to the people, at a time when the people are engaged in a vibrant debate on that question. And it answers that question based not on neutral principles of constitutional law, but on its own "understanding of what freedom is and must become." . . . I have no choice but to dissent.[6]

Windsor and *Obergefell* will go down as among the most controversial cases of their time. They addressed an explosive issue that had divided the nation for decades. Hence, the justices could not have been shocked, or even surprised when their rulings elicited cries of joy, bellows of anguish, calls for celebration, and threats of recrimination. It takes courage for public officials to enter the political fray and resolve divisive issues that, regardless of what they decide, are sure to infuriate half of their audience—including the isolated, unstable zealot who might jeopardize the officials' safety.

That said, the nine justices who decided *Windsor* and *Obergefell* understood that for them, the consequences of their decision would be limited to wailing and gnashing of teeth. They knew that however they decided those cases, their jobs were safe. After those justices were nominated by the president and confirmed by the Senate, the U.S. Constitution guaranteed them tenure during "good behavior," which effectively means for life. The only way to remove a federal judge for bad behavior is via impeachment, a process that—despite multiple attempts—has never in 225 years and counting ousted a judge for making an unpopular or highhanded ruling. They could not have their pay docked—the Constitution prohibits that too. They could not be disciplined—there is no mechanism for that, at least with respect to justices on the high court (and even in the lower federal courts, judges are not subject to discipline for conduct related to the merits of their decisions). Their authority would remain intact: short-term damage to the Court's perceived legitimacy among conservatives angered by the majority's ruling would be offset by short-term gains among progressives, at a time when public support for same-sex marriage was rapidly gaining momentum. Isolated acts of defiance—most notably by a Kentucky county clerk who achieved brief national prominence for refusing to issue same-sex marriage licenses—would gradually subside. Congress could conceivably retaliate against the Supreme Court by cutting its operating budget, curtailing its appellate jurisdiction, or altering its size. Such manipulations, however, are quite unlikely, because they run counter to time-honored institutional norms against encroaching on the Court's autonomy—norms the Court has helped to preserve by picking its battles with care so as not to stray from public opinion so far or so often as to jeopardize the customary independence that the Court enjoys.[7]

The chapter that ended with the Supreme Court's decision in *Obergefell* actually began two decades earlier, in the state of Iowa, where evangelical conservatives launched a national campaign against same-sex marriage. Troubled by a recent Hawaii Supreme Court ruling that cast doubt on the constitutionality of laws prohibiting same-sex marriage, several fundamentalist Christian organizations hosted a rally on the eve of the 1996 Iowa presidential caucuses, where they solicited pledges from every Republican candidate to oppose same-sex marriage. Later that year, Congress passed and President Bill Clinton signed the DOMA, which *Windsor* would later invalidate. Soon thereafter, a flood of states enacted mini-DOMAs that the Supreme Court would ultimately declare contrary to the U.S. Constitution in *Obergefell*. Iowa passed its mini-DOMA in 1998, which amended its marriage statute to state that "[o]nly a marriage between a male and a female is valid."[8]

In December 2005—eleven years before *Obergefell* was decided—six gay couples filed suit in Iowa state court against a county recorder who denied them marriage licenses. The plaintiffs alleged that the statutory prohibition on same-sex marriage violated their right to equal protection of the law under the Iowa Constitution. So began the tale of a second judiciary. In 2007, the state district court ruled in favor of the plaintiffs, and in 2009, the Iowa Supreme Court affirmed, holding the state statute unconstitutional. In *Varnum v. Brien*, the Iowa Supreme Court anticipated the furor to follow, by going out of its way to emphasize that it was just doing its job and had no choice but to conclude as it did. Writing on behalf of the unanimous Court, Justice Mark Cady began by opining that the Court had a "responsibility" to exercise judicial review—a responsibility that the courts became duty-bound to shoulder after the plaintiffs filed suit challenging the constitutionality of the marriage statute. The responsibility to invalidate unconstitutional enactments, Justice Cady explained, sometimes required the Court to reach unpopular conclusions: "A statute inconsistent with the Iowa Constitution must be declared void, even though it may be supported by strong and deep-seated traditional beliefs and popular opinion."[9] Following an extended analysis of precedent under Iowa's equal protection clause, in which the Court took pains to show how the Iowa Constitution had long been interpreted to safeguard equal protection rights more vigorously than the U.S. Constitution, the Court ended where it began. "We have a constitutional duty to ensure equal protection of the law," the Court declared. "Faithfulness to that duty requires us to hold Iowa's marriage statute . . . violates the Iowa Constitution," and "to decide otherwise would be an abdication of our constitutional duty."[10]

Democratic governor Chet Culver stood by his opposition to same-sex marriage but did not favor amending the Iowa Constitution to overturn *Varnum*. In the General Assembly, Democrats agreed with the governor, and Republicans were unable to garner the votes needed to calendar a constitutional amendment for debate. As a consequence, for those angered by *Varnum*—and two-thirds of Iowans opposed same-sex marriage at the time—the target shifted from undoing the decision to undoing the justices who made the decision.

Unlike justices on the U.S. Supreme Court, justices on the Iowa Supreme Court are subject to periodic "retention" elections. In 1962, Iowa amended its constitution to adopt a system of judicial selection commonly called "merit selection," or the "Missouri plan" (Missouri being the first state to adopt such a system), among other names. Under the Iowa system, when a vacancy on the Supreme Court arises, a commission of lawyers and laypeople receives applications from judicial aspirants and creates a short list of candidates from the applicant pool that the commission deems qualified. The governor then appoints a justice from that list. The next year, the newly minted justice faces the electorate in a retention election to decide whether the justice stays or goes: thumbs up, and the justice wins an eight-year term; thumbs down, and the justice is ousted, and the process starts over again. Justices who wish to remain on the court after their first full term must stand for retention elections every eight years.

No justice on the Iowa Supreme Court had ever lost a retention election since Iowa's "merit selection" system had been adopted over fifty years earlier. That was about to change. Three of the Iowa Supreme Court's seven justices were up for retention election in 2010, the year after *Varnum* was decided. A million-dollar campaign to remove the incumbents for their votes in *Varnum*, bankrolled largely by organizations from outside the state, portrayed the three as activist judges who had legislated from the bench. That effort was countered by pro-retention organizations and the justices themselves. Pro-retention organizations raised less than half the funds as retention opponents, and ran a commercial that did not defend the court's decision in *Varnum*, but likened the justices to referees who should not be fired for making a bad call. As for the incumbents themselves, they did, well, almost nothing. Two journalists who covered the story later explained, "Ternus, Streit, and Baker made few public appearances and refused to campaign, or raise money to defend themselves," because "litigants, they agreed, should never have to wonder whose lawyer gave how much money to a judge's reelection campaign."[11]

All three justices lost their retention votes by substantial margins, with each garnering only around 45 percent support. Two voter focus groups were assembled after the election, to discuss the outcome. One observer's report noted: "We heard a lot of 'It may have been the 'right' decision based on the Constitution, but I just don't like it. So I voted them out.'"[12] A second observer's report stated: "Several expressed a frustration with the fact that they didn't know who the justices were, how they became justices, how they arrived at their decision, what gave them the right to make the decision, etc. There appears to be a great desire for more information . . ."[13]

The slogan of the Iowa opposition campaign—"It's we the people, not we the courts"—highlights a seeming paradox at the heart of the Iowa experience. In the Iowa retention elections, "we the people" removed three justices from office because those justices invalidated popular legislation that "we the people" enacted through the legislature. And yet, "we the people" also ordained and established a constitution in which the people delegated to the courts the authority and responsibility to invalidate unconstitutional legislation. Empowering courts to exercise judicial review in this way proceeds from the premise that constitutions are enduring embodiments of "we the people" that should trump inconsistent legislation, which is a more fleeting and temporary expression of popular will. In Iowa, did "we the people" fire three justices for doing what "we the people" directed them to do?

This apparent paradox can be reconciled if "we the people" removed those justices because they misapplied the law incompetently, or in a willful gambit to usurp power, legislate from the bench, and impose their own policy preferences as "we the court." But does the electorate possess the legal expertise to make such assessments? Is it problematic that voters may have opposed retention simply because they favored the statutory ban on same-sex marriage, regardless of whether the justices were correct in holding the statute unconstitutional? Or can we simply say that when state supreme courts make constitutional policy, "we the people" ought to have a voice in shaping that policy as voters, by removing incumbents who make unacceptable policy choices?

This tale of two judiciaries serves as a point of entry to the debate over how state judges should be selected that plays out like a game of tennis. Across state systems, judges are appointed and elected in different ways, with the election-appointment divide servings as a net between the adversaries. Unlike the typical tennis match, however, which concludes in a matter of hours, the judicial selection debate is now in its third century, with no end in sight. Some readers may have a difficult time separating their views on how judges should be selected from their views on how certain controversial policy issues ultimately play out. For example, those who are angry with the Iowa and U.S. Supreme courts for invalidating state and federal DOMAs may be more inclined to favor elective systems that empower voters to oust the incumbents than those readers who are happy with the decisions. To account for such bias in your capacity as spectators at the judicial selection tennis match, ask yourself whether your views on how judges should be chosen would change if the judges at issue had upheld laws banning same-sex marriage. We join the match, already in progress:

—In a representative democracy, those who govern are chosen by and held accountable to the people they represent in periodic elections. That should be no less true of judges than governors or legislators. When judges decide such fundamental questions as who may marry whom, they should be accountable to the people they serve for the choices they make. *15-love, elections.*

—Unlike legislators, judges do not make law on behalf of constituencies they "represent." Rather, judges independently and impartially interpret and apply the laws that others make, to the end of resolving disputes between the people judges serve. In *Obergefell* and *Varnum*, the plaintiffs asked judges to decide whether their right to equal protection of the law—a right that the people had ordained and established in their constitutions—guaranteed homosexuals the same legal right to marry as heterosexuals. Judges cannot be counted on to interpret the law impartially and independently in such controversial cases, if an unpopular answer will cost them their jobs at the next election. Hence, judges should be appointed. *Point, appointments: 15-15.*

—Appointed justices who are unaccountable to the electorate do not apply the law impartially: They apply their own ideological preferences. It is no coincidence that in *Obergefell*, the four liberal justices favored same-sex marriage rights, while the four conservatives opposed, and the Court's moderate justice cast the deciding vote and wrote the opinion for the majority. Insofar as courts are making constitutional policy, it is better for that policy to reflect the preferences of the people judges serve than the idiosyncratic preferences of the judges themselves. That can best be accomplished if judges are elected. *Point, elections, 30-15.*

—Judges are trained and acculturated to take law seriously beginning in law school. That is why, when the law is clear, liberal and conservative judges will reach the same conclusion, which helps to explain why nearly half of the cases that the U.S. Supreme Court hears are decided by a unanimous vote. When the law is ambiguous and subject to different, comparably plausible interpretations, judges are still committed to applying the law as they understand it to be written. But their background, experience, race, gender, and policy perspectives can affect which interpretation they find more persuasive. Elected judges are discouraged from giving us their best assessment of what the law is—regardless of whether the law is clear—whenever that best assessment could provoke a voter backlash that might cost judges their livelihoods, to the ultimate detriment of the rule of law. *Point, appointments, 30-30.*

—Regardless of whether judges mean well, they should not have unfettered freedom to do their jobs badly. Elections help to keep judges from running off the rails, by holding them accountable when their eccentric policy preferences lead them to misapply the law and reach a wrong result. In that way, elections foster both democracy and the rule of law. *Point, elections, 40-30.*

—Unlike governors and legislators, state law requires that judges be trained lawyers with legal expertise. Voters lack the time, interest, and competence to choose the most capable, qualified jurists with such specialized skills, let alone determine when they misapply the law. They will vote against judges who reach conclusions they dislike, regardless of operative law, as the Iowa experience suggests. Appointive systems avoid such problems by delegating the task of selecting judges to governors or commissions, who are better able to assess the specialized expertise of judicial candidates. *Point, appointments, 40-40.*

—Voter ignorance is a problem in all elections. If that is an argument for ending judicial elections, it is an argument for ending elections and democracy altogether. Moreover, competitive judicial elections educate and engage voters by incentivizing the candidates to campaign aggressively and provide voters with the information they need to make intelligent choices. In Iowa, the justices who lost have only themselves to blame for refusing to get out there and educate voters on their perspectives. To make matters worse, retention elections in merit selection systems (such as Iowa's) lack the horse-race intensity of contested elections that grab voter attention and encourage information-rich campaigns, the way that traditional, partisan elections do. *Advantage, elections.*

—To the extent that judicial campaign advertising reduces the information deficit for voters, the cure is worse than the disease. In a recent ten-year span, the financial support that buys advertising in state supreme court races increased nearly tenfold. This dramatic uptick in campaign contributions and spending has given rise to a widely held suspicion that those who lend significant financial support to a justice's campaign buy influence with the judge, to the detriment of the court's perceived legitimacy. *Deuce.*

—For the general public, the damage a court's legitimacy suffers from the perception that campaign contributions and spending buy influence is offset by legitimacy gains a court enjoys when its judges are accountable to the people in periodic elections. *Advantage, elections.*

—If we are concerned about whether judicial elections pose a threat to the judiciary's perceived legitimacy, we should not focus on the views of the general public, which ordinarily has too passive and remote an interest in the cases judges decide to think deeply about the problem, or act upon their views. Rather, we should focus on the views of the litigating pubic—parties to proceedings before the courts. They are the ones with skin in the game, and if they are unwilling to acquiesce to adverse rulings because they question the legitimacy of the courts that issued those rulings, the American judiciary is in real trouble. Parties will accept court rulings as legitimate only if they feel that they were given a fair hearing before a fair judge. Imagine yourself as a party in a controversial case before a judge who is in the midst of a re-election campaign. Your opponent has contributed significant sums to re-elect the judge, and angry voters might remove the judge if she decides the case in your favor. You could hardly be faulted for entertaining significant doubts about the fairness of the judge or the legitimacy of the process. *Deuce.*

—Obsessing over widespread suspicion that money buys influence is a waste of time when those suspicions are groundless. The perception and reality of influence are two different things. Ideologically aligned interest groups support candidates whose ideological predispositions are most compatible with theirs. Thus, money does not buy influence. Except in isolated cases of outright corruption, it merely buys support for like-minded candidates. That is democracy. The perception problem is best addressed by educating voters and parties to the reality that their perception is misperception. *Advantage, elections.*

—Even if interest groups sponsor judges who are predisposed to favor their causes, it does not mean that campaign support exerts no influence. When a judge knows that he may not win the next election without the continued support of an interest group that bankrolled his previous campaign, it transforms the judge's voluntary predisposition to favor the group's causes into a strategic need to keep the group happy. *Deuce.*

—Merit selection—with or without retention elections—is an appointive system that lessens problems associated with contested partisan and nonpartisan judicial elections. First, merit selection takes the politics out of judicial selection by delegating the task of screening judicial candidates to nominating commissions that have the expertise voters lack to choose capable and qualified judges based on neutral criteria. Second, retention elections in merit selection systems are best conceptualized as an augmentation of appointive processes that offers judicial accountability without spawning big money campaigns or jeopardizing judicial independence by putting judges at meaningful risk of losing their jobs for making unpopular decisions. The retention elections following the Iowa Supreme Court's decision in *Varnum* may have illustrated the perils of judicial elections in action, but were freakish exceptions to the general rule that retention elections are sleepy, incumbent-friendly afterthoughts. *Advantage, appointments.*

—Partisan election, nonpartisan election, and "merit selection" systems all produce judges with comparable credentials. There is evidence that nominating commissions do not use neutral criteria to screen applicants, and nothing stops governors from taking political criteria—such as a nominee's partisan affiliation or support for the governor—into account when appointing judges from the nominee pool. Moreover, the retention election feature of merit selection systems is useless at best. When retention elections are low-key, low-cost, non-threatening affairs—which is most of the time—they fail to create the voter interest needed to promote meaningful accountability, and are simply a rubber stamp for retention. On those rare occasions when retention elections catch fire, incumbents are ill-equipped to defend themselves because they have no opponent to compare themselves to, and because opposition campaigns can surface too late in the election cycle for incumbents to respond effectively. *Deuce.*

Talking about judicial selection in the context of the national debate on same-sex marriage illuminates points of contention in the never-ending fracas over whether judges should be elected or appointed. But it does not adequately explain why the subject is worth disputing, or why the disputants have persisted in an endless, unwinnable debate with no meaningful compromise on the table.

As to why the argument over judicial selection is one worth having, the answer boils down to this: We should care about how America picks its judges because we should care about who becomes judges and the decisions that those judges make. And we should care about the decisions judges make for at least four reasons.

First, judges, in their capacity as courts, are interpreters of constitutional meaning who are called upon to protect personal freedom from governmental encroachment by answering questions critical to the scope of individual rights and the limits of sovereign authority. May governments prohibit homosexuals from marrying? Bar women from having abortions? Restrict public possession of firearms? May governments implement affirmative action programs? Permit public school teachers to lead students in prayer? Require uninsured citizens to enroll in a national healthcare system? Insofar as answers to these questions are sought in the U.S. Constitution, the buck stops, or at least pauses, with the U.S.

Supreme Court. That helps to explain why public conversations about judicial selection often focus on Supreme Court justices and the federal appointments process.

Lost in this national fixation on the U.S. Supreme Court is the fact that state constitutions create myriad rights and responsibilities, some of which augment those found in the U.S. Constitution, others of which the U.S. Constitution ignores, and all of which are within the exclusive jurisdiction of state courts to interpret and apply. Such questions can be of vital importance to the people that state courts serve: How must public education be funded? How must water rights be allocated? What protocols must citizen initiatives follow to amend state constitutions, and when are those protocols violated? When state and federal constitutions do protect the same rights, the supremacy of the U.S. Constitution prohibits state constitutions from infringing on rights that the U.S. Constitution guarantees, but it does not prohibit state constitutions from guaranteeing their citizens greater rights than the U.S. Constitution requires. Suppose, for example, that in *Obergefell*, Justice Kennedy had switched sides and the Supreme Court had rejected the argument that state laws prohibiting same-sex marriage violate the equal protection clause of the U.S. Constitution. That result would not have affected the Iowa Supreme Court's decision in *Varnum*. That ruling would still have prohibited the Iowa legislature from enacting laws prohibiting same-sex marriage because such laws would still violate the equal protection clause of the Iowa Constitution.

A supreme court's interpretation of its constitution is not "final," in the sense that constitutions can be amended to override those interpretations. That vests ultimate control over constitutional meaning with the people and arguably diminishes the importance of courts as expositors of the constitution. As foundational charters for state and nation, however, constitutions render themselves arduous to amend. In the extreme case of the U.S. Constitution, there have been over ten thousand proposals to amend the Constitution since the Bill of Rights was ratified in 1791, of which only seventeen have succeeded (fifteen, if you think of Prohibition and its repeal as canceling each other out). And those seventeen amendments have overridden a total of only five Supreme Court decisions.[14] Many states make their constitutions less difficult to amend, but less difficult does not mean easy enough to blunt the enduring impact of judicial review on the meaning and development of state constitutions.

Second, we should care about the decisions that judges make because courts are interpreters of statutory meaning. Like constitutions, statutes can be ambiguous. The meaning of a given statutory section, clause, or term can be intrinsically unclear, or its meaning can be unclear in the context of a particular dispute. A statute may include gaps that leave unanswered questions crucial to its scope or operation. Some of those gaps may be the result of sloppy legislative drafting; others may be caused by the legislature's inability to foresee the future and all the circumstances in which the statute will apply; and still others may reflect a conscious choice by the legislature to punt, and let the courts resolve difficult or controversial issues that the legislature chose to avoid. Hence, the judgment courts exercise when interpreting statutes exerts a profound impact on the meaning and application of laws that legislatures make.

Statutes can be amended more easily than constitutions to override court rulings; a simple act of the legislature will do the trick. But legislatures are cumbersome decision-making bodies by constitutional design, with political agendas that can complicate or thwart legislative rewrites, for which reason "simple" acts of the legislature are rarely simple. For example, in *King v. Burwell* the U.S. Supreme Court was petitioned to resolve an ambiguity in the text of the Affordable Care Act—a centerpiece of the Obama administration—which, if read literally, would have undermined the statute's purpose.[15] A divided Court interpreted the text in a manner consistent with the statute's purpose, but had it done otherwise, the statutory scheme was so controversial that Congress would likely have allowed it to fail. In other words, the stamp that courts place on a statute's meaning may not be indelible, but is nonetheless difficult to remove—difficult enough to render judicial statutory interpretation an integral component of operative law.

Third, we should care about the decisions that judges make, because state judges make common law.[16] We can debate whether courts "make" or merely "apply" the law when they interpret their constitutions to protect rights previously unrecognized, such as that of gay couples to marry. But when it comes to the common law, there is no debate. Included with the baggage that settlers unpacked when they colonized North America was the English common law—a body of judge-made law in development for centuries, which supplied the substantive rules that courts applied in civil and criminal cases. Over time, state legislatures have replaced great swaths of common law with statutes, but judge-made common law continues to hold sway over significant segments of American law, most notably in the areas of property, contracts, and torts. Judges may be polar bears on a shrinking iceberg of common law, but it is their iceberg to control unless and until it melts away. And as explained in chapter 3, statutory reform of common law tort liability has been a pivotal issue in the changing landscape of judicial elections around the country.

Fourth, we should care about the decisions judges make for reasons having nothing to do with the role judges play in developing constitutional, statutory, or common law, but simply because they are powerful people who control the fates of parties who petition the courts to resolve their disputes. Judges decide which parent will be awarded child custody following divorce, whether a driver will lose her license for a traffic violation, whether to enforce the terms of a contested will, whether a drunk driver will be sentenced to probation or jail time, whether a landlord must return a tenant's security deposit, whether a debtor may declare bankruptcy, and how much money a taxpayer owes the government. In these examples, the operative law may be simple and clear, but the application of that law to the unique facts of the given case often requires the exercise of judgment and discretion. In a nation with twenty-five thousand judicial officers and over one hundred million annual case filings, the impact of the judgment and discretion that judges exercise on the lives of the people they serve is no small matter.

Accepting that there are at least four good reasons to care about the decisions judges make, it follows naturally that one should care about who those judges are. Randomly assigning to Barb, the auto mechanic, the task of parsing constitutions, codes, and cases could be even more ill-advised than randomly assigning to Supreme Court Justice Elena Kagan the task of replacing Subaru transmissions, because the ripple effects of the poor choices that Barb makes will be felt by an entire population for generations. That implies the need for a system that selects judges who possess the special skills and attributes required to administer justice well. Whether one system of selection is better suited than another to serve that purpose is thus a worthy inquiry, which leads to the question: Why has it been so difficult to reach consensus on whether justice is better administered by judges who are elected or appointed?

There is an easy explanation. By holding judges accountable to voters, electoral systems eliminate judicial independence from such accountability. Conversely, by shielding judges from electoral accountability, appointive systems render judges independent from that accountability. It is simple work to defend both judicial independence and judicial accountability as instrumental values: independence is important because it insulates judges from electoral pressure to do what is popular at the expense of what the facts and law require, and accountability is important because it empowers the public to thwart judges from acting on their personal predilections in derogation of applicable facts and law. Each system of selection promotes one instrumental value at the expense of the other—hence, the never-ending tennis match.

The trouble with this "easy" explanation is that it is a little too easy. First, the independence-accountability dichotomy does not map onto the appointments-elections dichotomy as well as the "easy" explanation implies. Appointive systems are truly independence-enhancing only if they do not subject their judges to meaningful reselection processes. For example, appointed judges subject to periodic reselection at the whim of legislators or governors may be as if not more "dependent" than their nominally elected counterparts in jurisdictions (or lower tiers of courts within jurisdictions), where the seats of elected incumbent judges are often uncontested. This raises a critical caveat: To the extent that elective systems constrain judicial independence more than appointive systems, it is because elective systems tend to subject judges to more a rigorous reselection process. Therefore, the independence-accountability dichotomy of greater magnitude may not be between elective and appointment systems, but between selection and reselection processes.

Second, if it were as simple as saying that we are in a perpetual state of equipoise between judicial independence and accountability, the sensible-seeming response would be to recognize that choosing a preferred selection system is a judgment call for which there is no correct answer. But that is not the tenor of the judicial selection debate, which remains binary and overwrought. Disputants, myself included, have picked their preferred core value, hunkered down in their respective trenches, and lobbed endless barrages of scholarly mustard gas in the general direction of their opponents.

This book seeks to transcend fruitless independence-accountability debates by taking a closer look at why judicial selection is such an intractable, contentious mess, and what to do about it. It examines past and present incarnations of the judicial selection conundrum. It presents the cases for elective and appointive systems. It explains why the arguments for each system are flawed, and it explores why it has been so hard for proponents of their preferred system to acknowledge those flaws. It proposes ways to narrow the divide between appointive and elective system proponents. It concludes, however, that the divide cannot be eliminated altogether, and that ultimately, which system is "best" will turn on which selection system's values take priority in a given place at a given time.

The focus of this book is on state judicial selection. The U.S. Supreme Court may be the rock star of the American judiciary, but it decides fewer than one hundred of more than one hundred million cases filed across the country each year. The federal courts may receive most of the media attention, but of twenty-five thousand judicial officers in the United States, fewer than nine hundred are Article III federal judges. Those nine hundred shoulder a scant 5 percent of the nation's court docket and leave the remainder to their state counterparts. When it comes to the day-to-day administration of justice in the United States, state systems are where the action is. Federal courts make occasional, cameo appearances in this book, to provide a basis for comparison to state courts; to bring findings of federal court studies to bear on issues relevant to state judicial selection; and (as illustrated by the discussion of *Obergefell* and *Windsor* at the beginning of this chapter) to serve as a proxy for appointive systems generally. But I do so sparingly, because the history, political culture, and institutional role of the federal courts are different enough to warrant caution when bringing the federal system into a conversation about state judicial selection.

Writing a book about state judicial selection is complicated by the fact that differences between and within states render overgeneralization a chronic risk. The selection process that different states employ may be similar enough to be classified as the same system, and yet vary in subtle but significant ways. States with identical selection systems have different histories, demographics, political cultures, and current events that can affect how the same system operates in different places. Within a given state, issues relevant to selecting supreme court justices may differ from election cycle to election cycle and between tiers of courts. As it turns out, these differences are critical to the conclusions I ultimately reach.

Chapter 2 places the current state of affairs in context, with a short history of judicial selection in the United States. That history expands on the metaphor of the judicial selection debate as an interminable tennis match in four ways. First, it shows that the game has been going on for centuries—disagreement over how best to choose judges predates the nation itself. Second, it adds an important nuance: the match features a series of rallies, in which different systems of selection have been introduced and gained a temporary upper hand during different periods of time. Third, it isolates the motivation common to these rallies: a desire to render judges more independent from the control of those who were responsible for the selection of judges in the predominant system. Fourth, it situates the current debate between rallies, when no system of selection is popular enough to catalyze sweeping reform, or unpopular enough to be systematically replaced. And to the extent that history repeats itself, it suggests that the time for a new rally may be approaching.

Chapter 2's historical overview of judicial selection sets the stage for chapter 3, which maps the current judicial selection landscape. It begins by describing a series of developments over a generation in the making that has altered the political environment of judicial elections in fundamental ways. These developments have transformed many state supreme court races into high-stakes referenda on how incumbents voted on an array of volatile issues, which has given rise to unprecedented increases in both direct financial contributions to judicial campaigns and expenditures in support of those campaigns by independent organizations. Mass infusions of campaign cash have bought advertising, including attack advertising, that has made judicial elections more competitive, antagonistic affairs. To compete more aggressively in this new environment, judicial candidates have raised constitutional objections to state-imposed ethical limits on their campaign conduct, with some success. Litigants have pushed back by demanding the disqualification of judges who receive significant campaign support from interested parties, likewise with some success. In states with contested judicial elections, groups angered by the perception that money is buying influence have agitated for merit selection. In states with merit selection, groups angered by the perception that activist judges are usurping power have advocated for contested elections, or a return to the federal model.

More recently still, spending in judicial races has begun to taper off. One possible explanation is that the arc of the new politics of judicial elections is past its apogee, and that the events described in this chapter will ultimately be remembered as little more than another blip in the history of judicial selection. A more likely explanation is that the forces driving the new politics have largely prevailed in their efforts to repopulate state supreme courts with judges to their liking, which suggests that we are not witnessing an end to the new politics, but a lull. Regardless, the new politics represent a pivot point in the history of judicial selection. Whereas prior movements in judicial selection aimed to promote judicial independence, the new politics aim to constrain independence by better ensuring that the decisions judges make do not stray too far from the preferences of those responsible for judicial selection.

Against this backdrop of the incendiary new politics of judicial selection, chapter 4 lays out the respective arguments for appointive and elective systems. It does so with reference to the research that social scientists have published, and the arguments that scholars, lawyers, judges, and policy analysts have made. The aim is twofold: to summarize what we know about different systems of selection, and to underscore (with exceptions) the starkly binary character of the judicial selection conversation.

Chapter 5 then revisits the arguments summarized in chapter 4, to the end of showing how and why arguments for and against each system are exaggerated, misleading, and wrong. Some disputants make arguments premised on factual assumptions that are unsupported by data and are based instead on anecdotes or the authors' signature blend of what they rationalize as common sense. Others rely on data generated by others, but cherry-pick the "good" data that support their claims and ignore the pesky facts that undercut their positions. Still others generate their own data and frame their research questions in ways that effectively ensure answers supportive of their pet arguments. Still other researchers announce conclusions putatively drawn from their data, which are dubious extrapolations that drive the square pegs of their factual findings into the round holes of their preferred policy conclusions. Chapter 5 concludes by offering several explanations for why participants in judicial selection showdowns have—for the most part, unwittingly—overstated or disregarded their claims in pursuit of normative agendas, which has impeded the path to consensus.

Chapter 6 begins by exploring two implications of chapter 5. First, we can come closer to consensus in the judicial selection debate by confronting and thereby overcoming the impediments to agreement that chapter 5 isolates. Second, while we can approach consensus, we can never actually achieve it. States can reduce the gap between elective and appointive systems—merit selection, for example, tries to do just that, by coupling commission-based appointment with periodic retention elections—but cannot eliminate that divide altogether. Ultimately, a state must choose to hold its judges accountable to the electorate or not. And that choice exposes an irresolvable conundrum at the core of American government: judicial independence from electoral accountability is both in tension with and essential to democracy.

Given this irresolvable conundrum, America's indecision over judicial selection should be viewed as a chronic condition to be managed, rather than a disease to be cured. One step toward managing this chronic condition is to pursue a course of deep interdisciplinarity by accounting for the different perspectives of judges, lawyers, law professors, political scientists, historians, psychologists, journalists, and policy analysts. Each has useful but incomplete perspectives to offer that taken together yields a more accurate composite that can inch the debate closer to consensus.

A second step is to better develop a middle ground that makes elected judges more independent and appointed judges more accountable, so as to render binary choices less stark. Of particular importance, one can explore ways to preserve electoral accountability while diminishing the threat to independence posed by reselection processes—which is where the most serious problems have arisen. To these ends, I propose a new "qualified election" model of selection that seeks to strike a better independence-accountability balance by preserving one-time elections for state supreme courts who serve a single, lengthy term without subjecting judges to re-election or other reselection processes.

A third step is to acknowledge that ultimate failure to achieve consensus is inevitable—and perhaps that is a good thing. The competing values underlying the choice between elective and appointive systems will remain in constructive and perpetual tension despite best efforts to make both systems better and diminish the distance between them. Moreover, the unavoidably binary character of the election versus appointment choice and the consequent inability to reach universal consensus may be a virtue, rather than a vice. It gives states the flexibility to accommodate changing times, changing circumstances, and changing legal cultures in different jurisdictions by keeping variations of two viable selection alternatives on the table. Which alternative is optimal will depend on which selection system's values take precedence in a given place at a given time.

That said, in choosing between elective and appointive systems, I make the case for appointment as the appropriate default. I argue that appointive systems are more compatible with the appropriate role of the judiciary in America's brand of representative democracy—at least when the courts are in good public standing. The peril of an appointive system is that the judiciary can lose its legitimacy if the general public suspects that its judges are abusing their independence and going rogue. Hence, there comes a tipping point, where the public ceases to trust its judges or those who appoint its judges, and where electoral accountability becomes necessary to preserve or restore legitimacy. At that tipping point, the default properly yields to an elective system. For states with elective systems, a return to the default position is justified when the perceived impact of elections on the litigating public and the rule of law outweigh the benefits of electoral accountability for the voting public that justified a departure from the default position in the first place.

Chapter 7 then looks to the future of judicial selection and brings the book to conclusion. The modern judicial selection debate is taking place when our time-honored "rule of law paradigm" is crumbling. That paradigm posits that independent judges will disregard extralegal influences on their conduct and uphold the rule of law. The paradigm has undergone significant erosion in recent decades. It is contradicted by social science research showing that judges are subject to ideological and other extralegal influences. Data notwithstanding, the bench and bar continue to defend the rule-of-law paradigm from attack. But politicians, pundits, political scientists, and public alike have become increasingly skeptical. This state of affairs counsels in favor of moving to a new "legal culture" paradigm, which proceeds from a different and more sustainable, twofold premise: First, that judges are acculturated by training and experience to take law seriously. Second, at the same time, law is often indeterminate, and in the context of a difficult case, extralegal influences—including a judge's legal philosophy and political ideology—can affect which of two comparably plausible arguments the judge finds more persuasive.

This legal culture paradigm better frames the judicial selection debate. It justifies a default in favor of appointive systems because we should begin from the premise that judges are predisposed to uphold the law—a premise that is better protected if judges are insulated from electoral pressure to disregard the law when the law is in tension with popular preferences. But by acknowledging that independent judges are subject to extralegal influences, the paradigm allows for the possibility that independence is subject to abuse by judges whose policy preferences trump their commitment to law or are otherwise unacceptable. Hence, there are circumstances in which a default in favor of appointment systems must yield. Viewed in this way, it is possible to manage judicial selection choices while conceding the inevitability and desirability of change and lack of consensus.

CONCLUSION

Ronald Coase is attributed with saying that "if you torture the data long enough, it will confess" to anything.[17] A complicated array of psychological phenomena is at work in leading well-intentioned lawyers, judges, law professors, policy analysts, political scientists, and others to torture their data, overstate their claims, and create an impasse in the judicial selection debate that this book explores. My ambition here is to diminish the clutter that has obstructed our approach to consensus, while recognizing, paradoxically, that ultimately reaching consensus is neither possible, nor desirable.

2

A SHORT AND POINTED HISTORY OF JUDICIAL SELECTION

We academic types love to begin our books with a bit of history. It is a ritual akin to washing up before dinner. As with washing up, that kind of history is often half-hearted, badly done, and unnecessary. I hope you will bear with me, though, because my objective here is less ritualistic than pointedly focused on three objectives.

First, I want to show that disputes over how independent and accountable judges should be, as reflected in disagreements over judicial selection and retention, are ancient in origin. Those disagreements reinforce a point emphasized in chapter 1—that the judicial selection debate has been perennial.

Second, I want to show that perpetual bickering over how best to select and retain judges has not remained in a steady state. Different systems of selection have had their heydays at different periods in time. To that extent, the five major systems of selection (each of which can fairly be described as a form of appointment or election) are aging rock stars, each with loyal followings, who seek to recapture former glory with an endless series of revival tours.

Third, I want this chapter to set up the next, by situating the current judicial selection landscape (as described in chapter 3) in a deeper historical context. The history of judicial selection has featured periodic waves of reform that have produced different systems for choosing and retaining judges. The common aim: an independent judiciary that is buffered from external sources of interference with its impartial judgment. Those selection processes remain the systems of choice in different states. The modern era of judicial selection falls between waves, at a time when no established or proposed system is gathering momentum. And, as discussed in chapter 3, the new politics of judicial elections embrace a different ethos that is less concerned about protecting judicial independence than constraining it.

The targeted history I provide here is incomplete by design. For devotees of American history who are interested in a more comprehensive account of judicial selection in the United States, I recommend Jed Shugerman's wonderful book, *The People's Courts: Pursuing Judicial Independence in America*.

COLONIAL RULE AND GUBERNATORIAL APPOINTMENTS

At of the turn of the seventeenth century, English judges were appointed by and served at the pleasure of the Crown. Sir Edward Coke (pronounced "cook") tested the limits of the king's pleasure during his tenure as chief justice of two different courts between 1606 and 1616. These confrontations did not end well for him, but they did lead to reforms that exerted a profound impact on judicial independence in England, and later, in the United States.

Coke was a true believer in the rule of law, and the authority of English judges—once appointed—to interpret and apply the common law without interference from the king. As a young barrister reporting on Jentleman's case, decided by the Court of King's Bench in 1583, Coke wrote that "The King may create a new court and appoint new judges in it: but after the Court is created and established, the Judges of the Court ought to determine matters in it."[1] Decades later, as chief justice of two different courts, Coke was in a position to practice what he had previously preached. He wielded the supremacy of the common law with unprecedented gusto, and in so doing crossed the king several times—one too many times, as it turns out.

In one episode, King James I interceded to arbitrate a jurisdictional dispute between the Ecclesiastical "Court of High Commission" and courts of common law. At their meeting, Coke contended that the common law was supreme within its jurisdiction, which served the interests of the Crown because "the common law protecteth the King."[2] "A traitorous speech!" James blustered, countering that "The King protecteth the law and not the laws the king."[3] Undeterred, Coke explained that "his Majesty was not learned in the laws of his realm," and that "long study and experience" enabled judges to "protect his Majesty in safety and peace" by trying cases competently.[4] "The King was greatly offended," Coke noted later, because Coke had implied that the king was subservient to the law, which, the king declared, "was treason to affirm."[5]

In a later altercation, Parliament challenged the king's practice of encroaching on legislative authority through frequent resort to royal proclamations that had the force of law. The Lord Chancellor warned Coke's court to "maintain the power and prerogative of the King."[6] Coke, however, was having none of it: "[T]he King cannot change any part of the common law," he declared, "nor create an offense by his proclamation which was not an offense before, without parliament."[7] In yet another confrontation, the king's attorney general, Francis Bacon, polled each of the judges on Coke's court to determine whether a preacher, whose confiscated notes attacked the king and advocated rebellion, had committed treason. Coke declined to give Bacon the answer his king sought, and "asserted boldly that no mere declaration of the of the King's unworthiness to govern amounted to treason."[8]

The king's gasket finally blew in an imbroglio that began when Bacon conveyed the king's "commandment" to Coke's court that it "put off" the disposition of a case concerning the king's power to make a disputed presentation of land to a bishop.[9] The court disregarded the king's request for postponement, which it interpreted as a demand for special treatment, and ruled against him on the merits of the underlying dispute. King James then summoned all twelve justices on the Court of King's Bench, and asked each a pointed, poison-tipped question: whether, when the king demanded to consult with them and "required . . . that they should stay proceedings in the meantime—they ought not to stay accordingly?"[10] Eleven judges whimpered their acquiescence. Coke, however, stood his ground, saying: "I would do that which an honest and just judge ought to do."[11] The King's Privy Council removed Coke later that year without a formal trial or impeachment proceeding.

Coke may have lost his battle for separation of powers, judicial independence, and the rule of law, but his travails became the cause célèbre of a more protracted campaign for greater judicial separation and independence from the Crown. Following the Glorious Revolution of 1688, King William and Queen Mary relinquished their power to establish courts. And the 1701 Act of Settlement afforded English judges tenure during good behavior and subjected them to removal only upon an address from Parliament.

This tectonic shift in the structure of English government gave judges greater job security and transferred powers relevant to judicial selection and removal from monarch to legislature, to the end of promoting a more independent judiciary. The quake it produced, however, was not fully felt in colonial America, where judges remained beholden to the king and his representatives, the colonial governors.

Some colonial legislatures and governors granted judges tenure during good behavior, presumably on the assumption that tenure protections guaranteed by the Act of Settlement extended to the American colonies. In a 1761 circular to the governors, King George III made it clear that they assumed wrong. First, the king declared that, "it does not appear to us that in the present situation and circumstances of our said colonies . . . the judges or other chief offices of justice should hold their offices during good behavior."[12] Therefore, the king announced his "express will and pleasure" that the governors "do not upon . . . pain of being removed from your government," acquiesce to any acts of colonial legislatures that sought to regulate judicial tenure. Moreover, the king's circular warned, the governors were to "take particular care" that any judicial appointments they made, be "granted during pleasure only," which was consistent with "the ancient practice and usage in our said colonies and plantations."

Judicial salaries likewise became a bone of contention in the colonies' power struggle with the king. In 1772, King George transferred control over Massachusetts Superior Court salaries from the legislature and governor to the Crown, ostensibly to increase them. The twofold effect of the move was to spark protests among the colonists, who argued that judges were thereby rendered subservient to the king, and to engender suspicion of the judges themselves, whose livelihoods were thereafter under the king's control.[13]

Episodes such as these contributed to pervasive disaffection with and distrust of the king, his appointed governors, and colonial judges under the governors' control. The colonists' anger reached its apogee in the Declaration of Independence, which included the grievance that King George "has made Judges dependent on his Will alone, for the tenure of their offices, and the amount and payment of their salaries."

EARLY STATEHOOD AND LEGISLATIVE APPOINTMENTS

Between 1776, when America declared its independence from England, and 1787, when the U.S. Constitution was drafted, most fledgling states adopted constitutions, and did so with the colonial experience fresh in their minds. That experience led the states to curb the excesses of executive power that the colonists had endured at the hands of the king and his colonial governors—excesses that included encroachments on the courts. Those encroachments, however, did not catalyze a movement to entrust judges with their independence—after all, the Crown's efforts to render colonial judges subservient, undermined confidence not only in the king but in the judges as well. Instead, the states sought to diminish executive branch power over judges and courts by transferring that power from governors to legislatures. The original thirteen states thus selected judges by one of two methods: gubernatorial appointment with confirmation by a legislative council (in five states) or legislative appointment (in eight states).[14]

In addition to delegating to legislatures greater responsibility over judicial appointments, state constitutions often vested legislatures with significant control over judicial tenure and retention. The full extent of the judiciary's resulting dependence became clear as state courts began to exercise judicial review and invalidated enactments near and dear to their legislatures' hearts.

The circumstances surrounding the Rhode Island Superior Court's decision in *Trevett v. Weeden* illustrate the control that early state legislatures sought to exercise over their judiciaries.[15] In 1786, the Rhode Island legislature passed a statute requiring merchants to accept paper currency as legal tender—a controversial move at a time when paper currency was devalued.[16] Presumably to ensure that angry citizens could not, in their capacity as jurors, nullify prosecutions by acquitting defendants who refused to accept paper currency, the statute denied defendants jury trials in such cases. In *Trevett v. Weeden*—a case widely cited as early precedent for the power of judicial review—the Superior Court of Rhode Island found that the statute was incompatible with the colonial constitution still in force (Rhode Island had yet to adopt a new constitution after becoming an independent state ten years earlier), which guaranteed citizens the right to a jury trial. The court therefore declared that the suit was "not cognizable," which effectively invalidated the statute as unconstitutional.

The Rhode Island legislature was infuriated. It summoned the Superior Court's judges to appear and explain themselves. When a majority of the legislature found the judges' explanation wanting, it initiated removal proceedings. The attorney general and others interceded on the court's behalf and the legislature suspended removal proceedings. But when the time came for the legislature to reappoint the judges of the superior court, four of the five members of the court found themselves out of work.

Episodic judicial dependence on governors during the colonial period, followed by episodic judicial dependence on state legislatures in the aftermath of the Declaration of Independence, gave rise to a moment of unprecedented consensus in support of judicial independence at the Constitutional Convention of 1787. At the Convention, there was spirited disagreement over whether federal judges should be appointed by the president, by the Congress, by the Senate, or, as they ultimately decided, by the president, with the advice and consent of the Senate. But there was no dispute that judges should be appointed. Even "Brutus," the pseudonym of Robert Yates, a prominent anti-Federalist critic of the proposed constitution, agreed that, "it would be improper that the judicial should be elective," because judges require specialized expertise in law, and because judges "should be placed, in a certain degree in an independent situation, that they may maintain firmness and steadiness in their decisions."[17] There was likewise universal consensus that once appointed, federal judges should hold their tenure during good behavior and receive a salary that could not be diminished, although some anti-Federalists worried that the judicial power to declare acts of Congress unconstitutional (without a mechanism for congressional override) could render federal judges too independent and powerful.

Within the span of a century, then, the pendulum of judicial tenure had swung from precarious to semi-secure first in England, and then in the United States. It would, however, be premature to bellow three huzzahs for judicial independence. The U.S. Constitution afforded judges tenure during good behavior, but arguably empowered Congress to manipulate judicial tenure by disestablishing lower federal courts, and impeaching federal judges—powers that partisan Jeffersonian Republicans in Congress wielded against disfavored Federalist judges at the beginning of the nineteenth century. Initially, most though not all state constitutions provided judges with tenure during good behavior, but state legislatures did not necessarily regard tenure during good behavior with any greater reverence than Congress had. And those states in which judges were subject to legislative reappointment after a term of years were even more vulnerable. Hence, in the early 1800s, legislatures in Kentucky, Ohio, and elsewhere sought to bring their judiciaries to heel, by instigating impeachment proceedings against targeted judges, disestablishing wayward courts, and manipulating judicial terms of office.

JACKSONIAN DEMOCRACY AND ITS AFTERMATH: THE RISE OF PARTISAN JUDICIAL ELECTIONS

As the nation's democratic republic entered its second generation, confrontations between legislatures and courts sowed the seeds for a more populist strain of democratic judicial accountability that began to blossom with the election of President Andrew Jackson in 1828. Prior to the 1830s, there had been isolated experiments with elected judiciaries in Vermont, Georgia, and Indiana. But Jacksonian democracy paved the way for a more sustained debate over the merits of judicial elections by pairing public suspicion of judicial power with an almost reflexive enthusiasm for electing pretty much everybody.

Article VI of the U.S. Constitution requires that all state and federal officials take an oath to support the Constitution. Therefore, presidents, governors, legislators, and judges all swear to act within the scope of their constitutional authority, as they understand it. The power of judicial review, however, hands the judiciary a trump card. When Congress and the president, or legislatures and governors, combine to make and execute a law that judges deem unconstitutional, those judges, in their capacity courts, can second-guess the choices that the other branches of government make and invalidate the law. This form of so-called "judicial supremacy," did not sit well with President Jackson, who declared that: "The opinion of the judges has no more authority over Congress than the opinion of Congress has over the judges, and on that point the president is independent of both."[18] The State of Georgia took Jackson's war of words a step further, by executing a Cherokee prisoner in open defiance of a U.S. Supreme Court order, on the grounds that the Court had no business intruding on the affairs of a sovereign state.[19]

States imbued with Jacksonian populist zeal sought to curb judicial power by moving away from tenure during good behavior and toward fixed and shorter renewable terms.[20] For some, however, an additional source of ambivalence over judicial power was that judges were unelected. Frederick Robinson, who would later become president of the Massachusetts Senate, delivered a speech on the 4th of July in 1834, which captured the emerging sentiments of ardent Jacksonian populists: "Judges should be made responsible to the people in periodical elections," he argued. "The boast of an independent judiciary is always meant to deceive you," he warned: "We want no part of a government independent of the people. Those who are responsible to nobody ought to be entrusted to nobody."[21]

Jacksonian-era support for elected judiciaries was not especially sophisticated and did not try to reconcile the desire for democratic accountability with the view that judges needed to be independent and impartial enough to uphold the law in the teeth of popular pressure to do otherwise. That said, it would be a mistake to explain the rise of judicial elections with primary reference to Jackson and his followers, because the partisan judicial elections movement did not take off until the 1840s, after Jackson had left office and his cohort had lost influence.

The continuing appeal of democratic accountability generally may have buoyed support for elected judiciaries after Jackson's movement had lost momentum. The view that governmental legitimacy derives from electoral accountability is, of course, core to all democracies. Many states embraced that principle with unprecedented enthusiasm throughout the middle decades of the nineteenth century, as they drafted and redrafted their constitutions to elect a widening array of public officials. As a delegate to the Kentucky Constitutional Convention of 1850 grumbled, "We have provided for the popular election of every public officer save the dog catcher, and if the dogs could vote, we should have that as well."[22]

But the lawyers who populated constitutional conventions that adopted elected judiciaries were not Jackson devotees. Nor were they hostile to courts or judicial independence. They did not promote an elected judiciary for the primary purpose of empowering voters to purge the bench of judges who had the temerity to issue unpopular rulings.[23] They promoted an elected judiciary because they were supportive of courts and thought that judges would be better respected and more independent-minded if they derived their authority from the people they served than if they were hand-picked cronies of governors, or sycophants of legislatures.[24] The perceived need for a strong and independent judiciary became more acute in the aftermath of banking crises in the late 1830s. Those crises were widely attributed to the excesses of state legislatures, and in the minds of reformers, state judiciaries would be better able to keep legislatures in check via judicial review if judges were less dependent on the body whose legislation they were reviewing.[25]

Jacksonian Democrats (including Jackson himself) may have favored judicial elections as a means to curb judicial power. Ironically, however, states that inaugurated the movement toward elective systems over a decade later did so as a means to increase judicial power in relation to legislatures. Mississippi, which provided for the popular election of all its judges beginning in 1832, is rightly hailed as the first state to do so. But it was not until the latter half of the 1840s that the partisan judicial elections movement caught fire, beginning with New York's adoption of judicial elections in 1846. By 1900, thirty-three of the forty-five states had either entered the Union with constitutions that selected judges by means of partisan elections, or had amended their constitutions to replace appointive systems with elective ones.[26]

As of the late 1800s, states selected judges by one of three means: Gubernatorial appointments, legislative appointments, or contested partisan elections. Each system had a different origin story, and each would have its moment in the sun eclipsed by a new method of selection, in the perennially restive world of judicial selection. Gubernatorial appointments processes ceded turf to legislative appointments processes in the aftermath of independence, and both yielded primacy to partisan election processes beginning in the mid-nineteenth century. Partisan judicial election processes, in turn, would have their dominance challenged by the nonpartisan election movement of the Populist and Progressive Era at the turn of the twentieth century.

THE ADVENT OF NONPARTISAN AND RECALL ELECTIONS IN THE POPULIST-PROGRESSIVE ERA

The Populist and Progressive Era ushered in a protracted period of intense anti-court sentiment. Industrialization gave rise to a new working class that Progressives sought to protect via legislation to limit corporate power generally and to regulate the workplace in particular. Employers pushed back. They took the issue to court, and argued that legislation regulating hours, wages, and working conditions interfered with the freedom of employers to contract with their employees, which deprived them of their property without due process of law in violation of the Fourteenth Amendment to the U.S. Constitution. In *Lochner v. New York*, decided in 1905, the U.S. Supreme Court sided with the employers.[27] During the so-called *Lochner* era that ended in 1937, the U.S. Supreme Court invalidated as many as two hundred state laws (recent historical scholarship disputes the number) and some state supreme courts followed suit.

Populists and Progressives raged against state and federal judges who, in their minds, were indifferent to the plight of the people and had elevated laissez-faire capitalism to the status of a constitutional edict. The Progressives' reform agenda aimed to deter judicial excesses by subjecting judicial selection, retention, and decision-making to greater political control. As one legal historian elaborated: "[T]he Populist-Progressives during the early decades of the century sought to infuse judicial institutions with elements of popular democracy, to alter the substance of judicial decisions, to change the selection of federal judges, and to circumscribe their power and the jurisdiction of their courts."[28]

The partisan judicial elections movement had sought to wrest control of judicial selection and retention from politicians and vest it in the people themselves. But in the minds of Progressive-Era reformers, partisan elections served only to transfer political power from governors and legislators to party bosses, who controlled the nomination process and thus the electorate's choices. To loosen the grip of party control, Progressives proposed that judges be chosen in nonpartisan elections, in which the candidates' party affiliation would not appear on the ballot.

North Dakota adopted a nonpartisan election system in 1910, and by 1927, eleven more states had done likewise.

Partisan election processes arguably aimed to strengthen judicial independence by diminishing the dependence of judges on the governors and legislators who appointed (and sometimes reappointed) them. In the same way, nonpartisan election processes arguably aimed to strengthen judicial independence by reducing the dependence of judges on the political party leaders who would otherwise nominate them. For ardent Progressives, however, the true peril of *Lochner* era courts lay in the courts' perceived disdain for the will of state legislatures and their allegiance to corporate overlords. It was a peril that nonpartisan elections could diminish, insofar as party strongmen who hand-picked judicial nominees in partisan systems were in the thrall of big business. But for reformers, more was needed to deter judges who, once elected, "can and do usurp legislative functions" by invalidating popular Progressive legislation.[29] To keep corporate influence at bay, these reformers proposed recall elections.

Recall elections worked like this: If enough voters signed a petition, they could demand a special election to recall a public official from office before his term expired. Reformers proposed recall procedures for elected officials in all three branches of government. As applied to judges, Progressives defended recall as a boon to independence that would diminish judicial subservience to business interests. As recall proponent, and later Minnesota congressman, James Manahan argued, "A fearless judge would never fear the people. A cowardly judge would fear the people less than he would the political boss and big business men who made him."[30] Oregon adopted a judicial recall procedure in 1908, and by 1926, five additional states had done the same.

Recall elections were the point of the spear in the Progressive campaign to control *Lochner* era courts. The Progressives' claim that judicial recall sought to promote judicial independence from special interests, candy-coated their more hostile ambition to bend judges to popular will. As Manahan explained in private correspondence, " 'Fear of the stout fist of the people', was 'the only antidote' to the "poison injected into the arm of the law," by the 'powerful and insidious influence', of big business and the wealthy."[31]

The specter of recall elections frightened conservatives, who sought refuge in the courts from what they regarded as ill-considered legislation of the Populist-Progressive rabble. For conservatives such as U.S senator George Sutherland of Utah, recall elections rendered judges dependent on voters in a way that reflected "a complete misconception of the nature of the relationship . . . between the people and the judge." A judge "is not a political agent to declare the *wishes* of a constituency," Sutherland argued, but "a self-responsible arbitrator to decide the *rights* of contending parties, bound by the most solemn of covenants to consider nothing but the law and the facts and to obey no voice save the compelling voice of his own instructed conscience."[32]

The competing worldviews of Progressives and conservative-traditionalists collided in Arizona's application for statehood. In 1911, the proposed constitution that Arizona submitted to Congress in its petition to become a state included judicial recall procedures. In a joint resolution, Congress approved Arizona's petition subject to the condition that Arizona consider an amendment to eliminate judicial recall. Republican president Taft went further and vetoed the resolution, because it would have allowed Arizona to reject the amendment and enter the Union with the recall procedure intact. As the president explained: "This provision of the Arizona Constitution . . . seems to me so pernicious in its effect, so destructive of independence in the judiciary, so likely to subject the rights of the individual to the possible tyranny of the majority, that I must disapprove of a constitution containing it."[33]

Arizona relented, resubmitted a constitution that did not include judicial recall, and in February of 1912, President Taft signed off on Arizona's admission to statehood. Weeks later, Arizona's governor told his state legislature that "the people of Arizona have twice declared their belief in the righteousness of the power to discharge, through the medium of the recall, dishonest and unfaithful public servants," and that exempting judges would make them "more than human."[34] That April, the legislature proposed a constitutional amendment to reinstate judicial recall that was pointedly identical to the one Taft vetoed. Arizona voters approved the amendment at the next election.

Judicial recall never became the weapon that Progressives had hoped and traditionalists feared. Gathering enough signatures to petition for a recall made the process too cumbersome for regular use. But it brought into bold relief the role that elections could play in purging the judiciary of bad judges who usurped power and disregarded the law, or good judges who upheld the law in favor of unpopular parties or causes—depending on whom one asked.

THE MERIT SELECTION MOVEMENT IN THE TWENTIETH CENTURY

In the breakout role of his illustrious academic career, Roscoe Pound (who would later become dean of the Harvard Law School) delivered a seminal address to the American Bar Association in 1906, entitled "The Causes of Popular Dissatisfaction with the Administration of Justice." Over the course of a lengthy speech, he enumerated the sources of public disaffection for the courts, and proposed reforms. In his fourth and final category of causes, which he labeled "causes lying in the environment of our administration," he included "[p]utting courts into politics and compelling judges to become politicians," a reference to judicial elections, which "in many jurisdictions has almost destroyed the traditional respect for the Bench."

Pound's address signaled the arrival of a new breed of reformer. These new reformers were protective of the judiciary's autonomy and opposed Progressive attacks on *Lochner*-era courts. They nonetheless took popular critiques of the courts seriously and were receptive to alternative reforms that brought the special expertise of bench, bar, and academy to bear. In 1911, Charles Boston, a prominent New York attorney who would later become ABA president, conducted a national survey of lawyers and laypeople. He found that judge-related complaints were focused not on judicial review run amok, which was the target of Progressives' ire, but on a lack of competence and integrity. Boston noted that the problem was most pronounced in places where political party bosses controlled judicial nominations.[35]

For these new reformers, judicial elections were a problem because they politicized courts to the detriment of public confidence, jeopardized judicial independence from political parties and temporary majorities of the electorate, and produced unqualified jurists. Nonpartisan elections offered one way to diminish the role of party politics in judicial selection. But the new reformers were concerned that nonpartisan elections would not produce capable and qualified judges because voters were ill-equipped to assess judicial qualifications. Northwestern law professor Albert Kales made the point bluntly: "The electorate does not fail to choose simply because the party leaders have taken that choice from it," Kales argued. Rather, "the party leaders rule because the electorate regularly goes to the polls too ignorant politically to make a choice of judges." Such ignorance, Kales asserted, "is due to the fact that the office of judge is inconspicuous and the determination of who are qualified for the office is unusually difficult, even when an expert in possession of all the facts makes the choice."[36]

Because voters in nonpartisan systems have no basis upon which to cast an intelligent vote, Kales predicted that political parties will, "after a period of chaos and readjustment," re-emerge to exploit the informational vacuum. Each political party, Kales anticipated, will "have its slate of candidates." Those slates "would be distributed at the polls, and the voters would . . . as now, take the list of that organization he was loyal to . . . and vote the names upon it no matter where they appeared upon the ballot."

In 1913, Pound, Kales, and others founded the American Judicature Society, which new reformers established to improve the administration of justice by capitalizing on the special expertise of judges, lawyers, law professors, and others. The next year, Kales, writing in an American Judicature Society bulletin, devised a "Nonpartisan Court Plan" to address the problems that like-minded reformers had identified. Kales proposed that a council of judges create a pool of qualified candidates to fill judicial vacancies. The chief justice would then appoint judges from that pool. After a period of years, the judge would then be subject to a retention election in which voters would decide whether the judge should remain in office. If the electorate voted in favor of retention, the judge would remain in office for an additional term; if not, the chief justice would appoint a replacement from a new candidate pool created by the judicial council.

In 1926, British political scientist Harold Laski proposed that judges should be appointed by the governor rather than the chief justice, from a candidate pool created by a committee of judges and lawyers, rather than the judicial council imagined by Kales.[37] Laski recommended tenure during good behavior or until a specified age, instead of retention elections, because "the qualifications for judicial office are not such as an undifferentiated public can properly assess."[38] In 1928, the American Judicature Society endorsed a Nonpartisan Court Plan, but tweaked the Kales and Laski proposals to provide that the governor appoint judges from a list that the bar compiled.[39] And in 1931, the Grand Jury Association of New York suggested that non-lawyers be included in nominating commissions.

In 1934, California became the first state to jettison contested judicial elections in favor of an appointive system. The impetus for reform had been a campaign led by then district attorney (and later chief justice of the United States) Earl Warren to combat crime. Proponents argued that Proposition Number 3, as the judicial selection plan was known, would create a corps of capable, qualified, and professional judges who would do their part to remediate the state's crime problem by administering justice more efficiently and expeditiously. As originally conceived, California's Proposition No. 3 proposed a system akin to that developed by Kales, Laski, and others, in which governors would appoint judges from a pool of candidates screened by a nominating board. But before it went to the voters, Proposition Number 3 was amended to replace the nominating board with a "commission on qualifications" that would, in effect, confirm judges whom the governor nominated. The net effect was to give the governor significantly greater control over judicial selection than the Nonpartisan Court Plan contemplated, and to render the

California selection process a hybrid gubernatorial appointment model that would not be widely emulated.

In 1937, the American Bar Association cobbled together a composite proposal from the varied Nonpartisan Court Plans to date. The only unequivocal component of the ABA proposal was that judges be "appoint[ed] by [an] executive or other elective official or officials ... from a list named by another agency, composed in part of high judicial officers and in part of other citizens, selected for the purpose." The proposal added that "if further check on appointment be desired," states could provide for legislative confirmation. Finally, the proposal recommended that judges be subject to periodic reappointment or retention elections.

In 1940, over a quarter century after it was first proposed, Missouri adopted a Nonpartisan Court Plan. In Missouri, as in California, reformers capitalized on an anti-crime campaign, arguing that commission-approved judges would be better qualified than their elected counterparts to administer backlogged criminal court dockets. But in Missouri, these relatively sterile, good government arguments for efficient and expeditious administration of justice were paired with a more urgent campaign to rescue judicial selection from the clutches of political party leaders. In this way, the Nonpartisan Court Plan engine that had been putt-putting along as an intellectual exercise, would receive its first infusion of rocket fuel.

One of the bellwether events that propelled the Missouri reform movement was a brazen effort by notorious Democratic Party boss Tom Pendergast to manipulate the composition of the state supreme court. In 1937, Democratic governor Lloyd Stark appointed Justice James Douglas to fill a vacancy on the Missouri Supreme Court. Soon thereafter, Douglas cast the deciding vote in an insurance case against a corporation in which Pendergast had an interest. Pendergast launched a hard-fought but ultimately unsuccessful campaign to replace Douglas with a candidate of Pendergast's choosing, which exposed the power and influence that political parties sought to exert over the Missouri judiciary.

A second catalyzing event in the Missouri campaign was the 1934 election of nominal lawyer, but mostly pharmacist, Eugene Padberg to the circuit court in St. Louis.[40] Padberg's slender credentials were supplemented by his not inconsiderable loyalty to the Democratic Party that ensconced him on the bench. The embarrassment reached a high-water mark when Padberg's inertia in presiding over a grand jury investigation of local voter fraud became so obvious that a fellow judge interceded to end the proceedings and discharge the grand jury. An editorial in the *St, Louis Post Dispatch* blared, in terms shrill enough to get the attention of *Time Magazine* that, "St. Louis is confronted with a reeking, stinking scandal, and Circuit Judge Eugene L. Padberg is sitting right in the middle of it."[41]

Missouri voters had had enough. They approved the Nonpartisan Court Plan in 1940. They rejected a proposal to defeat it in 1942, and in 1945, they enshrined the plan in their new constitution.

The Nonpartisan Court Plan movement took flight like an albatross, which is to say slowly and awkwardly, with a lot of preliminary, ineffectual flapping, but with considerable staying power once airborne. Successes in California and Missouri were offset by failures in Michigan and Ohio, and it was not until the 1950s that additional states began to adopt merit selection systems. Around that time, it dawned on the new reformers that "Nonpartisan Court Plan" was a stupid name, given how easily it could be confused with nonpartisan election plans that they opposed. As the Nonpartisan Court Plan began to proliferate, it was rebranded "Merit Selection" or "The Missouri Plan"; by the 1980s, over twenty states had adopted it in one form or another.

In his history of judicial selection, Jed Shugerman attributes the ultimate rise of merit selection to a complex array of factors. First, he notes that "in rural but industrializing states, business interests had grown strong enough to organize merit campaigns, but industry and labor had not yet produced unions or machines that could block businesses' efforts."[42] Second, he credits "opportunistic leadership," for making a difference in several states.[43] Third, he credits the sincerity of merit selection proponents for their ultimate success, noting that "many key actors in merit's spread chose judicial independence over their more direct political interests," which transformed those "key actors" from potential obstructionists into cheerleaders.[44]

CONCLUSION

The history of judicial selection in the United States is a centuries-long snipe hunt for an independent and impartial judiciary. That hunt has yielded five distinct methods of selection, each with sub-variations. Each of those five methods was conjured in a unique historical context that enabled a given method to achieve favored status for a period of time, until its weaknesses were exposed, and circumstances were right for its popularity to diminish and the hunt for a new quarry to resume.

In the United States, colonial rule put governors in charge of the colonies and judicial selection. The autocratic rule of the Crown and the governors under the king's control led the colonists to rebel, and to establish systems of selection that diminished judicial dependence on governors by delegating greater power to state legislatures. Populist suspicion of appointed judiciaries and the cronyism they enabled, coupled with economic crises that buoyed support for judiciaries that were independent enough to keep the excesses of legislatures in check, sparked a movement to diminish judicial dependence on governors and legislatures by selecting judges in partisan elections. Scandals that exposed the unchecked power of political party bosses led critics to argue that partisan judicial election systems rendered judges dependent on party leaders, which catalyzed a movement for nonpartisan judicial elections. And suspicion that nonpartisan elections did not produce qualified judges and simply drove judicial dependence on political party leadership underground, paired with a post-Depression era body politic that was receptive to delegating greater authority over judicial selection to experts, gave rise to the merit selection movement.

The history of state judicial selection chronicles a quest to diminish disfavored sources of control over judicial decision-making. As states have sought to exclude external sources of control over judicial decision-making, they have reduced the power of governors, legislators, political parties, and voters to put their thumbs on the scales of justice. This approach to reform has proceeded on the premise that judicial independence promotes judicial impartiality by rendering judges independent of influences that could interfere with their impartial judgment.

But here is the thing. As selection systems make judges more independent by eliminating external interference with their impartiality, those systems indirectly facilitate internal interference with judicial impartiality. Judges who are unaccountable to external actors—be they politicians, party officials, or voters—are liberated to indulge their own internal biases that external actors might otherwise keep in check.

The merit selection movement subsequently stalled out. The last state to adopt a merit selection system was Rhode Island, in 1994. Commission "experts" revered by the merit selection movement, have become "elites" reviled by merit selection critics.[45] Those critics have ridden a long-gathering wave of anti-elitism and distrust of government culminating in the 2008 vice-presidential nomination of Sarah Palin, the 2016 election of Donald Trump, and the emergence of the so-called alt-right."[46] In this skeptical, neo-populist environment, significant segments of the public have become increasingly loath to relinquish its control over judicial selection and retention at the ballot box, which is the primary means by which they can keep perceived judicial excesses in check.

With isolated exceptions, the history of judicial selection has been about "pursuing judicial independence in America," to quote the subtitle of Shugerman's book. As implied by the preceding paragraph and explained in the next chapter, however, in the modern era, the American judiciary has undergone a political transformation that has placed increasing emphasis on constraining independence and enhancing political control.

3

THE NEW JUDICIAL SELECTION LANDSCAPE

Five historical movements, described in chapter 2, gave rise to five different methods of initial selection currently in use across the country, as shown in Table 3.1. In five states, high court judges are chosen via gubernatorial appointment with legislative or commission confirmation. In two states, supreme court justices are selected by the legislature. Seven states choose their high court justices via contested partisan elections. Fifteen states do so by contested nonpartisan elections. In twenty-one states, governors appoint judges from a list of nominees selected by a commission (and in eight of those twenty-one, judges so appointed are subject to confirmation by a legislative body or executive council).

This means that high court judges come to the bench by way of contested popular elections in twenty-two of the fifty states. That data point must be qualified, however, to avoid overstating and understating the pervasiveness of elections as a means of judicial selection.

In the twenty-two states that select their supreme court judges via contested election, it is quite common for incumbents to retire, resign, or die prior to the end of their final term. That creates an interim vacancy

Table 3.1. Initial selection

Methods:	High Court	Intermediate Appellate Court	Trial Court
Gubernatorial appointment	California* Maine** Massachusetts*** New Jersey** Tennessee**	California* Kansas** Tennessee**	Maine ** New Jersey**
Commission assisted gubernatorial appointment (aka assisted appointment)	Alaska Arizona Colorado Connecticut Delaware** Florida Hawaii ** Indiana Iowa Kansas Maryland** Missouri Nebraska New Hampshire*** New York** Oklahoma Rhode Island** South Dakota Utah** Vermont ** Wyoming	Alaska Arizona Colorado Connecticut Delaware** Florida Hawaii** Indiana Iowa Maryland** Massachusetts*** Missouri Nebraska Oklahoma Utah** Vermont**	Alaska Colorado Connecticut Delaware** Hawaii** Iowa Massachusetts *** Nebraska New Hampshire*** Rhode Island** Utah** Vermont** Wyoming
Legislative appointment	South Carolina Virginia	South Carolina Virginia	South Carolina Virginia
Partisan election	Alabama Illinois Louisiana New Mexico North Carolina Pennsylvania Texas	Alabama Illinois Louisiana New Mexico New York North Carolina Pennsylvania Texas	Alabama Illinois Louisiana New Mexico New York Pennsylvania Tennessee Texas

(*continued*)

Table 3.1. Continued

Methods:	High Court	Intermediate Appellate Court	Trial Court
Nonpartisan election	Arkansas Georgia Idaho Kentucky Michigan (partisan nomination) Minnesota Mississippi Montana Nevada North Dakota Ohio (partisan primary) Oregon Washington West Virginia Wisconsin	Arkansas Georgia Idaho Kentucky Michigan Minnesota Mississippi Ohio (partisan primary) Oregon Washington Wisconsin	Arkansas California Florida Georgia Idaho Kentucky Michigan Minnesota Mississippi Montana Nevada North Carolina North Dakota Ohio (partisan primary) Oklahoma Oregon South Dakota Washington West Virginia Wisconsin
Mixed			Arizona Indiana Kansas Maryland Missouri

*With confirmation by commission
**With confirmation by Senate/legislature
***With confirmation by executive council

for the governor to fill until an election can be held, at which point, the new appointee runs for office as an incumbent (except in jurisdictions where the interim appointee is disqualified from doing so). The net effect: many judges in the twenty-two states with elective systems are initially appointed, and across the country, significantly more judges ascend the bench via appointment than election.

At the same time, confining the discussion to modes of initial selection understates the pervasiveness of judicial elections. As reflected in

Table 3.2, nineteen states subject their high court judges to contested reelection (four in partisan contests, and the remainder, in nonpartisan). In another nineteen states, supreme court justices stand for retention elections. Thus, thirty-eight states subject judges to reselection via election. Most judges may be appointed, but most stand for election too.

Moreover, election is not the only means of reselection, as shown in Table 3.2. Of the twelve states that do not reselect high court judges via election, those judges are reappointed by the governor with the approval of a legislative body or commission in six jurisdictions, and reappointed by the legislature in three more. In other words, forty-seven states subject judges to reselection processes, as compared to three that do not. In the binary election versus appointment squabbles introduced in chapter 1, election processes are typically characterized as accountability-enhancing and independence-constraining, and are pitted against appointments processes, which are characterized as independence-enhancing and accountability-diminishing. This traditional divide overlooks the possibility that the more meaningful dichotomy is between initial selection and reselection processes, and that reappointment can be as, if not more independence-constraining than reselection via contested or retention elections.[1]

Finally, confining the analysis to courts of last resort understates the extent to which states subject judges to contested elections, as reflected in Table 3.1. As compared to the selection of supreme court justices, more states choose their trial judges in contested elections, while fewer do so via gubernatorial appointment—commission assisted or otherwise.

This chapter tells the story of judicial selection in the modern era. It is as much a story about what has not happened, as what has. Chapter 2 recounted the history of state judicial selection as successive waves of reform that began with gubernatorial appointments, and gradually transitioned to include legislative appointments, partisan elections, nonpartisan elections, and merit selection. The merit selection movement that enjoyed significant success in the mid-twentieth century stalled out in the 1980s. Since then, no system of selection has generated the kind of energy and enthusiasm needed to kick-start a new movement.

Table 3.2. Reselection

Methods:	High Court	Intermediate Appellate Court	Trial Court
Nonpartisan re-election	Arkansas Georgia Idaho Kentucky Michigan Minnesota Mississippi Montana Nevada North Dakota Ohio Oregon Washington West Virginia Wisconsin	Arkansas Georgia Idaho Kentucky Michigan Minnesota Mississippi Ohio Oregon Washington Wisconsin	Arkansas California Florida Georgia Idaho Kentucky Maryland Michigan Minnesota Mississippi Montana Nevada New York North Carolina North Dakota Ohio Oklahoma Oregon South Dakota Washington West Virginia Wisconsin
Partisan re-election	Alabama Louisiana North Carolina Texas	Alabama Louisiana New York North Carolina Texas	Alabama Louisiana Tennessee Texas
Retention election	Alaska Arizona California Colorado Florida Illinois Indiana Iowa	Alaska Arizona California Colorado Florida Illinois Indiana Iowa	Alaska Colorado Illinois Iowa Nebraska New Mexico Pennsylvania Utah

Table 3.2. Continued

Methods:	High Court	Intermediate Appellate Court	Trial Court
	Kansas Maryland Missouri Nebraska New Mexico Oklahoma Pennsylvania South Dakota Tennessee Utah Wyoming	Kansas Maryland Missouri Nebraska New Mexico Oklahoma Pennsylvania Tennessee Utah	Wyoming
Gubernatorial reappointment with senate or legislative approval	Connecticut Maine New Jersey Delaware* New York*	Connecticut Delaware*	Connecticut Maine New Jersey Delaware*
Nominating commission retention	Hawaii	Hawaii	Hawaii
Legislative reselection	South Carolina Virginia Vermont	South Carolina Virginia Vermont	South Carolina Virginia Vermont
Mixed reselection methods			Arizona Indiana Kansas Missouri
No reselection	Massachusetts New Hampshire Rhode Island	Massachusetts New Hampshire Rhode Island	Massachusetts New Hampshire Rhode Island

* Includes nominating commission review

Proponents of merit selection have been thwarted in their struggle to export the Missouri Plan to additional states. Since the 1990s, Arkansas, Mississippi, and West Virginia became disgruntled enough with their partisan election systems to give nonpartisan systems a try, but those reforms lacked the kind of evangelical zeal that inspires nationwide campaigns. Tennessee and Kansas swapped out merit selection in some of their courts for gubernatorial appointment paired with legislative branch confirmation. Meanwhile, North Carolina moved from partisan elections to nonpartisan and back.

In other words, judicial selection reform is in a trendless lull. This is not to imply that we are entering an era in which judicial selection warriors have reached their Valhalla, and are at peace with their current selection systems. To the contrary, the prevailing sentiment may be better captured by a former Texas chief justice, who is credited with saying that "no judicial selection system is worth a damn."[2]

To explain what has not happened since the 1980s, one must understand what has happened; and what has happened is a series of developments in judicial politics that have altered the judicial selection landscape and rendered judicial elections "noisier, nastier and costlier," to borrow the widely quoted phrase of a long-time observer of judicial races.[3] The net effect of these developments has been to fuel arguments for and against alternative selection systems, with the engines of political and economic power set against each other in ways that have thwarted momentum in any one direction. In addition, the elevated stakes in judicial races have spawned constitutional litigation over the rights and responsibilities of judges, judicial candidates, campaign supporters, and litigants, which has yielded conflicting outcomes with uncertain consequences that contribute to reform paralysis.

This chapter surveys recent changes in judicial politics to the ends of describing this new era of judicial elections, and setting the national stage upon which competing arguments for elective and appointive systems (as discussed in chapter 4) play themselves out. I begin by discussing the contributing causes to the new politics of judicial races, followed by a discussion of their consequences.

Before delving into those causes and consequences, it bears emphasis that the national trends I summarize in this chapter do not signify an unvarying landscape. Although judicial elections in the modern era are fairly characterized as "noisier, nastier, and costlier" (a wave that shows recent signs of cresting), the accuracy of that generalization varies across the states. There is variation between states with the same selection system: nonpartisan races in Idaho or North Dakota have not, on average, been as contentious or hotly contested as nonpartisan races in Mississippi or Wisconsin. There is variation between states with different selection systems: for example, the frequency with which incumbent judges are challenged tends to be higher in states that select their judges in partisan elections than nonpartisan. There is variation between tiers of court: supreme court contests tend to be more heated than intermediate appellate court races, which are typically more active than elections for trial courts, where it is not unusual for incumbents in states with contested election systems to run unopposed throughout lengthy judicial careers. Finally, there is significant variation between elections for judges on a given court within a given state: a slugfest in one supreme court race can be followed by a sleeper in the next.

The critical point for purposes here and later, is that while the national trends described in this chapter reveal the changing landscape of judicial selection, these trends are not uniform between or within the states. Insofar as these variations can be explained with reference to the different selection processes different states employ, they fuel arguments for and against elective and appointive systems discussed in chapter 4. But to the extent that these variations exist between states with the same selection system, or within the same state between elections, it implies a possibility explored in chapter 6: different states have different political cultures, different histories, and different current events and controversies, which produce different experiences with judicial elections. Those differences not only complicate narratives that seek to describe judicial selection trends in monolithic terms, they may ultimately undercut normative claims that a given selection system is inevitably optimal for all states at all times.

THE NEW POLITICS OF JUDICIAL ELECTIONS: CONTRIBUTING CAUSES

The politics of judicial elections have been ramping up for decades. The explanation is multifaceted, as elaborated upon in the paragraphs that follow. First, the decline of Democratic Party control in southern states has given rise to intensified competition between the parties in elections generally that has spilled over into judicial races. Second, controversial decisions by state supreme courts have energized judicial campaigns. There are several contributing causes to this second development. The rise of discretionary review by courts of last resort has limited state supreme court dockets to fewer and often more controversial cases. Lawyers and litigants committed to sometimes controversial civil rights and civil liberties agendas have shifted focus from federal to state courts. Judges have been called out for being enemy sympathizers in the so-called wars against crime and drugs. Moneyed interests have elevated the profile of tort reform as a controversial issue in judicial campaigns. Finally, the American judiciary has simply become a more political place in which judges are held accountable at the ballot box for their views across a broadening array of issues.

The Fall of the "Solid South"

In the aftermath of the Civil War, so-called Radical Republicans in Congress undertook to reconstruct the former Confederate states as they re-entered the Union, which bred resentment among southern whites. In the 1870s, as Reconstruction ended, the Republican Party ceded political control of southern states to the Democrats, and in 1876, former Confederate general John Singleton Mosby described this emerging political bloc of Southern Democrats as the "solid South." In the generations that followed, southern states remained solidly Democratic, united by the determination of white southerners to preserve their sociopolitical culture by enacting and enforcing "Jim Crow" laws that reversed the civil rights gains Reconstruction had achieved for African Americans.

The first chink in the wall of the solid South appeared in the 1940s when Democratic president Harry Truman desegregated the military, which angered southern Democrats, and prompted a third party presidential campaign by "Dixiecrat" Strom Thurmond, who won four southern states in the 1948 election. In the mid-sixties, Democratic president Lyndon Johnson's civil rights agenda further alienated southern Democrats. In the 1968 presidential race, the southern states split their allegiance between Republican Richard Nixon and third-party candidate (and former Alabama governor) George Wallace, with the Democratic nominee Hubert Humphrey winning only Texas and West Virginia. And in the 1980 election, Republican presidential candidate Ronald Reagan swept every southern state except West Virginia and incumbent president Jimmy Carter's home state of Georgia. These trends in southern presidential politics gradually percolated their way down to the state and local level. The rise of the popular "Reagan Revolution" in the 1980s effectively ended the southern Democrats' century-long monopoly on state political power and introduced a new era of two-party competition.

As the solid South liquefied, state supreme court elections became more heated. In Texas, for example, until the 1980s, every justice who served on the state supreme court dating back to Reconstruction had been a Democrat, which rendered supreme court elections "sleepy, low key affairs."[4] The Democratic Party's lock on the Texas Supreme Court ended in 1988. Amid a series of scandals that impugned the court's integrity, Chief Justice John Hill proposed a move to merit selection, which created such controversy on and off his court that Hill resigned. Bill Clements, the first Republican governor in over a century, appointed Republican Tom Phillips to fill the vacancy. That same year, six of the nine seats on the Texas Supreme Court were on the ballot, all of which were contested. Phillips headed a "clean slate" of Republican candidates who ran on a "reform" platform.[5] On election night, three of six Republican candidates (including Phillips) emerged victorious.

The Texas experience was replicated throughout the south. In his comprehensive study of judicial elections, Herbert Kritzer found that beginning in the 1980s, the southern states experienced "very substantial changes, both in the decline of unchallenged incumbents ... and in the increase in competitive elections and incumbent losses," which occurred "as the South transitioned to a two-party system."[6]

The Rise of Discretionary Supreme Court Review and the Decline of Mundane Cases

A second cause contributing to the changing politics of judicial elections in the modern era is that state supreme courts have made controversial decisions that have energized judicial campaigns for and against judges who participated in those decisions.[7] There are several explanations for this new wave of controversy.

One explanation has to do with changes in the structure of state appellate courts. Although the U.S. Supreme Court has never held that state court litigants have a constitutional right to appellate review, virtually all states guarantee access to appeal.[8] As explained in a report of the National Center for State Courts, appellate review serves "two primary roles": "to review individual decisions of lower tribunals for error and to interpret and develop the law for general application in future cases . . . ."[9] The role of appellate review in error correction is not especially controversial: Trial courts make bad calls because of honest mistakes, incompetence, bias, or in rare cases, corruption, and appellate courts step in to fix the problem. The role of appellate review in developing the law has the potential to be more problematic. Reviewing courts can be called upon to make new and controversial common law, and resolve important and undecided questions about what ambiguous statutes require. Of particular concern, courts can invalidate popular laws that, in the view of the judges comprising those courts, are inconsistent with what the constitution demands—and in novel contexts, do so unguided by precedent.

When the nation was young and cases were few, state court systems were typically limited to two tiers: trial courts and a supreme court. As populations grew, so did court case filings, to the point where the opportunity for state supreme court review became compromised by docket congestion. To relieve backlogs on their high courts, a trickle of states introduced a third tier of intermediate appellate courts, beginning in the 1890s. The press of burgeoning caseloads turned that trickle into a surge in the 1950s. As of 1957, thirteen states had provided for intermediate courts of appeals; by 1993, that number had grown to thirty-nine, with forty-one in place today.[10]

Adding a middle tier of appellate courts could not achieve the goal of reducing supreme court backlogs, unless a significant number of appeals ended with the newly minted appellate courts. To reduce double appeals, most states have granted litigants the right to an appeal before an intermediate appellate court, but have given their supreme courts the discretion to limit the appeals they will hear from decisions of the intermediate appellate courts. Supreme courts have generally exercised that discretion by "selecting the cases they review in order to address novel legal issues, reformulate decisional law, and maintain consistency in lower court decisions."[11]

The effect of these developments has been threefold: First, limiting the number of cases that supreme courts review has elevated the political profile of those cases if only because there are fewer of them. Second, the division of responsibility between appellate and supreme courts has, in effect, made the intermediate appellate courts the courts of last resort in routine cases of error correction. Third, and following from the second, supreme courts are no longer courts of error correction, but for the most part have become courts of law clarification and lawmaking only. Gone from many supreme court dockets is the high volume of noncontroversial cases in which an often unanimous court methodically corrects trial court mistakes—a baseline of mundanity that kept the occasional controversy in perspective. Instead, supreme court dockets are increasingly top heavy with novel and difficult policy-laden questions that have divided the state's lower courts, which can foment controversy in judicial races.[12]

The Migration of Civil Rights and Civil Liberties Campaigns to State Courts

In the 1950s and 1960s, amid the liberal Warren Court era, interest groups with civil rights and civil liberties agendas sought to pursue their goals via litigation in federal courts. Such a strategy was a controversy-breeder by design. It began with a minority of the population who could not persuade state and local governments—and the majorities they represented—of the rightness of their cause. This disgruntled minority then sought to convince courts to give them what their state and local governments would not, by declaring state and local laws and actions unconstitutional. The NAACP's decades-long campaign to dismantle Jim Crow laws throughout the south, by filing an orchestrated barrage of civil suits in federal courts, served as a template for later campaigns on other issues.

In the 1968 presidential campaign, Republican nominee Richard Nixon promised to dismantle the Warren Court, if elected. After he was elected, President Nixon made four new appointments to the Supreme Court in his first term, including Warren Burger, who was appointed to replace Earl Warren as chief justice. Justice William Brennan, a liberal holdover from the Warren Court, became frustrated by the conservative turn of the Burger Court. In 1977, Justice Brennan wrote a famous law review article (which sounds like an oxymoron, but there it is), in which he exhorted liberal interest groups and their lawyers to take their campaigns to state courts.[13] He did so on the premise that many state constitutions offered greater protection for civil rights and liberties than the U.S. Constitution.

Five years later, Justice John Paul Stevens made a similar point when writing the opinion of the Court that included Justice Brennan, in *City of Mesquite v. Aladdin's Castle, Inc.* There, the Court concluded that a Texas ordinance did not violate the due process clause of the Fourteenth Amendment to the U.S. Constitution, and that the Court lacked the jurisdiction to decide whether the ordinance violated the Texas Constitution. After noting that the operative protections of the Texas Constitution were "arguably significantly broader than . . . the corresponding federal provisions," Justice Stevens pointedly added that "a state court is entirely free to read its own constitution more broadly than this Court reads the Federal Constitution, or to reject the mode of analysis used by this Court in favor of a different analysis of its constitutional guarantee."[14]

In other words, the states are prohibited from doing less than the U.S. Constitution requires of them, but they are free to do more, by adopting constitutions that protect the same rights more fully, or that enshrine new and different rights altogether.

These invitations from Justices Brennan and Stevens caught the attention of state judiciaries. In an article entitled *Reincarnation of State Courts*, Wisconsin justice Shirley Abrahamson (who would later become its chief justice and later still, president of the Conference of Chief Justices) extolled the virtues of the "new federalism" that Brennan and Stevens advocated.[15] In 1986, Justice Brennan wrote a sequel to his earlier article, which included a report card of sorts: between 1970 and 1984, he noted, state courts "handed down over 250 published opinions holding that the constitutional minimums set by the United States Supreme Court were insufficient to satisfy the more stringent requirements of state constitutional law."[16]

The downside risk of the new federalism, however, was not lost on state judges. As Justice Abrahamson observed, "many state judges ... fear that state courts cannot take the heat that comes from deciding tough individual rights cases," because placing that onus on state courts "puts the constitutional issues closer to the public who will become hostile to state court judges." She quoted a California state judge as saying that he was " 'frightened by the reaction of the lay person,' " and that "popularly elected state judges ... may have trouble resisting the popular and political pressures that may be adverse to individual rights."[17] Given that California chief justice Rose Bird and two of her colleagues would lose their retention elections four years later after putatively upholding the rights of criminal defendants in a series of death penalty cases, the concerns of this unnamed state judge would seem to have been validated. And as discussed in chapter 1, the fact that three Iowa justices lost their retention elections in 2010 after concluding that same-sex couples had the right to marry under the Iowa constitution suggests that the path of the by then not-so-new federalism remains perilous.

Judges as Enemy Combatants in the War on Crime

"War" as a metaphor for a national initiative to control crime dates back at least as far as the Franklin Roosevelt administration. President Nixon, however, was the first to make the "war on crime" a centerpiece of his policy agenda. After a brief hiatus during the Ford and Carter administrations, the issue returned with a vengeance during the presidency of Ronald Reagan, who vowed to "get tough" on crime and wage a "war on drugs."

After President Reagan took office in 1980, he assembled an advisory board to guide him. Upon reviewing the data, the board discovered that the rate of serious and violent crimes was in remission, if not decline, which would seem to diminish the urgency of the president's anti-crime platform. That led the board to what one scholar describes as an "uncomfortably ambiguous conclusion": it recommended that the administration's anti-crime initiative emphasize the fear of crime, instead of crime itself.[18] Rather than seeking to diminish fear by publicizing the declining crime rate, the administration would allay public fear with an aggressive anti-crime agenda. And so, during his eight years in office, the extremely popular President Reagan signed five major anti-crime bills into law, and issued eight executive orders relevant to crime control.[19]

Such exclusive focus on public fear helps to explain the durability of crime as a campaign issue. If the public fears—or can be made to fear—crime, then anti-crime campaigns can retain momentum despite declining crime rates and despite rising costs associated with increased appropriations for police, prosecutors, and prisons. Moreover, crime is more than a practical problem—it is a moral one, which can provoke a kind of outrage that transcends pragmatic considerations and fosters ambivalence if not disdain for individual rights that impede law enforcement. Because it is the responsibility of judges to interpret and uphold those rights in the context of judicial proceedings, rulings in favor of criminal defendants can render judges the targets of public ambivalence and disdain in judicial elections.

In 1977, California's Democratic governor, Jerry Brown, appointed Rose Bird chief justice. During her tenure, Bird heard sixty-one capital cases and never once voted to uphold the death penalty. As discussed in chapter 2, California has a hybrid judicial selection system dating back to the 1930s, in which judicial candidates are nominated by the governor, confirmed by a Commission on Judicial Appointments, and later stand for periodic retention elections. Brown's successor, Republican governor George Deukmejian, opposed Bird's retention because of her votes in capital cases, and warned two of Bird's fellow justices that he would oppose their retention too if they did not vote to uphold more death sentences.[20] Deukmejian later announced his opposition to all three justices; all three lost their retention elections in 1986, and Deukmejian appointed their replacements the next year.

In an era that began with a "war" to eradicate the fear of crime, the charge that judges were "soft on crime" became an enduring and effective campaign issue. In 1990 and again in 1992, justices on the Mississippi Supreme Court lost their seats to opponents running "tough on crime" campaigns.[21] In 1994, all three judges on the Texas Court of Criminal Appeals lost their elections after reversing a conviction in a high-profile capital case.[22] In 1996, Tennessee justice Penny White lost her retention election in the wake of an opposition campaign that focused on her vote in a death penalty case; that same year, Nebraska justice David Lanphier lost his retention election over two opinions he authored, one of which reversed a murder conviction.[23] A four-state study of the 2000 supreme court elections found that crime control was the most frequent theme of television advertising.[24] In 2004, West Virginia justice Warren McGraw lost his election after an aggressive campaign by the organization "And for the Sake of the Kids" portrayed McGraw as soft on sex offenders.[25] A report on the 2006 supreme court races found that criminal justice ranked third of the twelve most frequent themes in campaign advertising (behind "traditional justice" and "conservative values").[26] And a report on campaign spending in the 2013–2014 election cycle found that "[a]ds discussing criminal justice issues—including describing a candidate as being tough or soft on crime, highlighting a candidate's history of putting criminals behind bars, or showcasing their support of victims' rights—made up an incredible fifty-six percent of all ads that ran this cycle."[27]

Although crime control has been a potent campaign issue for the voting public in judicial elections, those who sponsor campaign advertising that targets judges for being soft on crime often harbor a different agenda.[28] For example, the campaigns that culminated in the defeat of California chief justice Rose Bird in 1986, and West Virginia justice Warren McGraw in 2004, were financed by individuals and groups that had no obvious affinity for criminal justice issues. Rather, their opposition to the justices they targeted for defeat could best be explained with reference to the incumbents' record on economic and business issues, which were adverse to the interests of the groups that organized to oust the judges on the ballot.[29] These economic and business issues do not necessarily energize the electorate, which explains why groups with business agendas would attack judges they sought to defeat by provoking public ire over the judges' records on hot-button criminal justice issues.

State Courts and the Battle for Tort Reform

If you were asked to identify the five most pressing issues of our time, "tort liability" might not make your list—unless you run a business, a trade association of businesses or physicians, an insurance company, or a union, or are a lawyer who defends or sues them. What these groups and individuals have in common is an economic self-interest in tort liability, and the financial resources necessary to make tort liability a pivotal issue in judicial campaigns by throwing money at candidates who share their perspectives and priorities. And so tort liability has become a controversial issue that has transformed judicial elections, despite the issue's seeming lack of resonance with ordinary voters. That explains why, as discussed in the preceding section, interest groups seeking to elect business-friendly judges have resorted to shadow campaigns that attack opponents for being "soft on crime."

Beginning in the middle third of the twentieth century, state courts led a revolution in the personal injury arena that transformed the common law of torts to accommodate victims of injury in the post-industrial age.[30] Courts moved away from traditional "privity of contract" restrictions that had barred consumers from suing manufacturers directly for injuries caused by products that those consumers had purchased from retailers.[31] Courts devised new theories of tort liability that held manufacturers strictly liable for injuries caused by defectively dangerous products.[32] Punitive damages—damages that aimed to punish and deter defendants over and above damages that sought to compensate plaintiffs for losses caused by their injuries—had long been a part of the common law but were brought to bear with heightened frequency and ferocity.[33] And court systems developed the class action and related mechanisms, which enabled a multitude of plaintiffs to sue a defendant en masse for injuries resulting from a common cause.[34] Businesses sought relief from state legislatures in the form of "tort reform" legislation that limited tort liability in various ways.[35] Plaintiffs' trial lawyers pushed back, filing claims in state courts that challenged the validity of tort reform legislation under state constitutions, and their efforts met with some success.[36]

These developments led forces sympathetic to the interests of the business community to take a new tack: change tort liability by changing the judges who make the common law of torts and who review tort reform legislation. As with many firsts in the modern era of judicial elections, the rise of tort liability and reform as a controversial issue in judicial races began in Texas. The 1988 Texas election cycle was a watershed in the new politics of judicial elections, as discussed earlier in this chapter. It was then and there that two-party competition for supreme court seats in a southern state resumed for the first time in the modern era. The substantive issue that divided the candidates: tort liability. The impetus came from businesses and physicians groups that saw an opportunity to change the composition of a supreme court that they regarded as biased in favor of consumer-plaintiffs—a court that Democrats had controlled for over a century. Business-friendly Republican candidates, backed by business and physician groups, squared off against consumer-plaintiff-friendly Democratic candidates, backed by trial lawyers. Ten million dollars later, a split decision: candidates supported by the new wave of Republican tort-reformers won three of the six supreme court seats up for grabs in the 1988 race.[37] Given, however, that no Republican candidate had won in the previous century, it was a major breakthrough for tort-reformers.

Beginning in the 1990s, the U.S. Chamber of Commerce emerged as a leader in a multistate campaign to replicate the Texas experience and elect more business-friendly judges on other supreme courts that, in the Chamber's view, had become dominated by judges with pro-consumer-plaintiff prejudices. Contentious judicial campaigns focused on tort liability and reform, pitting rival interest groups against each other in multimillion-dollar battles to reorient the composition of supreme courts in Alabama, Illinois, Michigan, Mississippi, Ohio, Pennsylvania, and West Virginia.[38]

The Changing Landscape of the American Judiciary

To this point in the chapter, I have highlighted specific structural changes, strategic developments, and hot-button issues giving rise to controversies that have transformed the landscape of judicial elections. But this list of particulars is best understood in the context of a more general observation: the American judiciary itself shows signs of becoming a more controversial place in jurisdictions with appointive and elective systems alike.

There have been cycles of anti-court sentiment throughout American history, often triggered by a regime change in which those who brought a new administration into power have sought to intimidate or remove holdover judges associated with the prior regime. Hence, controversy is hardly new to the history of judges and courts. In 1801, Thomas Jefferson's cohort went on the attack against judges John Adams had appointed. Beginning in the late 1820s, Andrew Jackson's populist followers challenged the supremacy of the aging Marshall Court. After the Civil War, newly elected "Radical Republican" congressmen threatened to "annihilate" the holdover Supreme Court if it interfered with their Reconstruction agenda. When Progressive Era reformers came to power in the early twentieth century, they went to war against conservative

"*Lochner*-era" judges who obstructed their agenda. In the 1930s, Franklin Roosevelt proposed packing the Supreme Court with additional justices to neutralize the impact of conservatives appointed by his Republican predecessors. In the 1960s, Richard Nixon was swept into power on a platform that committed him to replacing the liberal Warren Court with "strict constructionists." And in the 1990s, the Republican Party regained control of Congress and embarked on a campaign against the "judicial activism" of Carter and Clinton appointees.

It is easy to mistake cyclical issues for something new or to overlook relevant history and claim that an event is unprecedented when it is not. For that reason, I proceed cautiously here. But there are a number of developments more sustained than cyclical attacks can explain, which may not bear on judicial elections specifically, but which contribute to the conclusion that judicial politics are becoming more contentious and controversial in the modern era.[39]

There is a new politics of federal judicial appointments. The ideological orientation of a Supreme Court nominee's future decision-making became an issue in Senate confirmation proceedings beginning in the late nineteenth century, increased in salience throughout the twentieth century, was the sole issue at stake in the Senate's rejection of Supreme Court nominee Robert Bork in 1986, and has since become the focus of circuit and sometimes district court confirmation proceedings as well.[40]

Transformative developments in mass media have likewise created a more partisan, polarized environment in which news about judges, courts, and judicial decisions are reported.[41] Traditional media increasingly report Supreme Court decisions with reference to ideological alignments on the Court and the political party affiliation of the presidents who appointed the justices authoring opinions for the majority and dissent. The advent of infotainment journalism has diminished the role of "hard" news in television broadcasts and reduced coverage of courts to shorter, more impressionistic sound bites. Ideologically aligned cable television news stations have emerged, which provide commentary highlighting partisan, political disagreements over Supreme Court decisions. So-called citizen-journalists who lack formal training in journalism and are unencumbered by journalism's professional norms, have created websites that monitor judges and courts. Those sites publicize events—often with an unapologetically ideological slant—to a worldwide audience that previously would have remained local news and reported, if at all, in local newspapers. More recently, the Trump administration has attacked mainstream media, calling into question the integrity of traditional news sources relative to their openly partisan counterparts.

There is a new politics of court practice and procedure. Congress passed the Rules Enabling Act in 1934, which authorized the federal courts to promulgate nationwide rules of practice and procedure for the federal courts. Congress did so on the premise that judges would bring their expertise to bear in developing neutral, process-oriented rules that did not implicate substantive rights in ways that required the active participation of legislators. Beginning in the 1970s, however, with the development of the Federal Rules of Evidence, it became clear that rules of procedure were fraught with substantive implications. Whenever a "procedural" rule is created or amended that makes it easier or harder for parties to achieve their substantive goals, it implicates policy questions that can generate controversy. For example, a hypothetical rule that makes it easier to certify class actions would enhance access to courts for plaintiffs who do not have the resources to sue individually, at the expense of increasing defendants' potential liability in a single action to the point where they could feel pressured to reduce the risk of catastrophic loss by settling even meritless claims. As the substantive implications of procedural rules became clearer, partisan, ideological alignments akin to those in the tort reform arena have emerged. Groups associated with business interests and the Republican Party have pitted themselves against groups associated with consumer interests and the Democratic Party, in a chronic struggle for influence over rule content.[42]

The law of judicial disqualification has likewise become infused with controversy. The ironclad presumption of impartiality that judges enjoyed in early English common law has gradually eroded. In its place, a network of rules has developed that articulates the circumstances under which a judge's impartiality can be challenged and the judge removed from cases she is assigned. Those circumstances run from the very specific, such as when denominated relatives of the judge are parties, to the very general, when the judge's "impartiality might reasonably be questioned." As the judiciary has become a more political place, open-ended disqualification standards have bred new controversies. Interest groups have clamored for the disqualification of justices on the U.S. Supreme Court because of their personal friendships, their prior affiliations, and their spouses' political activities. Other interest groups have agitated for the disqualification of justices on state supreme courts because of the campaign support those justices have received. And there is often room to argue that those interest groups are less concerned about the judges they target being partial, than being unsympathetic to case outcomes the interest groups favor.

Finally, there is a new politics of judicial conduct and discipline. Prior to the 1960s, there were no binding state codes of judicial conduct and no formal means to sanction wayward state judges short of removal via cumbersome mechanisms specified in state constitutions, such as impeachment or legislative address. Today, the judiciaries in all fifty states have adopted codes of conduct and have established processes that subject judges to disciplinary sanctions ranging from reprimands to removal. The federal system likewise had no code of conduct prior to the 1970s and no disciplinary process prior to 1980 (and still has neither a code nor a disciplinary process applicable to the U.S. Supreme Court). Because they are administered by and for judges, state and federal codes of conduct and disciplinary processes have not become sites for politicized battles over the ideology of judicial decision-making. But they have created another venue for controversy over judicial conduct of interest to policymakers, the media, and disgruntled litigants. Congress periodically showcases episodes of under-regulation in oversight hearings, and proposes reforms. Interest groups have agitated for the Supreme Court to bind itself to a Code of Conduct, and Chief Justice John Roberts has resisted those proposals as unnecessary because the justices already "consult" the code applicable to the lower federal courts.[43] In state systems, the media have publicized judicial misconduct complaints, which has fomented controversy when disciplinary processes fail, as in Wisconsin, where ideological fractures and mass recusals led to stalemates in disciplinary actions against two members of the supreme court.[44]

I do not mean to imply that the American judiciary has ever been apolitical or controversy-free. But the disparate developments recounted here reveal how the landscape has changed in ways that have made judicial politics more volatile. Witness President Trump's attacks on "so-called" federal judges whom he has characterized as "disgraceful," and "so political," for decisions adverse to the administration's agenda.[45] In this controversy-prone environment, judicial elections have become a kind of crucible in which the decisions judges make are attacked and defended. As a consequence, the controversies sparking election year battles have not been confined to crime and tort-reform. They have run the gamut from school funding and water rights, to abortion and same-sex marriage.

That said, it is important to keep the "new politics" in perspective. There have been significant changes in the judicial selection landscape, as recounted here, but the rates at which supreme court seats have been contested, and the competitiveness of those contests has not increased uniformly across the states to the extent that alarmist proclamations suggest.[46] This implies the need to be cautious about categorical claims and to be alert to interstate variations—a point that will later prove critical to the argument I make in chapter 6 that no one system of selection is optimal for all jurisdictions at all times.

THE NEW POLITICS OF JUDICIAL ELECTIONS: CONSEQUENCES

The multifaceted causes of a more contentious judicial election landscape have yielded multifaceted consequences.

The Rise of Big Money: Campaign Contributions

The confluence of events heralding the modern era of judicial elections is focused in the latter half of the 1980s. That is when electoral politics in southern states became more competitive, when being soft or tough on crime emerged as a galvanizing issue in judicial races, and when business interests began to flex their muscle and challenge incumbent judges they regarded as consumer-plaintiff friendly. Unsurprisingly, then, that is also when campaign contributions to judicial races began their long, slow rise.

The Brennan Center for Justice, the National Institute for Money in State Politics, and Justice at Stake issued jointly authored, biannual reports on "The New Politics of Judicial Elections" covering judicial races, beginning with the 2000 election cycle.[47] Those reports tracked increases in judicial campaign contributions and spending over time. They were also advocacy pieces that take a dim view of the developments they chronicle, but for purposes here, I focus on the underlying data and reserve a discussion of their policy perspective, for chapter 4.

Campaign contributions to supreme court races increased dramatically throughout the 1990s. Judicial candidates raised a total of $5.9 million during the 1989–1990 election cycle. That was followed by $9.5 in 1991–1992; $20.7 million in 1993–1994; $21.3 million in 1995–1996; $27.3 million in 1997–1998; and $45.9 million in 1999–2000.[48]

Beginning in 2000, two additional patterns began to emerge. First, contributions to judicial races in presidential election years outstripped contributions in off years. That is presumably due to the strategic desire of campaign supporters to capitalize on heightened voter interest and participation during presidential election cycles, and to the increased cost of advertising during presidential campaign years. Second, direct contributions to supreme court campaigns began to stabilize and decline. Thus, during non-presidential election cycles, judicial campaign contributions increased from $29.7 million in 2001–2002 (after a dramatic drop from $45.9 million in the prior, 1999-2000 presidential election cycle), to

$33.2 million in 2005–2006, down to $27 million in 2009–2010,[49] and down again to $20.6 million in 2013–2014.[50] In presidential election years, judicial spending remained close to 1999–2000 levels in the 2003–2004 and 2007–2008 cycles—hovering between $45 and $46 million—before declining to $30.6 million in 2011–2012.[51]

Contested partisan elections are, on average, more expensive than contested nonpartisan elections. That makes sense. The supreme court seats incumbent justices occupy are more frequently contested and seriously challenged in states with partisan elections, followed by nonpartisan elections.[52] And for challengers, every 1 percent more they spend translates into a 1.8 percent decline in electoral support for their incumbent opponents.[53] Insofar as partisan elections are more competitive affairs, and spending can affect outcomes in competitive races, it is unsurprising that partisan elections would tend to generate higher levels of campaign support.

When it comes to judicial campaign spending, contested elections in partisan and nonpartisan systems have been where the action is. Cumulative data from the first decade of the twenty-first century shows that of the twenty states that spent the most on judicial races, all selected their judges via partisan or nonpartisan contested elections, or hybridized systems that provide for initial selection via those methods. None employed retention elections in merit selection systems. This is not particularly surprising. Incumbents facing retention elections in merit selection systems are often foreclosed from forming campaign committees and soliciting contributions unless and until an opposition campaign surfaces, and serious opposition campaigns have been infrequent events. Unless the judge is unusually vulnerable, the advantages of incumbency can be insurmountable without a challenger in place to make a race of it. And if would-be opponents mount no opposition campaign because they regard the effort as futile, retention will follow with little or no money spent.

In a new era when controversies are more common and judges are more vulnerable, however, retention elections show signs of becoming a bit less soporific. In the aftermath of the 2010 cycle, when three Iowa justices lost their retention elections because of their ruling in a same-sex marriage case, as discussed in chapter 1, spending in retention election campaigns (in states with and without merit selection systems) has been on the rise. Average spending in retention races increased tenfold between 2009 and 2014, with a total of $6.5 million spent in the 2013–2014 election cycle.[54] Partisan and nonpartisan elections remain the elephant in the room of judicial campaign spending, but retention elections show signs of becoming a mouse consequential enough to make the elephant uneasy. Once again, however, interstate variation is significant, which counsels against categorical conclusions or predictions.[55]

The Rise of Big Money: Independent Expenditures

The decline in direct contributions to the candidates themselves, which began in 2000, has been offset by an increase in independent expenditures on the candidates' behalf. If you are a group or individual with the desire and resources to play a significant role in judicial races, there are several strategic advantages to plowing your financial support into an independent campaign on your candidate's behalf, instead of contributing to that candidate's campaign committee directly. First, if you organize the independent campaign that you bankroll, you control your campaign's message; when you contribute directly to a judge's campaign, in contrast, the campaign committee retains ultimate control over the campaign's communications. Second, your direct contributions to judicial campaigns are subject to state-imposed contribution limits. Independent expenditures on a candidate's behalf, in contrast, are unlimited, because the U.S. Supreme Court has held that statutory limits on campaign spending violate the First Amendment rights of the spender. Third, the advertising that you disseminate as an independent organization is not subject to ethics rules that prohibit the candidates themselves from running ads that make misleading statements or comment on pending or impending cases. Fourth, your direct contributions to judicial campaigns are subject to public disclosure, as are independent expenditures by political action committees, or PACs. But if you wish to conceal your relationship to the candidate you are bankrolling, federal tax laws enable independent groups to spend "dark money" on judicial races by structuring themselves as nonprofit, social welfare organizations, which are not required to disclose their donors.[56]

Non-candidate spending in supreme court races—by independent organizations, individuals, and political parties—increased ninefold between the 2001–2002 and 2011–2012 election cycles.[57] In 2010, the U.S. Supreme Court invalidated federal restrictions on independent expenditures by corporations in election campaigns, in the famous, if not infamous case of *Citizens United v. FEC*, which lifted additional barriers to corporate participation in the electoral process. In the 2011–2012 election cycle, independent interest group expenditures as a percentage of total spending in judicial campaigns reached an all-time high at 27 percent—a record that was eclipsed again in 2013–2014, when the figure rose to 29 percent.[58]

The tale of costlier judicial races in the modern era having been told, a cautionary note is in order. There are signs that spending in judicial races has crested and begun to taper off.[59] This could imply that groups and individuals interested in the business of the courts have begun to lose their appetite for bankrolling judicial campaigns, or that claims of sea change in the politics of campaign spending are overstated. At least, as if not more likely, it could simply signify that the latest battle has been won. The Republican Party has gained control of supreme courts in southern states. Business interests have, for the most part, prevailed in their efforts to transform state high courts into more business-friendly places. To that extent, the new politics of judicial elections are not over but in a lull, pending the arrival of new controversies.

The Rise of Attack Advertising

All that new money flowing into state supreme court races via direct contributions and independent expenditures does not just sit there in a burgeoning pile. It buys stuff—including advertising. In her award-winning book, *Attacking Judges: How Campaign Advertising Influences*

State Supreme Court Elections, Melinda Gann Hall reports that as of 2002, television advertising was purchased in about 43 percent of contested supreme court races.[60] In the election cycles since, that number has jumped and then remained between 61 percent and 74 percent.[61] That uptick has coincided with the ascension of well-funded independent campaigns, described in the preceding section, "The Rise of Big Money: Independent Expenditures."[62]

Television advertising is used more frequently in nonpartisan supreme court races than partisan, which is curious because spending in partisan races is, on average, higher than in nonpartisan, and television advertising is expensive.[63] The best explanation may be that without partisan labels, candidates in nonpartisan races perceive a greater need to gain name recognition and differentiate themselves from their opponents, which can best be achieved by devoting a higher percentage of their campaign budget to television advertising.

Not only has the percentage of supreme court campaigns featuring television ad campaigns risen, but the tenor of that advertising has changed. Attack advertising—advertising that criticizes the favored candidate's opponent—has increased from about 18 percent of the television ads produced, to between 21 and 29 percent in the succeeding three election cycles.[64] And as a proportion of total commercial airings (which measures how frequently a given ad appeared on television), attack advertising increased from 7.6 percent in 2002, to between 19 and 22 percent of the total in the three election cycles that followed.

The latest data suggest a recent decline in the prevalence of attack advertising, which accompanies recent declines in spending. This latest turn toward fewer attack ads in judicial campaigns belies shrill claims that the sky is falling, but may signify only that the tort reform battle giving rise to the new era of negative advertising has been won. If so, the recent peace could simply be a calm that precedes the next storm.

In the modern era of judicial elections, infusions of campaign cash have enabled candidates and their supporters to buy bigger megaphones with which to deliver a meaner message. Whether this is a bad thing that undermines the rule of law, or a good thing that embodies American democracy in action, will be explored in chapter 4. For purposes here, and subject to the latest data suggesting that we may be entering a lull, it is enough to say that it is a thing.

The Due-Processing of Judicial Campaign Conduct

A final consequence of more contentious judicial elections in the modern era is that the new politics of judicial campaigns have resulted in litigation challenging the constitutionality of how state judicial campaign conduct is regulated. The U.S. Constitution establishes and organizes the national government, specifies and circumscribes its powers, and guarantees individuals certain rights in relation to the national government. It does not have as much to say about state governments and the limits of their authority. One important exception, however, is the due process clause of the Fourteenth Amendment, which declares that no state shall "deprive a person of life, liberty, or property without due process of law." And the U.S. Supreme Court has interpreted the due process clause to prohibit states from depriving individuals of procedural rights to a fair hearing and selected substantive rights enshrined in the U.S. Constitution, including the First Amendment freedom of speech.

As the new era of judicial elections emerged, individuals and organizations began to challenge campaign-related state actions that implicated their Fourteenth Amendment due process rights. The U.S. Supreme Court responded in a series of controversial rulings—all decided by five to four votes. These decisions have proved to be both consequences of the new politics, and in some cases, contributing causes that have stoked the fire.

Republican Party of Minnesota v. White, decided in 2002, concerned an ethics rule promulgated by the Minnesota Supreme Court, which prohibited judicial candidates from announcing their views on legal issues they would decide as judges.[65] The U.S. Supreme Court held that the rule violated the candidates' First Amendment's right to freedom of speech incorporated into the due process clause of the Fourteenth Amendment.

The 2009 case of *Caperton v. A.T. Massey Coal Co.*, concerned a West Virginia Supreme Court justice who declined to recuse himself from a case in which he had recently received substantial campaign support from the defendant's CEO, and then cast the deciding vote in the defendant's favor.[66] The U.S. Supreme Court held that the support the justice had received was so substantial as to create a probability of bias, and that by failing to withdraw from the case he had violated the plaintiff's due process rights.

In 2010, the Supreme Court decided *Citizens United v. FEC*, in which the majority held that the First Amendment prohibited Congress from restricting independent expenditures by corporations in political campaigns.[67] *Citizens United* did not concern state actors, judicial elections, or the Fourteenth Amendment, but as noted, the Fourteenth Amendment's due process clause incorporates the freedom of speech. Hence, many assume that the First Amendment analysis the Court brought to bear in *Citizens United* would apply to state-imposed restrictions on corporate expenditures in judicial races.

Finally, in *Williams-Yulee v. Florida State Bar*, decided in 2015, the Florida Supreme Court disciplined a judicial candidate for violating an ethics rule that required judicial candidates to solicit contributions through their campaign committees and forbade them from soliciting such contributions themselves. The U.S. Supreme Court upheld the rule on the grounds that it was narrowly tailored to serve the compelling state interest of preserving judicial integrity. In so holding, the majority explained that judges were different from other public officials in ways that justified heightened regulation of their campaign speech. "Judges are not politicians, even when they come to the bench by way of the ballot," the Court declared, "and a State's decision to elect its judiciary does not compel it to treat judicial candidates like campaigners for political office."[68]

Recent due-processing of judicial conduct has created unpredictable cross-currents in the politics of judicial elections, with varied consequences. On the one hand, *Republican Party of Minnesota* liberated judicial candidates to transform judicial races into referenda on decisions they made or will make as judges, which in the minds of some has contributed to the new wave of contentious judicial campaigns. In addition, the Court's decision in *Citizens United* coincided with a rapid rise of independent expenditures in judicial election campaigns, which has led some to infer cause and effect.

On the other hand, the majority opinion in *Williams-Yulee* proceeded from the premise that judges are different enough from other public officials to justify state-imposed restrictions on the speech of judicial candidates that would not be tolerated in races for executive or legislative branch offices. Does that imply the possibility that *Citizens United* might not apply with equal force to judicial races on the theory that there is a special need to preserve judicial integrity and impartiality? More important, might this "special need" justify restrictions on corporate expenditures in judicial campaigns that would be unacceptable in other races? And what of *Caperton*? Is disqualification a new, post-election antidote for the influence of big money in judicial races? Or is it a remedy reserved for cases too extreme and exceptional to be useful? Can a litigant's due process right to an impartial judge dull the point of affording judicial candidates the right to tell voters how they are likely to vote in future cases, if sharing their views exhibits a probability of bias that will require disqualification later?

For someone who gets a bang out of constitutional law, there is considerable temptation to follow these questions down their respective rabbit holes. But pursuing answers to these questions is beside my essential point here, which is that the politics of judicial elections in the modern era has given rise to multiple rounds of constitutional litigation. And the impact of the U.S. Supreme Court's sharply divided opinions in these hotly contested cases has been like dousing a grease fire with water: it has extinguished the flames targeted, while expanding the conflagration in new and unpredictable ways.

CONCLUSION

Judicial elections have undergone a seismic shift in the modern era. Judicial races have transformed from sleepy, routine, and inconsequential affairs to often high-stakes, high-profile contests: more contributions, more spending, more advertising, more attack advertising, and more constitutional litigation. These developments, in turn, have attracted the attention of reformers, scholars, and the media. Reducing the explanation for complex phenomena such as these to a single cause is a consummation devoutly to be wished, because doing so simplifies the narrative, and gives it punch. But complex phenomena, being complex, are often uncooperative in that regard, and such is the case here. Rather, the new politics of judicial elections is attributable to a confluence of events, decades in development. Two-party politics have expanded their reach. The cases that many state supreme courts hear have become fewer in number but more controversial in nature. State courts have become more attractive forums for civil rights and civil liberties campaigns. Judicial races have impressed incumbents into the service of "wars" on crime, by threatening the tenure of those who are not good soldiers. The business community has discovered that throwing money at judicial candidates sympathetic to their cause is an effective strategy to reduce tort liability. And the American judiciary itself has become a more political place. Taken together, these developments have raised the stakes in judicial selection, and made selection reform a hot topic for discussion.

It is critical, however, to end this chapter on a cautionary note. Latest trends suggest that campaign spending has begun to level off. The latest cycles of campaign advertising have been less negative. And there are significant variations between states in virtually every facet of the "new politics" under study. These recent developments do not necessarily imply that the new politics is much ado about nothing. To the extent that the big-money drivers of the new politics have taken the pedal off the gas because they have won their race to repopulate state supreme courts with business-friendly judges, it would be premature to suggest that nothing of importance has just happened. But recent developments coupled with widespread variation across the states underscore the need to avoid over-generalization. If we are, in fact, entering a ceasefire in the new politics, it presents a unique opportunity to consider the future of judicial selection in a more dispassionate environment under a flag of temporary truce.

4

THE ARGUMENTS

Chapter 2 recounted the history of judicial selection. It chronicled the states' centuries-old efforts to promote an independent and impartial judiciary, and described the different systems of selection that have emerged over time. Chapter 3 then surveyed the modern judicial selection landscape and highlighted the ways in which judicial elections have become more contentious and expensive affairs, oriented less toward promoting judicial independence than curbing it. Having thus described the past and present of judicial selection across the states, this chapter takes a turn for the normative by exploring the arguments for and against the selection systems in use.

There are at least five selection systems in play among the states (not counting sub-variations): gubernatorial appointment, legislative appointment, partisan contested election, nonpartisan contested election, and merit selection (commission-assisted gubernatorial appointment), with or without retention election.[1] There are perennial skirmishes over the relative merits of these five systems, but the entrenched battle line is drawn between elections and appointments, and whether contested popular elections ought to be the primary means by which judges are chosen. In effect, that pits gubernatorial appointment and merit selection systems against partisan and nonpartisan election systems (with the two states that still employ legislative appointment processes making infrequent bids to join the fracas). A peril to this binary approach is that it overlooks important distinctions between partisan and nonpartisan election systems on the one hand, and merit selection and traditional appointive systems on the other. To keep it simple, in this chapter I retain the election versus appointment dichotomy, but to avoid overgeneralization, I flag distinctions between sub-regimes, as necessary. Another peril to the elections-appointments dichotomy is that it pays inadequate heed to the difference between initial selection and reselection processes. The implications for judicial independence and accountability are quite different when a judge is initially elected or appointed, and when she is reappointed, re-elected (or not) in light of her past performance on the bench. I revisit this issue in chapter 6.

The sections that follow organize and summarize the dueling arguments with reference to three core issues: the role of the judge in American government, the particular merits and demerits of elective and appointive systems, and the case for incremental reform.

THE ROLE OF THE JUDGE IN AMERICAN GOVERNMENT

The Brief for Appointed Judiciaries

In the United States, the people have ordained and established constitutions in which they delegate to the legislative branch the power to make laws, subject to limits that their constitutions specify. Through their constitutions, the people have delegated to the executive branch the power to implement and enforce laws that the legislature makes. And they have assigned to the judicial branch the power to interpret and apply those laws in the context of cases filed by parties who petition the courts to interpret the law in their favor. Included among the laws that the courts interpret is the constitution itself, which puts courts in the position of upholding the constitution by invalidating other laws that exceed the constitutional authority of the legislative branch to make or of the executive branch to enforce.

This state of affairs, in which adversaries square off against each other in front of a judge who officiates the contest by applying a preexisting body of rules to the end of declaring a victor, conjures an obvious sports analogy. The American Bar Association's Division on Public Education explains that "[j]udges are like umpires in baseball or referees in football or basketball."[2] "Like the ump," the ABA elaborates, judges "call 'em as they see 'em, according to the facts and law—without regard to which side is popular (no home field advantage), without regard to who is 'favored', without regard for what the spectators want, and without regard to whether the judge agrees with the law." In his 2005 Senate confirmation testimony, Chief Justice John Roberts likewise analogized judges to umpires, for the purpose of highlighting the limited role judges play in adjudication. "Umpires don't make the rules," then-judge Roberts cautioned; rather, "they apply them." Thus, in his view, "[t]he role of an umpire and a judge is critical," because "[t]hey make sure everybody plays by the rules. But it is a limited role."[3]

If judges are like umpires, then subjecting judges to popular election is incompatible with their role. In 1996, U.S. Supreme Court Justice John Paul Stevens gave a speech in which he likened the practice of electing judges to "allowing football fans to elect referees"—a practice that he condemned as "profoundly unwise."[4] If we want umpires to "call 'em as they see 'em," then letting the fans decide whether an ump keeps his job is a bad idea because it will motivate umpires to make popular calls, rather than correct ones. The same goes for judges: If we want judges to "make sure everybody plays by the rules," then subjecting judges to popular election is a bad idea because it will motivate them to disregard the rules whenever the rules dictate an unpopular outcome that could jeopardize the judges' tenure.

Social science data support the conclusion that impending elections influence the decisions judges make. One Pennsylvania study found that judges running for retention imposed sentences on criminal defendants for periods of incarceration that were, on average, several months longer than at other times.[5] This occurred in liberal and conservative voting districts alike: judges are at no meaningful risk of losing elections for being too tough on crime, and so risk-averse judges with upcoming elections err on the side of severity, even in liberal districts where the risk of voter backlash for leniency is lower.[6] One study found that supreme court justices in nonpartisan election states are more responsive to voter preferences than in partisan election states in abortion cases—the theory being that in nonpartisan election states, judges have no formal party affiliation to signal their ideological compatibility with voters, and convey that information via their decisions in ideologically charged cases.[7]

In contested election states the threat posed by a challenger substantially increases pressure on incumbents to mollify voters. Hence, during the campaign season, judges subject to partisan elections impose harsher sentences on criminal defendants than judges subject to retention election.[8] In states with noncompetitive retention elections, judges appear to take a "better safe than sorry" approach and issue rulings that align more closely with the liberal or conservative orientation of their voters as elections approach.[9]

In short, judicial elections do not motivate judges to "call 'em as they see 'em." Judicial elections motivate judges to call 'em as voters want 'em. That is as it should be for governors, mayors, legislators, and city council members. Public officials in the legislative and executive branches make and implement public policy on behalf of the constituents they represent. Being responsive to the preferences of those constituents is perfectly compatible with good government in a representative democracy.

But judges are different. "Unlike their counterparts in the political branches," Supreme Court Justice Ruth Bader Ginsburg has explained, "judges are expected to refrain from catering to particular constituencies." [10] Rather, "[t]heir mission is to decide 'individual cases and controversies' on individual records" by "neutrally applying legal principles, and, when necessary, 'stand[ing] up to what is generally supreme in a democracy: the popular will."[11] Unlike other elected officials, judges are not supposed to do what the electorate wants them to do. Hence, judges have been subject to a ubiquitous ethics rule dating back nearly a century, which states that they "shall not be swayed by public clamor or fear of criticism." In a like vein, ethics rules add that judges "shall not permit... political... or other interests or relationships to influence the judge's judicial conduct..."[12]

If the legislature enacts a new statute that violates the supreme law of the state constitution—a constitution that the people adopted generations earlier to protect the rights of those that the new law abridges—then it is incumbent on judges to strike the statute down, regardless of how popular it may be. If voters are unhappy with the result, they can petition their elected representatives to amend the constitution or (if possible) fix the statute. Judicial elections, however, enable the electorate to take the additional step of firing judges who make unpopular rulings—a step that cannot peacefully coexist with the expectation that judges will stand up to popular will. As the American Bar Association's Commission on the 21st Century Judiciary explained, "if the law is to protect the one as well as the many—it is imperative that the administration of justice not become a popularity contest. We need judges who will tell us what the law is and how it applies in individual cases without regard to what the results of the latest opinion poll are...."[13]

The role of unelected federal judges in desegregating the South during the civil rights era offers a classic illustration of "countermajoritarian," appointed courts in action. After the Civil War, the U.S. Constitution was amended to ban slavery, grant African Americans citizenship, extend voting rights to African American men, and guarantee due process rights to all. The Southern states then proceeded to entrench racial segregation in the "Jim Crow" era that followed, via laws that preserved nominal equality between the races. During the civil rights movement of the mid-twentieth century, southern federal courts began to invalidate state and local laws that perpetuated racial inequality through segregation, culminating in the U.S. Supreme Court's decision in *Brown v. Board of Education*, which declared that racial separation was inherently unequal. Those federal judges issued rulings in the teeth of extreme and sometimes violent opposition that would have been insurmountable had the local electorate possessed the power to vote them from office.[14] But for independent, unelected federal judges, Jim Crow laws could have flouted the Constitution's Civil War amendments indefinitely.

The Brief for Elected Judiciaries

Eighteenth century civics imagined independent judges aloft on benches and clothed in ermine robes symbolizing their purity of purpose, who issued crystalline divinations of law that sparkled unobscured by baser influences that cloud the thinking of mere mortals. We have learned some things in the intervening centuries, among them that this is a crock.

First, American judges are not above the political fray but part of it. They are powerful people, whose decisions are fraught with policy implications that affect our lives, liberty, and property. Judges breathe meaning into ambiguously worded laws. Their interpretations of legislative enactments can take statutes in directions their makers never intended. Their interpretations of constitutions can obliterate the validity of statutes altogether. Their decisions have prompted vituperative partisan debate, sparked generations of political protest, and catalyzed civil war.

Second, the law is not mathematics, in which case outcomes are dictated by mechanical application of clear rules to known facts. The reason parties litigate cases "all the way to the Supreme Court" is because the relevant facts and law are uncertain enough to support differing results. Hence, the rulings judges issue in difficult cases—and the resulting legal policies judges make—are not a matter of science, but art, that require the exercise of discretion and judgment.

Third, judges are not mathematicians, but people. As people, judges have varying perspectives on the world that they develop over the course of their lives—perspectives that guide their moral compass, inform their conception of justice, and fuel their ideological inclinations. Those perspectives are influenced by myriad factors, including their upbringing, education, life experience, religion, race, gender, ethnicity, and political affiliation. And the evidence is overwhelming that the policy perspectives unelected judges cultivate over the course of their lives inform the discretion and judgment that they exercise when deciding cases.

In the words of one political scientist, "[t[ ]he assumption that independent judges use their freedom to decide impartially according to law is contradicted by the empirical evidence."[15] Bluntly put, independent judges are policymakers in robes. Political scientists who have generated and reviewed the data have coined the phrase "myth of legality" to characterize stubborn and persistent adherence to the debunked proposition that independent judges disregard extralegal influences and follow the law.[16] And many of those same political scientists have developed an "attitudinal model" to show that the rulings judges make are better explained with reference to a judge's ideological attitudes than operative law.[17]

Chris Bonneau and Melinda Gann Hall punctuate the point concisely, when they write: "Although it is the modern equivalent of declaring that the emperor has no clothes to say so, politically astute observers fully recognize that the basic political preferences of judges influence their votes."[18] It is all fine and well to celebrate the federal courts for dismantling Jim Crow laws during the civil rights era. But if federal judges were truly "countermajoritarian" decision-makers who uphold the law unsullied by their own ideological preferences, they would have ended Jim Crow generations earlier.

Given the inevitability of ideological and other extralegal influences on judicial decision-making, independence from electoral accountability does not free judges to uphold the law; it untethers them to do whatever they damn well please. Insofar as the law has intrinsic meaning, appointed judges are liberated to disregard that meaning and act upon their personal feelings and ideological preferences. Insofar as the law lacks intrinsic meaning and is all in the eye of the beholder, appointive systems dictate that the eye of the elites trumps the eye of the electorate, which is antithetical to the principles of a representative democracy.

Judges are called upon to resolve unanswered questions about ambiguous spaces in the law. When judges fill those spaces by declaring what the law is, they make public policy, and the policy they make should be acceptable to the people they serve to no less an extent for judges than for policymakers in the other branches of government. And the only way to ensure that the public supports the policies judges make is to subject judges to periodic elections.

Social science data reveal that judges decide cases differently in the shadow of impending elections, which shows that judicial elections work as intended. The specter of future elections influences judges to exercise their judgment and discretion with reference to the policy preferences of the electorate, instead of their own idiosyncratic ideological biases that would otherwise hold sway. This state of affairs, in which judges check their own impulses and take the views of their voters into account when making legal policy—or face the consequences—is democracy in action, and wholly compatible with the rule of law. As Bonneau and Hall conclude: "We think it far better for justices to draw upon public perceptions and the prevailing state political climate when resolving difficult disputes than to engage in the unfettered pursuit of their own personal preferences. In fact, strategic contingencies should bring justices into line with the rule of law rather than negate it."[19]

Consider, for example, the defeat of California chief justice Rose Bird in her 1986 retention election, which, as discussed in chapter 2, was a bellwether event in the new politics of judicial elections. In ten years as chief justice, Bird heard sixty-one appeals from death penalty cases and voted to uphold the death penalty in precisely none of them. The operative law that she had taken an oath to uphold provided for the imposition of capital punishment. By refusing to uphold the death penalty across an uninterrupted line of cases, Bird disregarded the law and systematically imposed her own ideological bias against capital punishment in the teeth of the public's policy preferences to the contrary. But for periodic elections, Bird could have flouted the law and the will of the people indefinitely. Conversely, had Bird factored Californians' support for the death penalty into her decision-making, she could have retained her seat. That is not intimidation; that is representative democracy.

THE PARTICULAR MERITS AND DEMERITS OF ELECTIVE AND APPOINTIVE SYSTEMS

The Brief for Appointed Judiciaries

Beyond the core problem that subjecting judges to electoral accountability undermines the umpire-judge's ability to make independent, impartial, and sometimes unpopular calls consistent with the operative facts and law, is the related concern that voters are ill-equipped to hold umpire-judges accountable in acceptable ways. The problem is twofold. First, voters lack the competence to evaluate judicial candidates adequately. Second, voters are too apathetic about judicial races to participate meaningfully.

Evaluating the competence of doctors, lawyers, and other professionals who receive years of specialized training requires expertise. That helps to explain the need for expert witnesses in lawyer malpractice litigation: lay jurors lack the skills to ascertain and apply standards of professional competence unassisted. Most candidates for public office do not need specialized legal training. A good policy analyst with people skills can be a fine legislator without going to law school. A good administrator with leadership skills can be a terrific governor without holding a license to practice law. Thus, the electorate needs no special skills to evaluate those candidates. Voters can listen to the candidates, learn their agendas, and decide for themselves which candidates possess the qualities needed to best represent them and their views.

Judges are different. Judges do not represent the views of their constituents or advocate agendas. They must decide cases between adversaries who argue for opposing interpretations or applications of operative law. It therefore falls to judges to parse relevant language in constitutions, statutes, ordinances, administrative rules, and case precedent, to determine—as impartially as possible—what the law requires before applying that law to resolve disputes between parties. And that requires specialized legal training and experience. Every state establishes the minimum qualifications necessary for judicial officers, and every state requires that judges of general jurisdiction be lawyers.

Without legal training to make an independent assessment of whether judicial candidates exhibit the skills necessary to interpret and apply the law competently, voters must rely on their general knowledge of courts and judges, and the more specific information they can glean about a given race. Their general state of knowledge is woeful. One author has summarized the litany of deplorables in an article about voter ignorance in judicial elections:[20] Fewer than 20 percent of Americans can name the three branches of government—fewer, one infamous survey reported, than can name the Three Stooges. Two-thirds of the public cannot identify a single member of the U.S. Supreme Court and fewer than 3 percent of American teenagers can identify the chief justice. Most survey respondents are unable to identify any state judge at any level of their court system. And a majority is unaware that their state even has a constitution.

Given their lack of specialized skills and general knowledge necessary to evaluate judicial candidates competently, voters are uniquely positioned to make puzzling choices. Consider the example of Alabama chief justice Roy Moore.[21] Shortly after his election in 2000, Moore installed a 2.6-ton granite monument to the Ten Commandments in his courthouse rotunda, and arranged for a Christian television ministry to film the event. Federal courts ordered Moore to remove the monument on the grounds that the display established a religion in violation of the U.S. Constitution, but Moore refused. The debatable issue of whether installing the monument was unconstitutional was beside the inarguable point that by openly disobeying a direct court order, Moore had flouted his oath to follow the law. In 2003, Moore's fellow justices voted unanimously to remove the monument, and later that year, the Alabama Court of the Judiciary voted unanimously to remove Moore from office for misconduct. In 2012, Alabama voters elected Moore to another term as chief justice. In 2015, Moore, acting in defiance of the U.S. Supreme Court's recent ruling in *Obergefell*, directed the state's probate judges to deny marriage licenses to same-sex couples, as discussed in chapter 1. Then, in 2016, the Alabama Court of the Judiciary voted unanimously to suspend Moore for the remainder of his term. The Moore affair may be an outlier, but there is data to support the propositions that appointed judges are disciplined less frequently than their elected counterparts, and that merit selection systems do a better job of weeding out marginal candidates.[22] It is all but inconceivable, for example, that a merit selection nominating commission would deem a former judge, who had been removed for misconduct, qualified to occupy the highest judicial office in the state.

Justice Moore's imbroglio is an extreme example. He became a household name after making a national spectacle of himself—meaning that Alabama voters had plenty of information on hand before they made a puzzling choice. More typically, state judges operate below the electorate's radar. Thus, when it comes to what information voters acquire about judicial races in the new politics of supreme court elections, the usual answer is: what they learn from campaign advertising. But as discussed in chapter 3, campaign advertising often applauds or excoriates judges for the outcomes of cases they decide with little or no regard for whether those outcomes were warranted or required by applicable law. As a consequence, badly informed voters are left with no meaningful basis upon which to distinguish judges who are bungling rogues from those who are blameless messengers, and must shoot indiscriminately.

Highly motivated voters can overcome their information deficit by acquainting themselves with basic civics; consulting judicial candidate voter guides that some jurisdictions publish, reviewing judicial performance evaluations conducted by bar organizations and court systems, seeking out the opinions of legal experts, basing their votes on an assessment of the candidates' qualifications and credentials, and resisting the siren's song of campaign commercials that implore voters to punish incumbent judges for unpopular rulings regardless of applicable law. But "highly motivated" does not describe the average voter in judicial races. In addition to lacking the requisite expertise to evaluate judicial competence, many voters lack the requisite interest in judicial elections to participate. On the typical ballot, judicial races appear toward the bottom, after voters choose their president, senator, congressperson, governor, mayor, and so on. By the time voters reach the "down-ballot" judicial races, there is a well-documented "roll-off," in which an average of 25 percent of the voters who appear at the polls do not cast a ballot in the judicial races.[23]

One common explanation for roll-off is "ballot fatigue," which is a polite way of saying that after standing in the booth for two minutes, voters do not regard the judicial races as important enough to merit an additional thirty seconds of their lives. A second explanation is that voters forgo participating in judicial races because they have not gone to the trouble of acquiring enough information about the candidates to make an intelligent choice. Either way, the result is the same: when the average voter turnout of around 60 percent in years when presidential candidates are on the ballot, and 40 percent in years when they are not, is diminished by an additional 25 percent roll-off in judicial races, it means that a majority of eligible voters can rarely if ever summon the enthusiasm to vote in judicial races. That minority of voters contracts even further if one discounts for those who voted only in the technical sense by flipping levers randomly without knowing whom the candidates were.

Insofar as highly competitive judicial races have the potential to grab voter attention and diminish roll-off, they do so at the expense of the judiciary's legitimacy. As discussed in chapter 2, in 1906, Roscoe Pound criticized judicial elections for "compelling judges to become politicians," which "in many jurisdictions has almost destroyed the traditional respect for the Bench." Pound attributed the phenomenon to "an age in transition," and predicted that the problems it created "will take care of themselves."[24] He predicted wrong. Populist and Progressive Era attacks on federal and state courts would eventually subside, and in many states, the partisan election systems that Pound critiqued would be replaced by nonpartisan election and, later, merit selection systems. But the age of transition never ended, and a century later, the deleterious impact of "compelling judges to become politicians" has, if anything, worsened, as chapter 3 discusses.

Former U.S. Supreme Court justice Sandra Day O'Connor has described judicial elections in the modern era as "tawdry and embarrassing," and has warned that "[t]he public is growing increasingly skeptical of elected judges in particular," whom it has come to regard as "just politicians in robes."[25] As Justice O'Connor added, this bodes ill for the legitimacy of the judiciary generally, because "distrust of the judiciary in any jurisdiction becomes distrust of the judiciary in all jurisdictions."

Two specific features of competitive judicial races in the modern era exacerbate underlying legitimacy problems. First, in the aftermath of the U.S. Supreme Court's decision in *Republican Party of Minnesota v. White*,[26] judicial candidates have a right to campaign like ordinary politicians by taking positions on the issues they will later decide as judges. When judges telegraph how they will decide future cases before the parties are heard, the facts are adduced, or the law is analyzed in the context of the case that is ultimately filed, those judges undermine public confidence in the integrity of the judicial process and the impartiality of the judges involved.

Second, competitive elections are bankrolled by campaign contributions and independent expenditures from individuals and groups with a vested interest in the outcomes of cases that the candidates will decide as judges. There is a widely documented correlation between the campaign support judicial candidates receive and the decisions they later make. One study of 470 justices spanning 28,000 cases across multiple states found that for "judges elected in partisan elections, contributions from various interest groups have a statistically significant relationship with the probability that judges vote for litigants that the interest groups favor."[27] Other studies have replicated these results in states that select judges via partisan and nonpartisan elections, including Alabama, Georgia, Kentucky, Louisiana, Michigan, Montana, Ohio, Pennsylvania, Texas, and Washington.[28] One researcher described the correlation he found as "remarkably close;"[29] another concluded that the contributions judges receive "directly affect judicial decisionmaking,"[30] and two more inferred a "quid pro quo relationship between contributors and votes."[31]

When interest groups give candidates piles of money to win their elections, and those candidates later cast votes in favor of their benefactors, one need not be pathologically suspicious to think that something fishy is going on. And so 76 percent of the public and a surprising 46 percent of judges themselves think that judges are influenced to varying degrees by the campaign contributions they receive.[32] As Justice O'Connor has warned, "This crisis of confidence in the judiciary is real and growing.... Left unaddressed, the perception that justice is for sale will undermine the rule of law that the courts are supposed to uphold."[33] It is telling, that in the aftermath of a bruising $9 million Illinois Supreme Court race, the victor himself commented on the money spent, that "Basically, that's obscene for a judicial race... How can people have faith in the system?"[34]

In my first article on judicial selection, entitled "Why Judicial Elections Stink," I sought to distill the litany of problems associated with judicial elections down to their ironic essence, in a four-part "Axiom of 80."[35] Up to 80 percent of registered voters do not vote in judicial elections. Up to 80 percent of the public that does vote in judicial elections cannot identify the candidates for whom they voted. Up to 80 percent of the public think that the campaign contributions in judicial elections influence judicial decision-making. And yet 80 percent of the public still supports judicial elections. On the last point, however, I predicted that the legitimacy-threatening features of judicial elections would lead public support to erode over time.

This profusion of problems with elected judiciaries disappears if judges are appointed. Once appointed, judges retain the independence necessary to call balls and strikes without fear of reprisal for making unpopular calls. The task of appointing judges is vested in the hands of elected officials or commissions with the time, interest, and expertise to select capable and qualified men and women for the job. And without judicial races to bankroll, interest groups are denied the opportunity to peddle influence via campaign support.

The Brief for Elected Judiciaries

Given the role of elections in promoting judicial accountability, it should come as no surprise that a significant majority of the American public favors an elected judiciary. Political scientist James Gibson has shown that elections enhance the judiciary's legitimacy: the public is more likely to accept judicial decisions with which it disagrees if those decisions are made by elected judges.[36] Conversely, research has revealed that appointments processes can damage the judiciary's legitimacy: in the federal system, fractious confirmation battles diminish public respect for the courts to the extent that they cast judicial nominees as naked political actors.[37]

Then there are claims pressed by the election-phobic, that the judiciary's impartiality and legitimacy will be undermined by the Supreme Court's decision in *Republican Party of Minnesota v. White*. *White* will spawn a new generation of campaigns, critics of the decision argue, in which candidates lock themselves into positions on cases that will come before them as judges before those cases are heard. Such claims are, in a word, mistaken. Studies show no meaningful increase in contestation and competition among state supreme courts after *White*, and a comprehensive study of trial court races after *White* concluded that "[d]espite repeated claims of certain segments of the American Bar Association and the legal community," there is "simply no evidence that the speech environment in these races has devolved into nasty attacks."[38] Thus, the study authors conclude, "partisan elections are not contributing to an unhealthy campaign environment in trial court races."[39]

The new politics of judicial elections has enabled judicial races to realize their potential more fully. Demographic changes—most notably the decline and fall of Democratic Party control in southern states—have created new opportunities for interparty competition. State courts have become forums of choice for litigating contentious social issues. Changes in appellate structure have limited state supreme court dockets to fewer, often more controversial cases. The trial bar and business community have made state courts a battlefield in their struggle to control tort liability and reform. These developments, when coupled with the role of courts in helping or hindering the "war on crime," have elevated the political profile of state courts and the cases they decide. That, in turn, has heightened political interest in judicial races, which has generated more competition for judicial seats, which has funneled more money into judicial races, which has bought more advertising to better inform the electorate about the races, which has piqued voter interest in supreme court elections, which has decreased voter roll-off at the polls.[40] All good. Moreover, research reveals that voters draw relatively sophisticated distinctions between the candidates, by favoring quality candidates with prior judicial experience in races for open seats (where support for the more experienced candidate cannot be attributed to the advantages of incumbency).[41]

When it comes to judicial elections and the role they play in promoting democracy, partisan systems deserve special mention. A candidate's party affiliation conveys a package of information about the candidate's philosophy and ideological orientation that assists voters in making informed choices and reduces roll-off relative to nonpartisan races. Partisan races tend to be more competitive, with fewer uncontested seats, and a higher rate of incumbent turnover, which are hallmarks of a healthy democratic process. Nonpartisan races do not serve their intended purpose of eliminating political party control over judicial selection; rather, they are often nonpartisan in name only and subject to partisan influence and control behind the scenes. As a consequence, stripping candidates of party identifiers serves only to disable candidates from differentiating themselves with voters.[42]

In short, partisan systems deserve credit for promoting hotly contested, highly competitive, democracy-enhancing judicial races. But judicial elections have an important role to play even if races are uncontested, inconsequential affairs much of the time. When incumbent judges do their jobs well enough to remain popular, generate no controversy, and avoid attracting viable opponents, the electorate should not be faulted for remaining disengaged, under-informed, and voting in fewer numbers. But when judges step out of line, elections afford the public an important right to intercede and oust the rogues, which encourages good conduct and deters bad. This may be especially true of trial judges, whose relative anonymity makes their "races" sleepy, often uncontested affairs—unless and until something goes wrong. Two examples that captured national headlines illustrate the point.

In 2016, Santa Clara County judge Aaron Persky sentenced convicted rapist and former Stanford University swimmer Brock Turner to three months of incarceration, with the explanation that the longer prison term prosecutors had recommended would have a "severe impact" on Turner.[43] The sentence provoked national outrage. As the president pro tempore of the California Senate argued, "Judge Persky has put the interest of convicted abusers ahead of interests for victims of sexual assault. To me, it shows he is fundamentally unfit to serve on the bench." The judiciary investigated a complaint against Persky, but declined to discipline him. The remaining avenue available to address the judge's conduct was the electoral process. Persky had recently won uncontested re-election, and with his next election six years off, angry Californians petitioned for a recall election, as authorized by California law, and removed him from office. Although few states provide for judicial recall, the essential point is to underscore how elections can be an antidote to unacceptable judicial conduct when an otherwise indifferent electorate becomes energized.

Likewise in 2016, in Las Vegas, Nevada, Justice of the Peace Conrad Hafen ordered a public defender handcuffed and seated next to inmates who were awaiting their hearings, to teach her "a lesson" for interrupting him after he cut off her argument on behalf of her client. While there was room to argue that the public defender spoke out of turn, subjecting her to such public humiliation was widely regarded as an abuse of power, with sexist overtones.[44] Shortly thereafter, Hafen stood for re-election and was defeated in a landslide, garnering just 24 percent of the vote—a result attributed to voter disapproval of Hafen's conduct earlier that year.[45]

Appointive systems, in contrast, fail at every turn. First, and perhaps foremost, so-called "merit selection" systems do not produce judges who are measurably more meritorious. One study from the 1980s found no discernible differences in the quality of judges chosen by different selection systems.[46] In a more recent and extensive study of the subject, Greg Goelzhauser reached a similar conclusion: "Election underperforms merit selection and appointment on certain measures of educational quality and performance," but overall, "the empirical results suggest that selections yield similarly qualified state supreme court justices."[47] One study conducted by a trio of distinguished law professors found that elected judges wrote more opinions and were more independent.[48] "In other words," Bonneau and Hall conclude from this study, "judges chosen in elections, particularly in partisan elections, are *better* than judges chosen by other methods."[49]

Second, merit selection systems have failed in their efforts to keep the politics out of judicial selection. Merit selection systems delegate to unaccountable commissions the task of creating a candidate pool from which governors select judges—commissions typically dominated by lawyers and judges, who deliberate in black boxes impervious to public scrutiny. Researchers have found that these commissions are subject to a variety of political influences. An early study found evidence of "panel-stacking," in which commissions forced the governor's hand by creating candidate pools limited to one viable choice; and "log-rolling," in which commissioners traded their support for a fellow-commissioner's preferred candidate in exchange for reciprocal favors.[50] A substantial minority of commissioners has reported that their commissions were subject to political influences,[51] and a majority of commission chairs have indicated that politics entered into their deliberations at least "infrequently."[52] One study has shown that lawyer-controlled nominating commissions produce a disproportionate number of liberal judicial nominees, which the author attributes to the liberal-leaning predilections of the bar.[53]

Third, to the extent that merit selection systems seek to preserve the pretense of accountability with periodic retention elections, it is no more than that: a pretense. Retention elections are dreary by design. Who wants to go to the racetrack to watch a solitary horse run a time trial to see whether he qualifies to do it again next year? Nobody—and in the context of retention elections, that means nobody is energized enough to jeopardize incumbency. As consequence, voter roll-off in retention elections is substantially higher than in contested elections.[54] And the average support incumbents receive in retention elections is a whopping 75 percent—far more than the 55–60 percent that would qualify as competitive enough to promote accountability.[55]

THE CASE FOR INCREMENTAL REFORM

Incrementalists are a motley crew of judicial election skeptics, devotees, and agnostics. The judicial election skeptic would concede that elections have been a fixture of the American judicial selection landscape since the 1840s and as dreadful as they may be, are here to stay. For the skeptic-incrementalist, reforms can make the horrors of judicial elections a little less horrible. The judicial election devotee, in contrast, is at peace with an elected judiciary. But for the devotee-incrementalist, the wonders of judicial elections can be made even more wonderful by the occasional tweak. Judicial election agnostics include the occasional, true nonbeliever, and nominal agnostics whose preferences peek out between cracks in the studied neutrality they seek to preserve in an effort to maintain the appearance of objectivity. The agnostic-incrementalist is a pragmatist who seeks to take whichever system she is handed and make it better, with reforms that stand a realistic chance of implementation.

Incrementalists have advocated numerous reform proposals, three of which have gained at least some traction. First, several states have experimented with systems for publicly financing supreme court elections as a means to diminish the delegitimizing if not corrupting influence of special interest money on judicial races. Judicial candidates have a First Amendment right to solicit financial support from groups and individuals in privately funded campaigns, but candidates may agree to refuse campaign contributions from private sources in exchange for public monies with which to campaign. The American Bar Association's Commission on Public Financing of Judicial Campaigns endorsed public financing, concluding that "[t]he more money judges receive from public sources, the less they will have to raise from private groups and individuals who are interested in the outcomes of cases the judges decide, which will reduce the potential for campaign contributions to influence judicial behavior and address the public perception" of such influence.[56]

Second, many states have sought to address concerns over the real or perceived influence of campaign contributions on judicial decision-making by imposing campaign contribution limits and disclosure requirements. Modest campaign contributions in amounts too low to create a reasonable suspicion of influence peddling are harmless, and serve no purpose beyond showing support for the candidate and the judiciary of which the candidate is or may become part. Contribution limits restrict campaign finance to these innocuous displays of support. Disclosure requirements, in turn, dull the blade of influence peddling by keeping voters apprised of who is contributing to which candidates, so that voters might hold candidates accountable when the risk of influence becomes unacceptable.

Third, all states have recusal or disqualification rules that can require judges to withdraw from cases for campaign-related bias.[57] If eliminating elections is a guardrail at the top of the cliff that protects judges from independence, integrity, and impartiality-damaging plunges, then a rigorous disqualification regime is an ambulance at the base of the cliff that deals with the mess after plunges occur. Put another way, disqualification rules can alleviate problems that arise when campaign-related events compromise a judge's impartiality in later cases, by forcing the judge to withdraw from those cases.

One such problem has arisen when an issue comes before the court that the judge, as a judicial candidate, pre-committed to decide in a particular way. For example, in 2010, a West Virginia Supreme Court justice disqualified himself (albeit after adverse publicity, and angrily) from a case that challenged the constitutionality of tort reform legislation. As a judicial candidate, when asked for his views on the legislation, he declared, "I will not vote to overturn it. I will not vote to change it. I will not vote to modify it."[58] The justice may have felt that he could be impartial notwithstanding his prior statements, but from the perspective of an outsider looking in, it seems unlikely that a party challenging the law could get a fair shake from a judge who had committed himself to rejecting the claim before it had even been filed. Hence, the American Bar Association's Model Code of Judicial Conduct provides that if a judge, while a candidate, "commits or appears to commit . . . to reach a particular result or rule in a particular way" in a future case, the judge is later disqualified from hearing that case when it comes before the court.[59]

A second problem that disqualification addresses has arisen when judges are assigned to hear cases in which a party—or someone closely affiliated with a party—has given significant financial support to the judge's election campaign. In *Caperton v. A.T. Massey Coal Co.*,[60] the U.S. Supreme Court ruled that a West Virginia Supreme Court justice violated a party's constitutional right to due process of law when he refused to disqualify himself from a case in which the justice had received campaign support from the opposing party's CEO in amounts sufficient to create a probability of bias. The Court took pains to emphasize that states could avoid due process problems through the simple expedient of establishing their own disqualification rules that subjected judges to recusal before problems reach constitutional magnitude. And virtually every state—including West Virginia—has done just that, by adopting rules requiring judges to disqualify themselves when their "impartiality might reasonably be questioned."[61] Some states have gone further and crafted specific disqualification rules applicable to judges who receive campaign support from parties or their lawyers under circumstances that cast doubt on the judge's impartiality.[62]

CONCLUSION

The case for appointments proceeds from the premise that judges are umpires who can be counted on to call 'em like they see 'em and follow the law only if they do not have voters breathing down their necks, poised to fire judges who make unpopular calls. The case for elections proceeds from the premise that judges are politicians in robes who can be counted on to disregard the law and impose their own ideological preferences unless the electorate is there to keep them in check. In the judicial selection holy wars, the two sides defend their causes with a religious fervor to the end of enlightening their adversaries, or failing that, dominating them by force. This unyieldingly binary debate all but cries out for an answer to the question: Whose cause is righteous? As chapter 5 aims to show, the answer is: both and neither.

5

WHY EVERYONE IS WRONG

Chapter 4 laid out the arguments for and against elective and appointive judiciaries. Those arguments offered differing and sometimes contradictory perspectives on a host of issues. This chapter revisits those arguments to show that both sides make claims that are exaggerated, specious, unfounded, or simply incorrect to varying degrees. Demonstrating the ways in which that is so is one thing. Understanding why it is happening is another, and acquiring an appreciation for why disputants have defended problematic claims so tenaciously is critical to transcending the binary debate that has dominated the judicial selection landscape for generations.

I do not contend that everyone is wrong about everything. To the contrary, there has been a significant volume of superb work that gets it right, and aids in exposing exaggerated claims as such. Even work that overstates its claims can make important contributions to the literature and would be dead right if only it dialed back on its conclusions. My focus here, however, is on work that seeks to support or refute claims contributing to the binary arguments that dominate the public discussion of judicial selection—work that is most vulnerable to being overstated in the service of winning debates. I include in this category social scientists who profess not to make arguments at all, but aim simply to pursue the truth wherever it leads. When an author's "truth" vindicates one side in the debate and trounces the other, authors can become vested in defending the veracity of their conclusions in ways that are all but indistinguishable from "arguments."

DECONSTRUCTING THE ARGUMENTS

The arguments for and against appointed and elected judiciaries, summarized in chapter 4, can logically be divided into four groups: (1) arguments encircling the foundational issue of how to conceptualize judges and their roles, (2) arguments about the specific merits and demerits of elective systems, (3) arguments about the specific pros and cons of appointive systems, and (4) arguments over incremental reforms. The point I seek to make is simple: many of us—myself included—have been wrong to varying degrees.

The Foundational Dispute over Judges and Their Roles

Devotees of appointive systems have argued that judges are like umpires who will impartially apply the rules if insulated from electoral pressure to make calls popular with the public. Proponents of elective systems, in contrast, characterize judges as politicians in robes who will disregard the rules and act on their own ideological predilections unless they are held accountable to the people they serve in periodic elections. I do not mean to suggest that all disputants embrace these metaphors as if they were team mascots. Some do; some do not. My point is that participants in the debate differ on the core question of whether judges who are not subject to electoral accountability are more likely to follow the law or follow their fancy, and that both sides exaggerate the strength of their respective claims.

Proponents of appointive systems who claim categorically that independent judges apply the law like umpires call balls and strikes usually do not encumber their arguments with recourse to facts. Like Chief Justice John Roberts, they are stating principles. They are quoting the Federalist Papers. They are quoting each other. The inconvenient facts reveal that these claims are overstated. The so-called "legal model," which proceeds on the premise that independent judges set extralegal influences aside and apply the law, has been tested in studies of the U.S. Supreme Court and has not fared well. Research shows what 70 percent of the public already believes[1] Supreme Court justices are profoundly influenced by their ideological predilections. In a fascinating study of man versus machine, researchers pitted a computer model against a battery of legal experts and challenged them both to predict the outcomes of cases in the U.S. Supreme Court's upcoming term. Armed with a handful of factors aimed primarily at assessing the ideological and otherwise extralegal tilt of the cases without regard to the specific legal question at stake, the computer predicted 75 percent of case outcomes correctly, compared to 59 percent for the experts.[2]

Ironically, judges may be more like umpires than Chief Justice Roberts would care to admit. In easy cases, when a wild pitch hits the batboy, there is no room for discretion or disagreement and the pitch will be called a ball, which may help to explain why nearly half of the cases before the Supreme Court are decided by unanimous vote. But in close cases (and the Supreme Court's docket is top-heavy with them), when pitchers strive to paint the corners of the plate, the game demands that umpires make judgment calls. In those situations, calling balls and strikes is, as one major league umpire put it, "like [interpreting] the Constitution. The strike zone is a living, breathing document."[3]

Insofar as independent judges exercise discretion influenced by their policy preferences, it lends credence to the argument of election proponents that judges are policymakers in robes who, like policymakers in other branches of government, should be constrained by the people they serve. Election opponents point to data showing that state judges decide differently when elections approach, as if that is a flaw of elective systems when it may be a feature. Who is to say that the rule of law is not better served when elections are impending and judges are motivated to think strategically; set their idiosyncratic, ideological predilections aside; and allow the views of the many to inform the views of the one?[4] Partisan elections in particular can better ensure informed accountability by fostering competitive campaigns that grab voter attention and align candidates with their party affiliations, which offers voters access to basic information about the candidates' philosophy and ideology.

But this pro-election argument is also overstated. First, it proceeds on the problematic assumption that we can generalize from studies of U.S. Supreme Court justices to conclude that appointed judges categorically are driven by their ideological predilections and unconstrained by law.[5] Unlike U.S. Supreme Court justices, other appointed judges, including federal judges in the circuit and district courts, and state judges at all levels in jurisdictions with appointive systems are not at the apex of the organizational chart, but occupy "lower courts." As such, they are foot soldiers constrained by the precedent of the U.S. Supreme Court itself, and by a legal culture that assigns lower courts a different role in law-making relative to the U.S. Supreme Court. Researchers have found that the influence of ideology on judicial decision-making is significantly less for federal circuit judges than for justices on the U.S. Supreme Court.[6] They have likewise found that U.S. Supreme Court precedent exerts a "tremendous influence" on the decision-making of state supreme court justices—elected and appointed alike.[7] In short, law operates as a constraint on the decision-making of appointed judges in lower courts in ways that it does not for justices on the U.S. Supreme Court. Reliance on studies of the U.S. Supreme Court to support the claim that appointed judges in state systems are unfettered by law exaggerates that argument.

Second, the claim that electoral pressure promotes the rule of law is counterintuitive and contradicted by data. States require judges to have legal training because knowing how to parse legal texts in relation to each other and assimilate a body of law in the context of deciding specific, fact-sensitive cases requires specialized skills. The notion that voters, unskilled at law and armed only with information acquired from campaign advertising, could better assess the rule of law in cases that experienced state supreme court justices decide only after reading the briefs, reviewing the transcripts, hearing the arguments, and researching the law, herniates credulity. Because voters are ill-equipped to know what the operative facts and law are, the political pressure they bring to bear on judges in the shadow of elections is not to follow applicable law, but to follow voter policy preferences, applicable law notwithstanding. One study has found that partisan elected supreme courts are twice as likely as their appointed counterparts to overturn existing law in the form of established precedent.[8] Another study has found that state supreme courts followed binding U.S. Supreme Court precedent less frequently than federal circuit court judges, and attributed the difference to state courts making choices "less likely to garner public disapproval."[9] And as discussed in chapter 1, focus groups of voters who ousted three members of the Iowa Supreme Court for upholding the right of same-sex couples to marry objected to same-sex marriage without regard to the merits of the constitutional question that the Court decided by unanimous vote.[10]

Third, ardent judicial election proponents arguably overstate the accountability-enhancing features of partisan election systems. One important study found that judges were more likely to align their rulings with voter preferences in nonpartisan elections than partisan. The researchers speculated that because nonpartisan judges could not rely on their party affiliations to win voter support, they conveyed their alignment with voters via rulings that were more sensitive to public opinion. This finding led the researchers to conclude that, "partisan labels inhibit democratic accountability."[11]

Such a conclusion, however, may also be overstated. Partisan elections focus on voter choice in greater relation to the candidates' party affiliations and the philosophical differences those affiliations connote. Nonpartisan elections focus on voter choice in greater relation to the high-profile cases those judges decide. Both promote democratic accountability, but in different ways. Moreover, partisan elections arguably improve democratic accountability relative to nonpartisan by increasing voter interest and participation. And, of course, for election skeptics, the so-called virtues of democratic accountability that both systems tout are better characterized as vices that compromise the ability of elected judges to disregard public clamor and uphold the law, as their oaths of office and codes of conduct require.

Put simply, judges are neither umpires nor politicians in robes, and they are both. With exceptions, disputants in the binary judicial selection debate have opted against coming to terms with such complexity in favor of characterizing judges as cartoonish balloons in the service of arguments that are easy to inflate and puncture. That has yielded conversations colorful and festive, but results that are not especially durable.

The Specific Arguments for and against Elective Systems

Beyond the foundational question of whether judges are more like umpires who should be protected from intimidation by the fans, or politicians who should be accountable to their constituents, is a cluster of more specific arguments relevant to elections. Is the electorate too incompetent, ignorant, and apathetic to hold judges accountable in desirable ways? Does the electoral process undermine the judiciary's legitimacy, when judicial candidates are forced to campaign like ordinary politicians, take positions on issues they will decide as judges, and raise money from individuals and organizations with business before the courts? Team appointments shouts "yes!" Team elections bellows "no!"

Once again, the disputants exaggerate their claims. When arguing that voters are too unknowledgeable to hold judges accountable in meaningful ways, opponents of judicial elections rely on studies that distort the extent of voter ignorance, with a one-two punch. First, those studies often ask open-ended questions that require respondents to recall information from memory, which is much more difficult than closed-ended questions that ask respondents to recall information from a list of options.[12] Second, researchers can be unduly exacting in the criteria they impose for a "correct" answer. For example, one study, which found that only 10 percent of the public knew that William Rehnquist was the chief justice of the United States, coded as "incorrect" responses that identified him as the "main guy" or "head honcho" on the Supreme Court.[13] When these methodological flaws are corrected, the results change: A subsequent study found that solid majorities of the American public know that Supreme Court justices are appointed, that they serve life terms, and that they exercise the power of judicial review.[14] These findings led the authors to conclude that the public knows "far more" about the Supreme Court than is typically supposed, and that "the American people may in fact know enough about law and courts to be able to perform their assigned function as constituents of the contemporary judicial system in the United States."[15]

Bringing the research closer to home, studies of voter choices in state supreme court elections challenge claims (I, among others, have made) that voters are too ignorant to make intelligent choices. Chris Bonneau and Melinda Gann Hall found that in judicial races for open seats (where neither candidate possessed an incumbency advantage), candidates with prior judicial experience performed "almost five percent better than their inexperienced counterparts," leading them to conclude that "voters in state supreme court elections make fairly sophisticated candidate-based evaluations."[16]

These comparatively optimistic assessments of voter knowledge and acumen, however, are exaggerated too. The basic fact that the U.S. Supreme Court is comprised of life-appointed judges who exercise judicial review is foundational, and constitutes about as little as one can know about the Supreme Court and claim to know anything. When knowledge of that fact is tested by vivisecting the question into three subparts—Are the justices appointed? Do they receive life tenure? Do they exercise judicial review?—a majority of respondents can answer each subpart correctly, but only 44 percent of respondents can correctly answer all three.[17] I do not begrudge the authors their optimistic, "glass is 44% full" outlook, but there is room to argue that this result falls short of repudiating concerns about voter ignorance.

Moreover, studies testing the public's knowledge of the U.S. Supreme Court tell us nothing about their knowledge of state courts, which are the only courts of relevance to a study of judicial elections. When one of the researchers who authored the U.S. Supreme Court study asked respondents the same three questions about their state supreme court, he found that 24 percent knew that their state's supreme court justices were elected, 33 percent knew that the justices served fixed terms, 46 percent knew that the court exercised judicial review, and just over 7 percent knew the answer to all three—figures that the author acknowledges are "dismally low."[18]

Pervasive public ignorance of basic facts about state court systems does not necessarily mean that voters are ignorant of issues relevant to judicial races—a counterpoint corroborated by Bonneau and Hall's study, which shows that the electorate favors "quality" candidates with prior judicial experience. But the authors climb out onto a limb of data too slender to support the weight of their conclusions. Their finding—that candidates with prior judicial experience garner nearly 5 percent more voter support than those without—refutes assertions that voter choices are utterly random. But whether that finding supports the conclusion that voters make "fairly sophisticated . . . evaluations" of candidate quality is another matter. We do no not know whether voters are even aware that the candidates they prefer have prior judicial experience. They may vote for those candidates simply because voters recognize the candidates' names,[19] or because those candidates are more accomplished campaigners by virtue of having run and won judicial races in the past—neither of which has anything to do with the candidate's judicial qualifications. Of those who are aware of a candidate's prior judicial experience, some may be misled into thinking that the candidate is the incumbent, making work experience more relevant than is the case.[20] In short, we know that candidates with prior judicial experience receive more voter support. Whether that is because voters make "fairly sophisticated" choices based on candidate "quality," or because candidates with prior judicial experience enjoy other tactical advantages irrelevant to their qualifications, we do not know.

Exaggerated claims likewise color the public discussion of voter apathy and indifference. A claim I made in an early article, that as much as 80 percent of the public lacks the enthusiasm to vote in judicial elections, is technically true in some races if one combines the percentage of eligible voters who appear at the polls but do not cast ballots in judicial races with the much higher percentage of eligible voters who do not show up at all. Conflating voter apathy generally with voter apathy in judicial races specifically yields a flashy data point that overstates the apathy for which judicial races can fairly be held responsible. The more relevant figure is the 25 percent average roll-off in judicial races, but even that is misleading insofar as it homogenizes dramatic variations in roll-off across the states by combining the data from partisan, nonpartisan, and retention election states. In partisan races, roll-off averages only 11.2% percent[21] which reveals an intuitive truth: voter apathy declines if election campaigns are more interesting; and expensive, hotly contested partisan races make election campaigns more interesting.

Before we roar three huzzahs for elections and declare the apathy problem solved, it is worth noting the extent to which the healing powers of the high-stakes, partisan election elixir can be overhyped. First, the capacity of big spending in judicial races to diminish roll-off is confined to state supreme courts; throwing more money at judicial races does not diminish roll-off in lower court contests, where candidates struggle to attract voter attention.[22] Second, one reason voter roll-off declines in states with partisan judicial elections is that in around half of those states, voters are permitted to vote a straight-party ticket, which enables them to cast their ballot for all the Republicans or all the Democrats on the ballot by pulling a single lever. The straight-ticket option is thus a default that decreases roll-off in judicial elections[23] for reasons having nothing to do with heightened voter interest in those races. Conversely, in states with nonpartisan or retention elections, the straight-ticket option increases roll-off by leading voters to leave the booth after pulling the master lever before voting in the down-ballot, nonpartisan races, which exaggerates the extent to which partisan elections diminish voter apathy relative to other systems.[24] Third, partisan elections decrease but do not eliminate roll-off. Voter apathy thus remains a legitimate if diminished concern, and raises the question of whether the benefits of the partial cure to voter apathy that fractious, partisan elections offer outweigh other costs that partisan elections impose.

Finally, claims relating to the impact of judicial elections on court legitimacy have also been skewed. The pervasive rant that the new politics of judicial elections undermines public confidence in the courts has, for the most part, been the product of ceiling vent analysis: Lawyers, judges, law professors, and policy wonks have leaned back in their office chairs, and speculated that the impact of money, attack advertising, and campaign promises on public confidence in judicial impartiality cannot be good. But these data-free observations often overlook an important and intuitively sensible point that research confirms: People have more confidence in governmental institutions over which they exert a measure of control. Hence, judicial elections enhance legitimacy. The judiciary's legitimacy can be diminished by attack advertising and the perception that campaign contributions buy influence, but a body of research reveals that these concerns do not override the legitimizing effects of elections.[25] With respect to campaign promises, one study has found that "promises to decide cases in specified ways have no consequences at all for the legitimacy of the institution."[26]

On the flip side, the body of research to which I alluded in the previous paragraph may have made too much of too little and overstated its conclusions as a consequence. That research has generalized from studies in only two states—Kentucky and Pennsylvania. A more recent, nationwide study suggests the possibility that when judicial races become too contentious, the delegitimizing costs of elections can exceed the legitimizing benefits, relative to appointive systems.[27] In the study finding that campaign promises had no adverse impact on legitimacy, respondents reacted to a hypothetical judge who promised to decide various issues "the way that most people...want them decided."[28] So vague a "promise" sidesteps the core concern campaign promises raise—that by precommitting to decide a specific issue in a specific way, the judge's ability to give that issue a fair hearing when it comes before the court appears compromised. As a consequence, the data shows only that the public is unperturbed by judges who promise to be popular,[29] and does not support the more sweeping conclusion that the public is unconcerned by "promises to decide cases in specified ways."

One important sub-argument in the legitimacy wars offers another example of mutual overreach. In 2002, the Supreme Court decided *Republican Party of Minnesota v. White*, in which the Court held that judicial candidates have a First Amendment right to announce their views on issues that are likely to come before the candidates as judges. Election opponents responded with predictions of impending catastrophe that judicial campaigns would devolve into a *Lord of the Flies* remake, as judges and their challengers would grapple to win votes by effectively announcing how they would rule on hot-button issues before the issues were briefed and argued.[30] For their part, election proponents have simply dismissed such claims as categorically wrong, because the dire predictions have never materialized.[31] Neither side, however, acknowledges a plausible alternative between these all-or-nothing claims: The dire predictions of *White*'s critics have never materialized, but perhaps that is because the predictions themselves served their purpose. The predictions were alarmist and overwrought, but those who made them were not social scientists stating hypotheses. They were lawyers, judges, and law professors issuing warnings. The subtext of those warnings was that one has a right to do things that are not right to do, and that in our legal culture it is not right for judges to announce their views on issues and cases before they are heard. Viewed in this way, the truth represents a triumph for neither election proponents nor opponents but for the persistence of a legal culture that responded to a threat by hunkering down and refusing to budge.

In short, when it comes to arguments for and against elected judiciaries, overstated and under-supported claims abound. As discussed in the next section, the same may be said of arguments for and against appointed judiciaries.

The Specific Arguments for and against Appointive Systems

Insofar as arguments for and against elected judiciaries are backhanded arguments against and for appointed judiciaries, the preceding discussion carries over here. There are, however, three additional issues specific to appointive systems in general and merit selection systems in particular. Do appointive systems (including merit selection) produce more qualified judges? Is merit selection a less politicized alternative to contested elections? Are the retention elections that merit selection systems employ preferable to contested elections? Proponents of appointive systems cheer "yes"; proponents of elective systems boom "no." Once again, the arguments on both sides are often overstated or unsupported, and sometimes simply wrong.

The essential argument for merit selection systems is one that those systems wear on their sleeves: Their judges are selected based on "merit," and are therefore more qualified than their elected counterparts. The historical basis for this claim is a "stands to reason" argument: Surely, judges chosen by expert commissions dedicated to identifying the best candidates will yield better qualified judges than elective systems, where undiscerning voters choose between candidates who made their way onto the ballot for reasons that have more to do with their skills as politicians than their credentials as jurists. But social science has exposed such claims as grossly overstated, if not false. The best evidence shows that with insignificant exceptions elected and appointed judges are, on average, comparably credentialed.[32]

That said, election proponents may overplay their hand when they reference this empirical evidence to support the more sweeping conclusion that "schemes other than partisan elections fail to improve the quality of the bench."[33] First, early research indicates that merit selection systems do a better job than contested election systems of producing a barrel with fewer bad apples, by screening out the least qualified judicial candidates.[34] Second, comparing resumes may be a convenient way to measure the "quality of the bench," but does not capture the intangibles of judicial temperament essential to good judging. Codes of conduct prohibit judges from being people-pleasers on pain of discipline. Judges must not be "swayed by public clamor or fear of criticism."[35] They shall not "make any public statement" that could affect a pending case.[36] Nor are they permitted to "make pledges, promises or commitments" concerning their future decisions as judges.[37]

Winning elections, however, is all about pleasing people, being responsive to clamor and criticism, maintaining open channels of communication with voters, and making campaign promises. This suggests that judicial aspirants who seek office via contested elections may struggle to preserve the necessary judicial temperament more often than their appointed counterparts. And there is some evidence from states with mixed systems (which appoint some judges and elect others) that elected judges are subject to discipline more often than their appointed counterparts.[38]

Finally, election proponents have gone too far by touting as "excellent"[39] and "breakthrough" a study upon which they rely to show that elected judges are "better."[40] In this study, the authors concluded that elected judges were more "productive" than appointed judges because elected judges wrote more opinions, and were more "independent" because they disagreed with "co-partisans" (fellow justices who share party affiliation) on their courts more frequently.[41] Critical to the conclusion that elected judges were more productive than their appointed counterparts was the finding that they wrote more concurring and dissenting opinions.[42] This conclusion is based on the contestable premise that writing fewer concurrences and dissents is the mark of a "lazy" judge,[43] when it is at least as likely the mark of a less quarrelsome judge who strives to promote productivity on a collegial court by forgoing digressive secondary opinions that fracture consensus unnecessarily. Accepting the dubious premise that a judge's relative independence is an appropriate "performance" standard (a premise that should be doubly doubtful to election proponents who condemn appointive systems because they afford judges too much independence), measuring judicial independence with reference to whether judges vote independently from each other[44] is problematic. The independence of relevance to judicial selection is the independence of judges from those who control judicial selection and tenure. When elected judges disagree with each other more frequently via concurrences and dissents, it seems more likely indicative of dependent judges strategically tailoring their views to preserve voter support in the shadow of impending elections.

Merit selection was devised as a mechanism to depoliticize judicial selection relative to preexisting methods. In lieu of the bare-knuckle politics of contested elections or the politics of cronyism inherent in traditional appointive systems, merit selection promised a new way: judicial selection by apolitical, expert commissions. The claim that merit selection systems take the politics out of judicial selection is rooted in the unsupported assumption that a commission of unelected lawyers, judges, and laypeople will make apolitical assessments of applicants for judicial office. What evidence we have shows that this assumption is flawed: as elaborated in chapter 4, there have been reports of vote-trading or log-rolling within commissions, and commission manipulation of candidate pools that effectively disempowered the governor by presenting him or her with a list of nominees that include only one viable choice. Moreover, commissioners have reported being subject to political pressure. In an early, multistate study of merit selection commissions, 49 percent of commissioners reported that political influences or considerations were introduced into commission deliberations at least infrequently.[45]

Election proponents expose the weaknesses of claims that merit selection depoliticizes judicial selection, but in so doing take their arguments a step too far in the opposite direction. In the most comprehensive and compelling argument to date for partisan election of state supreme court justices, the authors characterize the claim that "appointments schemes take the politics out of judicial selection" as a "myth," adding that "appointment systems merely relocate politics from the electorate to political elites."[46] The one modern example they discuss in support of this conclusion is the U.S. Supreme Court.[47] Such an argument proceeds on the tenuous and data-free assumption that the partisan politics in play when the U.S. Senate confirms the president's nominee to serve on the most visible and powerful court in the nation are the same as when the Maine Senate confirms the governor's nominee for the state supreme court.

Even if traditional appointive systems are as politicized as this argument implies, the limited evidence we have suggests that the same may not be true of merit selection systems. In the early study discussed above, only 12 percent of commissioners reported that political considerations entered into their deliberations "always" or "frequently."[48] Moreover, of the 49 percent who reported that such considerations entered into their deliberations at least infrequently, only 7 percent (3 percent of the total) thought that those considerations were of "decisive importance" on those occasions when they were introduced.[49]

One study, often cited to show ideological bias in merit selection, found that "merit systems select judiciaries with ideological preferences to the left of those that would have been selected by the public or its elected representatives."[50] The author postulated that because lawyers were more liberal than the general population, lawyer-dominated selection commissions favored liberal-leaning applicants;[51] hence, merit selection did not "remove[] politics from judicial selection," but "simply move[d] the politics of judicial selection into closer alignment with the ideological preferences of the bar."[52]

But here is the problem: The study does not compare the ideological makeup of the applicant pool to the ideological makeup of the nominees selected from that pool. If the author's assumption is correct—that lawyers are more liberal than the general population (and there is some empirical support for that assumption)—then one would expect the applicant pool, comprised entirely of lawyers, to be more liberal than the general population as well. Hypothetically, if 55 percent of the applicant pool is liberal, and 55 percent of commission nominees are liberal, it does not imply that nominating commissions are playing politics—it implies that politics played no part in commission review. Under these circumstances, one may still fault merit selection systems for failing to nominate a disproportionate percentage of conservative applicants to compensate for ideological imbalance in the applicant pool. If so, however, the fault lies not in merit selection's failure to take the politics out of judicial selection, but its failure to put the politics back in.[53]

Finally, proponents of merit selection argue that the retention election component included in many merit selection regimes offers the best of both worlds: Meaningful accountability to the electorate without meaningful encroachment on judicial independence values. The unsupported claim that retention elections offer meaningful accountability is belied by the data, which show that non-retention events are on a par with credible Bigfoot sightings: rare, bordering on apocryphal, with non-retention rates hovering at 1 percent.[54] At the same time, research reveals that unwarranted fear of non-retention nonetheless compromises judicial independence by leading judges to align their votes with electoral preferences as elections near (albeit to a lesser extent than their counterparts facing contested elections).[55] Hence, retention elections offer the worst of both worlds: dependence without accountability.

So despairing a conclusion, however, may go too far in the opposite direction. A measure of electoral accountability is achieved if the threat of non-retention leads judges to be mindful of the electorate's preferences—which studies show to be the case—even if actual non-retention rates are low.[56] And while that responsiveness evidences a measure of judicial dependence, it is a lesser measure than in contested elections. Moreover, recent trends suggest that spending in retention elections is on the rise, which implies the possibility that retention elections may become more meaningful affairs. To that extent, retention elections may be less like heaven or hell on earth than they are purgatory.

Arguments over Incremental Reforms

Finally, there are arguments over the merits of incremental reforms. Will public-financing, contribution limits, or disclosure requirements diminish the perception, if not the reality, that justice is for sale in judicial elections? Can a rigorous disqualification regime preserve the integrity of the judicial process by forcing judges to withdraw from cases in which campaign-related events call their impartiality into question? Reformers say yes; others have their doubts.

Public financing proposals can fairly be characterized as wishful thinking. Several states have implemented public financing regimes, and none have succeeded. There is chronic public ambivalence over using tax dollars to finance the electioneering of judicial candidates in amounts sufficient to support competitive elections. Moreover, public financing regimes cannot abridge the speech of individuals and organizations by preventing them from spending astronomical sums on independent campaigns in support of their preferred candidates. In the infamous case of *Caperton v. A.H. Massey Coal Co.*, for example, the defendant's CEO contributed a modest sum to a West Virginia Supreme Court candidate's campaign committee (while the CEO's company had a case pending before the West Virginia Supreme Court), and funneled millions into a successful independent campaign on that candidate's behalf.[57] If West Virginia had a public financing system in place, it could have prevented the harmless direct contribution, assuming that the candidates agreed to accept public funding in exchange for their promise not to accept private contributions. But public financing could have done nothing to prevent the multimillion-dollar independent campaign that tainted the West Virginia Supreme Court's decision and tilted the outcome in the defendant's favor.

As long as the U.S. Supreme Court defines protectable "speech" to include offering financial support to judicial candidates, the ability of public financing systems to reduce the perceived influence of special interest money in judicial races will be limited to direct contributions. That said, it may be premature to bury public financing systems just yet. One study of public financing in North Carolina found that supreme court justices aligned their votes with the preferences of interest groups that campaigned independently on their behalf less frequently after public financing was introduced than before.[58] This implies the possibility that public funding creates psychological distance between judges and their supporters that may weaken their bond. In short, claims that public financing will cure what ails electoral judiciaries on the one hand, or are a complete waste of tax dollars that do nothing at all, on the other, are both overblown.

Disclosure rules promote openness in government by forcing donors to reveal themselves and the dollar value of their support. The utility of disclosure rules, however, is limited in two ways. First, thanks to the vagaries of campaign finance laws, campaign supporters can evade disclosure requirements by organizing themselves as nonprofit, social welfare organizations, which are not required to disclose their donors.[59] Second, to the extent such statutory gaps can be filled, it may be unduly optimistic to hope that ordinary voters will become aware of such disclosures in any but the most vigorously contested judicial campaigns. As with public financing, claims that disclosure is either a sure-cure, or so much snake oil, are both overhyped.

Disqualification is likewise no panacea. The ABA Judicial Division has thwarted efforts to amend the Model Code of Judicial Conduct to require disqualification when a judge receives significant independent campaign support from an individual or organization affiliated with a party who appears before that judge. The official explanation is that judges in the Judicial Division regard disqualification under such circumstances a matter of procedure rather than ethics, which has no place in the Model Code.[60] Such a position is difficult to square with the existing Code, which already requires judges to disqualify themselves from cases in which they have received direct contributions from parties or lawyers in excess of amounts left for the states to specify. Insofar as judges create a perception of bias when they preside over cases in which a party or lawyer has lent excessive support to the judge's election campaign—regardless of whether that support is provided via direct contributions or independent expenditures—the ethical problem is essentially the same.

The reality is that judges depend on campaign support to win elections, and interested individuals and groups lose their incentive to support the campaigns of like-minded candidates if that support will disqualify those candidates from hearing the cases that those individuals and groups want the candidates to decide. And so, state supreme court justices in states with hotly contested elections have sometimes exhibited continued reluctance to disqualify in the teeth of perception problems created when they hear cases of interest to their benefactors.[61]

Moreover, disqualification is a means to address perception problems after they arise, and does nothing to prevent those problems from arising in the first place. A pair of scholars has found that disqualification does not restore public confidence in the impartiality of the disqualified judge, which suggests that disqualification does not cure the taint that impartiality-damaging conduct creates.[62]

To show that disqualification is no cure-all, however, is not to show that disqualification is useless. Even if disqualification does not restore the public's confidence generally, it all but goes without saying that it improves the confidence of parties and their counsel, who would otherwise have their cases heard by a judge whose impartiality was in doubt. As with public financing and disclosure, the truth about disqualification regimes falls between exaggerated opposing arguments that they will achieve all or nothing.

WHY DISPUTANTS OVERSTATE THEIR CLAIMS

To this point, I have simply catalogued the array of flaws and exaggerations disputants in the judicial selection debate have made. In the remainder of the chapter, I offer four explanations for why participants in judicial selection showdowns have tortured or disregarded the data in pursuit of stated or implied normative agendas. What makes these explanations interesting is that none of them depends on disputants consciously misrepresenting the truth in the teeth of facts that undercut their claims. I do not deny the possibility that the isolated prevaricator has joined the judicial selection debate from time to time. Liars are out there, and purveyors of "alternative facts" and "fake news" are charlatans who must be exposed. But I take Abraham Lincoln's admonition to heart that "you cannot fool all of the people, all of the time"—meaning that one can neither sustain nor explain centuries of disagreement and uncertainty over how judges should be selected as the result of dissemblers perpetually disseminating disinformation.

PATH DEPENDENCE AND COMPETING NARRATIVES

Participants in the debates summarized in chapter 4 tend to employ one of two distinct narratives. The law narrative claims that judges are different from public officials in the other, "political" branches of government.

If afforded independence from the electorate, the law narrative posits, judges will make decisions based on the operative facts and law, rather than the whims of voters or the preferences of campaign supporters. Hence, appointed judiciaries are best. The politics narrative claims, in contrast, that judges are politicians in robes. If rendered independent from the electorate, the politics narrative asserts that judges will make decisions based on their own political or ideological preferences, rather than operative facts and law or the public's policy preferences. Hence, elected judiciaries are best.

The legal and political science communities both seek to understand and explain the decisions and conduct of judges and other public officials. Members of the legal community have opted into a culture that takes law seriously and proceeds from the premise that law is of central relevance to the choices judges make. Members of the political science community, in contrast, have immersed themselves in a culture that takes politics seriously, and conceptualizes judges as political actors whose legal rulings can best be explained in political terms. As a consequence, when it comes to judicial selection, law professors, judges, and lawyers (with exceptions) tend to align themselves with the law narrative. Political scientists and public officials without legal backgrounds (also with exceptions) tend to exhibit greater sympathy for the politics narrative.

The allegiance that disputants show for their preferred narrative may be attributable, at least in part, to what political scientists call "path dependence." Path dependence proceeds from the premise that "what happens at an earlier point in time will affect the possible outcomes of a sequence of events occurring at a later point in time."[63] Historical practice emerges over time to shape the thinking of decision-makers in ways that structure and limit the conclusions they are willing to reach. Those who begin on the path of the law narrative are led to the conclusion that elective systems are anathema. Those who begin on the path of the politics narrative are led to conclude that appointive systems are misguided. In that way, paths of analysis that an institution develops can become ruts that limit their perceived options. Although path dependence emerged as a way to explain the constrains under which institutions operate, two scholars—not coincidentally, both law professors and political scientists—have argued that the disciplinary divide between the legal and political science communities is attributable to a form of path dependence that has complicated the ability of each to see beyond the confines of their own paths, learn from each other, and seek common ground.[64]

Participants in the judicial selection debate are not limited to members of the law and politics camps. But those camps frame the issues for the public debate, and to that extent perpetuate a false dichotomy that renders consensus elusive.

MOTIVATED REASONING AND ASSIMILATION BIAS

Participants in the judicial selection debate may subconsciously interpret and resolve gaps and ambiguities in the applicable facts, in favor of whichever system of judicial selection they are predisposed to prefer. To understand how this works, I bring a better-studied analog into play: how judges subconsciously interpret gaps and ambiguities in applicable facts and law to favor case outcomes that align with their ideological preferences.

Political scientists who study judges have developed an "attitudinal model" of judicial decision-making, which has shown how judges are influenced by their attitudes or ideological predilections.[65] They have made that showing by coding parties and issues that come before the courts with reference to whether judicial rulings in favor of a given party on a given issue would yield a liberal or conservative outcome. Then, researchers compare those outcomes to the ideological orientation of the deciding judges. In the federal system, where most of this research has been conducted, a judge's ideological orientation is determined with reference to the party affiliations of the presidents who nominated them, together with other information available at the time of the judge's appointment. In the U.S. Supreme Court, which answers to no higher court and which has a docket largely limited to a small number of divisive, often politically charged cases, the influence of a justice's ideological orientation on case outcomes is profound.[66] The impact of ideological influence declines in the lower courts, but is still significant.[67]

An inference one could draw from this data is that federal judges are politicians in robes, who willfully disregard the law and issue rulings that further their ideological agendas to the extent they can get away with it. But judges emphatically and categorically deny that this is so, and swear allegiance to the rule of law[68]—which means either that judges categorically are bald-faced liars who consciously violate their oaths of office at every opportunity, or something else is going on.

One plausible, alternative inference, is that judges engage in "motivated reasoning," by subconsciously favoring legal arguments that resonate with their policy predilections when the operative facts or law are ambiguous enough to render the correct outcome unclear.[69] In easier cases, when the law and facts are clear, ideology plays less of a role, which helps to explain why attitudinal influences are less pronounced in lower courts. In hard cases, however, when the law or facts are ambiguous and the judge is confronted with two plausible legal arguments in support of opposite conclusions, the judge must make a judgment call as to which argument is correct or best. In such cases, the judge must bring her background, education, experience, common sense, and legal philosophy to bear in deciding which argument is the winner. That conservative and liberal judges would reach different conclusions in close cases is thus unsurprising, and is completely consistent with the proposition that judges give us their best assessment of what the law requires. But there is no denying that, at the margins, ideology influences their assessments in these cases.

The same may be true of social scientists, law professors (myself included), and others who think and write about how judges should be selected. We swear allegiance to facts, data, and science, much as judges swear to uphold the law. Confronted with two plausible judicial selection arguments in opposition, disputants are subconsciously motivated to resolve uncertainties in favor of arguments that are compatible with their preexisting attitudes. It is akin to what cognitive psychologists call "assimilation bias," in which people are predisposed to assimilate new information in ways that are consistent with their previously held views.

Thus, for example, the data shows that judges sentence criminal defendants more harshly when elections are impending. Election proponents assimilate this data by thinking of sentencing as a form of policymaking that is better done when the views of the public that judges serve are taken into account. Thus, the data shows that elections work magnificently. Election opponents assimilate this same data by thinking of sentencing as a form of legal judgment that is corrupted by voters who pressure judges to make popular choices. Thus, the data shows that elections are an abomination.

Research corroborates the common-sense suspicion that scholars are subject to the influence of biases akin to motivated reasoning.[70] And motivated reasoning may help to explain occasional departures from "path dependence," discussed in the preceding section on "Path Dependence and Competing Narratives." For example, insofar as merit selection systems are suspected to produce more liberal judges than election systems (as some research shows),[71] conservative groups within the legal community, such as the Federalist Society, may be motivated to support partisan election systems. In a similar vein, judges who prevail in states with contested elections may be predisposed to extol the wisdom of the electorate that selected them and support contested elections. Conversely, political scientists who study (because they value) procedural justice, and worry about the impact of judicial elections on the litigating public (as distinguished from the voting public), may part ways with the politics narrative.[72]

COPING WITH COGNITIVE DISSONANCE

The persistence of unyielding arguments for judicial appointments and elections in the teeth of evidence that such arguments are exaggerated and wrong may also be the result of a coping mechanism to relieve what psychologists call "cognitive dissonance."[73] Confronted with new information that contradicts their preexisting view on judicial selection, disputants seek ways to relieve the resulting dissonance. They could admit error and change their views, but in the context of a sharply divided, binary debate in which professional reputations rest on the rightness of previous conclusions, that pill can be difficult to swallow. The easier course is to rationalize the contradiction by marginalizing, qualifying, or disregarding the new information, or bolstering tenuous arguments compatible with preexisting views.

Cognitive dissonance and motivated reasoning/assimilation bias are related, in that both are means by which people reconcile competing claims in light of their preexisting perspectives. But assimilation bias, as I use it here, is a finer tool that leads people to analyze legitimate ambiguities between competing factual claims and resolve those ambiguities by subconsciously favoring claims that coincide more easily with whichever method of judicial selection they are predisposed to prefer. Avoiding cognitive dissonance is a blunter instrument that leads people to maintain allegiance to their preferred method of selection by dancing around or ignoring contradictory information, to the extent circumstances allow.

As detailed in chapter 4, when a study produces conclusions that support one side in the judicial selection scrum, those conclusions are often accepted uncritically and trumpeted to the hilltops by those whose argument the study helps. That same study creates cognitive dissonance among disputants on the other side, and is either ignored or scoured for flaws and rejected out of hand when flaws are found or manufactured. The most egregious offender may be the legal community. Many judges and lawyers persist in making strident claims about the deleterious effects of judicial elections generally and campaign financing in particular on public confidence in the courts, without engaging or even acknowledging the existence of data to the contrary—as if it is not there.

DUELING PUBLICS

Without focusing on it consciously, disputants often view selection from the perspective of different audiences. Election proponents usually take the perspective of the general or voting public, whose confidence in judges is promoted by democracy-promoting, accountability-enhancing elections. The politics narrative thinks of judges as policymakers who represent the body politic. In that light, there is nothing wrong and everything right with judges who take the views of the voting public into account when making legal policy.

Conversely, election opponents usually take the perspective of the litigating public, whose confidence in the judiciary is diminished when judges' perceived need to remain popular with the electorate is in tension with their duty to make fair and independent decisions under law. From the perspective of the litigating public, Pontius Pilate washing his hands of Jesus's fate after the crowd clamored for his crucifixion was not a shining example of democracy in action, but a miscarriage of justice at the hands of a craven judge. Thinking about judicial selection from a litigant's vantage point is consonant with the law narrative, which worries less about whether the result of a legal proceeding sits well with the viewers at home than whether the proceeding offered litigants a full and fair hearing, circumscribed by applicable facts and law.

Disagreements arise when disputants confuse or conflate these publics. For example, Justice Sandra Day O'Connor argues that, "elections . . . threaten the public's perception of judicial independence" because "[i]f I know I was litigating before a judge who received that kind of money from my opponent, I would not think I was getting a fair shake." Social scientists dismiss O'Connor's concern by pointing to survey research of the general public, which shows that the legitimacy-damaging impact of money in judicial races does not offset the legitimacy-enhancing benefits of judicial elections overall (although more recent research suggests that such a conclusion has its limits and may not hold in extreme cases).[74] But this counterpoint misses the mark, insofar as O'Connor is thinking about the perceived legitimacy of courts in relation to the litigating public rather than the voting public. A separate body of research finds that litigants will accept adverse court rulings if they feel that they received a fair hearing.[75] These latter studies would seem to give credence to O'Connor's concern that a litigant might doubt the fairness of a proceeding in which the judge received significant campaign support from her opponent. By the same token, generalizing about the voting public's perception of judicial elections with reference to the litigating public's perception is likewise ill-advised. For example, the litigating public may look askance at a judge who takes positions from the campaign stump that seemingly pre-commit her to reject a litigant's position before the case is heard. The voting public, in contrast, may have no problem with judicial candidates announcing their views on issues they are likely to decide as judges, and regard the practice as a benign and useful means for voters to educate themselves about the candidates.

CONCLUSION

The dichotomous and often shrill debate over whether to elect or appoint judges is packed with exaggerated claims. In the context of an isolated exchange, one could attribute such exaggerations to the simple, competitive desire to win an argument. Writ large, however, across centuries of disagreement, it would seem that more is at work here. This chapter has offered four explanations for this phenomenon: (1) Path dependence, in which disputants' backgrounds and training align them with competing narratives that explain judicial conduct in different ways that warrant different systems of selection; (2) Motivated reasoning and assimilation bias, in which disputants are subconsciously motivated to assimilate new, ambiguous information in ways that validate their preexisting views; (3) Coping with cognitive dissonance, in which disputants dismiss or disregard contradictory information that cannot coexist with their established policy perspectives; and (4) Dueling publics, in which disputants disagree as to which system of selection better promotes public confidence in the courts because one side is focused on preserving legitimacy of the legal process among litigants and the other side is focused on preserving the legitimacy of judges among voters. These impediments to consensus give rise to two possibilities that the next chapter explores. First, to the extent that these impediments are the products of oversight or subconscious bias, they can be acknowledged, confronted, and overcome. Second, to the extent that they are the products of competing core values, they are inevitable and unavoidable.

6

MANAGING THE SELECTION DEBATE

In summarizing contemporary arguments for and against different selection systems, chapter 4 showed how the new politics of judicial elections (described in chapter 3) have reframed the issues at stake in the perennial judicial selection debate. Chapter 5, in turn, explained how those competing arguments are exaggerated or wrong, and why such overstatements and errors occur.

This chapter begins by exploring ways to narrow the divide between disputants in the judicial selection debate, by lessening the impediments to consensus that chapter 5 isolates. Next, I argue that while we can thus approach consensus, we cannot achieve it because at the heart of judicial selection is an irresolvable conundrum: judicial independence from electoral accountability is both antithetical and essential to our democracy. A necessary implication of this conundrum is that America's ambivalence over judicial selection is ultimately a condition to be managed rather than a disease to be cured. No one system of selection will be optimal for all jurisdictions at all times. Accordingly, I conclude the chapter by offering a template for states to structure their selection choices.

INCHING TOWARD ROUGH CONSENSUS

Chapter 5 offered four explanations for the chronic divide between contestants in the judicial selection debate. First, the conclusions disputants reach can be influenced by their disciplinary paths: those with legal training are more likely to take law seriously and embrace a law narrative that leads them to see judges as akin to umpires whose independence is better protected by appointive systems. Conversely, those with backgrounds in politics favor a politics narrative, which characterizes judges as a subset of politicians who should be accountable to voters in contested elections. Second, people are naturally motivated to assimilate new and ambiguous information about judicial selection in a manner consistent with their preexisting views. Third, cognitive psychology teaches that when people confront new information about judicial selection processes that contradicts their preexisting views, one natural tendency is to resolve the dissonance by marginalizing or disregarding the contradictory information. Fourth, disputants in the judicial selection debate argue past each other with competing claims that public confidence in the courts is aided or hindered by hotly contested judicial elections, because election proponents tend to have the voting public in mind, while election opponents fixate on the litigating public.

These four obstacles to consensus are patently surmountable. Cognitive dissonance can be confronted and managed—disputants can be brought to the table and convinced to discard arguments that are demonstrably counterfactual and wrong. Motivated reasoning and assimilation bias occur subconsciously; their effects can be mitigated if disputants are alerted to their presence and committed to diminishing their influence. And reform agendas can consciously seek to better account for and accommodate law and politics narratives, for the benefit of both voting and litigating publics.

If this were as easy done as said, a generations-long impasse could be resolved with a couple of drinks and a group hug. But the four obstacles I have identified are inextricably intertwined, and comprise a tenacious whole that resists unraveling. The disciplinary ruts of path dependence run deep. Those who choose the path of law, like those who choose the path of politics, opt into different disciplines that bring deep-rooted norms to bear and lead to different conclusions when evaluating how judges should be selected. The law narrative fixates on the litigating public, because parties to court proceedings are the primary focus of lawyers and the legal process. The politics narrative, in contrast, fixates on the voting public—the "body politic" of primary concern to the political process. Path-dependent narratives that seek to further the interests of different publics entrench support for competing selection systems. Devotees of the politics narrative tend to favor contested judicial elections, which enhance the judiciary's legitimacy with the voting public, while aficionados of the law narrative tend to favor appointment systems, which are more protective of the litigating public. With support for competing selection systems so embedded, cognitive dissonance and motivated reasoning become powerful impediments to peace between pugilists predisposed to dismiss or rationalize away otherwise credible information that undercuts their preferred position.

Deep Interdisciplinarity and the Search for Middle Ground

Because leading arguments in the judicial selection debate are framed by path-dependent disputants whose disciplinary norms impel them in different directions, one way to diminish the distance between proponents of rival systems is to force their paths to converge on a course that is deeply interdisciplinary. In an ancient Asian folktale, blind men misdescribe an elephant by generalizing from whichever part of the animal that each touches. And so it is with those who study the judicial selection elephant. The judges, lawyers, law professors, political scientists, historians, psychologists, journalists, and assorted policy wonks who think about judicial selection each bring their respective disciplines to bear. Each has useful perspectives to offer that are incomplete in isolation, but that taken together yield a composite that is closer to accurate. Deep interdisciplinarity thus diminishes path dependence by encouraging cooperation, rather than conflict, between the law and politics narratives. By enriching those narratives with the lessons of history, psychology, and anthropology, deep interdisciplinarity adds nuance and depth to the discussion, thereby weakening the credibility of simplistic, strident claims and lessening the conceptual conflicts that often lead to cognitive dissonance and assimilation bias.

Deep interdisciplinary has already begun to work its magic in a related subfield of judicial politics. The so-called "legal model" of judicial decision-making, which the legal community has long defended, proceeds from the premise that when deciding cases, independent judges set extralegal influences aside and follow the law. Meanwhile, the so-called "attitudinal model" of judicial decision-making developed by the political science community in the mid-twentieth century posits that when deciding cases, independent judges disregard the law and impose their own "attitudes" or policy preferences. These starkly dichotomous visions of judicial decision-making proceeded on a rigid, parallel course for decades. More recently, however, a cadre of interdisciplinary scholars began to emerge.[1] They accused unyielding devotees of the legal model of unfortunate interdisciplinary ignorance,[2] and comparably inflexible proponents of the attitudinal model of not "taking law seriously."[3] The body of scholarship that followed intruded on the isolation of the opposing camps and led to a more nuanced exploration of the interplay between law and policy that narrowed the disciplinary divide and moved the debate closer to consensus.[4]

Path dependence helps to explain why opinion-leaders frame judicial selection arguments for public consumption in unrelentingly binary ways, and why the resulting landscape has become a thicket that disputants enter, never to re-emerge. Deep interdisciplinarity offers a common path out of the woods, by creating meaningful opportunities for each side in the debate to take the other seriously, adjust their own perspectives accordingly, and diminish—if not eliminate—the distance between them.

For lawyers, law professors, and judges whose paths track the law narrative, deep interdisciplinarity can lead them to reconcile their views with the data that social scientists have generated. In some cases, that means making concessions. For example, the data shows that subjecting judges to electoral accountability enhances the voting public's confidence in the courts most of the time.[5] Categorical claims that elective systems are bad because the perceived influence of money in judicial races delegitimizes the courts must be qualified or abandoned. At a minimum, it means that disputants must engage and critique the data. Lawyers who lack social science training may be ill-equipped to contest the details of a given study's methodology. But lawyers know loaded questions when they see them, and are well-positioned to assess whether a study's design has been crafted to foreordain the author's conclusions or whether those conclusions follow logically from the findings of a fair-minded study.

For social scientists and others who lack legal training, deep interdisciplinarity will call upon them to take the law narrative more seriously and reconcile their conclusions with that narrative in a non-dismissive way. For example, when confronted with studies showing that judges vote differently in the shadow of impending elections, some political scientists who defend contested elections point to these studies as evidence that judges abandon their idiosyncratic policy preferences and uphold the law when elections are impending. Such a conclusion proceeds on the counterintuitive, data-free premise that the voting public is better-positioned to say what the law is than judges who have decades of legal education and experience. A related argument is that law is essentially irrelevant to judicial decision-making, that what passes for "law" is just policymaking in drag, and that elections serve the salutary objective of pressuring judges to bring their policy preferences into closer alignment with their constituents. But here, recent interdisciplinary studies of judicial decision-making below the U.S. Supreme Court document the influence of operative law, belie forceful claims of law's irrelevance, and in so doing, reaffirm the utility of deep interdisciplinarity.[6]

Incremental Reforms

To the extent that deep interdisciplinarity softens the stridency of competing claims, it enables less pugnacious disputants to develop a broader array of middle-ground proposals for the benefit of a general public that has never been constrained by disciplinary ruts. States with elective systems may consider reforms that afford greater judicial independence for the benefit of the litigating public and the rule of law. States with appointive systems may consider reforms that enhance judicial accountability for the benefit of the general public and the judiciary's political legitimacy. By making judges in elective systems less dependent and judges in appointive systems more accountable, middle-ground reforms make binary choices less stark, and create a menu of options that increases the range of choices beyond the binary. Moreover, by virtue of their incremental character, middle-ground, intrasystem proposals are more feasible to implement between waves of reform, when the political will for sweeping, systemic change is absent.

Making Elected Judiciaries More Impartial and Independent

Incremental changes that could aid in rendering elected judges less dependent and more impartial include reforming campaign finance, amending disqualification rules, and lengthening terms of office. As discussed in chapter 5, the virtues of these reforms can be overhyped by their proponents, but are less objectionable when understood not as cure-alls, but as modest changes intended to make improvements at the margins.

Reforming Campaign Finance

Campaign contribution limits seek to ensure that the amounts donors are permitted to give to judicial campaigns fall below a dollar threshold that would create the perception that such contributions might buy influence with the judge. Most states already have judicial campaign contribution limits in place.[7] Those states that do not have such limits should consider adding them. States that impose incomplete contribution limits, by, for example, failing to include limits on corporations, individuals, or PACs, should consider more comprehensive limits. And states should review the dollar limits they impose to ensure that the caps are low enough to dispel reasonable perception problems.[8]

Imposing contribution limits can be like squeezing a balloon: To the extent that such limits constrict the financial resources that interested individuals and groups may give to judicial campaign committees directly, they create an incentive for those individuals and groups to shunt their resources into independent campaigns on the judges' behalf, which are not subject to contribution limits. One partial solution to this problem is to require entities with independent campaigns to disclose the sources of their support, which can alert voters to individuals and groups who may be seeking to peddle influence on the court. Insofar as federal law enables interest groups organized as nonprofit, "social welfare organizations" to avoid disclosure requirements—the source of the so-called "dark money" problem—the operative law can be amended. A more comprehensive but controversial remedy would be to explore spending caps on independent campaigns. The Supreme Court has invalidated such measures in political branch races, but the Court's analysis of judicial campaigns affords wiggle room to argue that the judiciary is different, and that the special need to preserve the judiciary's impartiality and integrity justify spending restrictions that are not warranted in races for other offices.[9]

More aggressively still, some have agitated to overturn *Citizens United* (and other campaign finance cases) via constitutional amendment, so as to enable legislatures to regulate campaign finance without First Amendment impediments. As discussed in chapter 3, *Citizens United* held that corporations enjoyed a First Amendment right to bankroll independent election campaigns on a candidate's behalf, because such financial support is a form of protected speech that Congress must not abridge. In the more than two centuries since its adoption, First Amendment freedom of speech has been revised by subsequent amendment precisely never. Without disputing the possibility that a sociopolitical sea change could spark constitutional reform, the more realistic prospect is for state campaign finance reforms to test and retest the limits of *Citizens United* over time, until the decision is overturned or the force of its holding is eroded as U.S. Supreme Court composition changes. For example, the Court could exempt judicial races from the reach of *Citizens United*, on the grounds that judges and courts are different, or create other exceptions in specific contexts where the government interest in restructuring or regulating independent judicial campaigns is particularly strong.

Public financing is a less promising campaign finance reform option. In theory, public financing enables judicial candidates to avoid privately funded campaigns and the legitimacy-damaging perception that they are subject to the influence of their campaign supporters when a case of interest to those supporters later comes before the candidate as a judge. In practice, public financing is helpless to prevent interest groups from redirecting their resources from direct contributions to a candidate, to independent campaigns on their candidate's behalf, which simply relocates legitimacy-threatening perception problems without eliminating them. And states that have implemented public financing regimes have found them difficult to sustain over time, as the philosophical appeal of holding supreme court elections unsullied by interest group influence gradually yields to a disinclination to spend taxpayer dollars on campaign commercials.

Amending Disqualification Rules

Disqualification rules are no panacea for what ails elected judiciaries, but they can still help in three ways. First, meaningful disqualification rules can lead judicial candidates to consider the consequences of their actions before they engage in conduct that will compromise their impartiality and force their disqualification as judges. Second, disqualification rules can protect the litigating public from judges who, as candidates, engaged in conduct that later undermines their impartiality as judges. Third, disqualification rules can reassure the voting public that judges will not be permitted to decide cases in which they, as candidates, received financial support from parties or lawyers in amounts sufficient to taint the proceedings.

With respect to the third point, the data shows that disqualification does not ameliorate the perceived taint that arises when judges are offered, but decline, contributions from would-be benefactors who later appear as parties or lawyers.[10] This, however, is a separate problem, better addressed in two other ways: First, by contribution limits, which prohibit direct contributions in excess of amounts that could create a reasonable perception of influence peddling, and second, by rules (recently upheld by the U.S. Supreme Court) that prohibit judicial candidates from soliciting contributions themselves and delegate the task to the candidate's campaign committee. The data likewise shows that disqualification rules do not fully restore the general public's confidence in the integrity of a judiciary tainted by the perception that campaign support buys influence.[11] But incremental increases in the general public's confidence, paired with the clear benefits to the litigating public (which is protected against having its cases decided by a judge whose impartiality is in doubt), render rigorous disqualification rules worthy of consideration for elective systems.

The ABA Model Code of Judicial Conduct includes three circumstances relevant to campaign conduct, in which judges must disqualify themselves: (1) when a party or lawyer appearing before the judge made aggregate contributions to the judge's campaign in excess of a threshold dollar amount; (2) when, as a candidate, the judge made public statements that appear to have committed the judge to rule a particular way in a case now before the court; and (3) as a general matter, when a judge's impartiality "might reasonably be questioned."[12] Among the states, the general rule is universally adopted; the specific rules are not. States that have not adopted the specific rules must evaluate campaign-related disqualification with sole reference to the general rule, which lacks the specificity and guidance instrumental to rigorous enforcement. Modest improvements to the perceived impartiality of elected judges within the litigating, if not the general, public might thus be achieved if states that have not adopted specific campaign-related disqualification rules did so.

Moreover, the Model Code includes no specific rule governing disqualification when a party or lawyer who appears before the judge sponsored an independent campaign on the judge's behalf, rather than contributed directly to the judge's own campaign. In *Caperton v. A.H. Massey Coal Co.*, the Supreme Court encouraged the states to adopt such a rule as a means to obviate federal court intervention on due process grounds.[13] The ABA's failure to follow the Supreme Court's lead has less to do with principled objections than self-interested squabbling within the ABA's ranks.[14] In the absence of ABA leadership, a number of state supreme courts have adopted rules of their own. Some have done nothing or taken a seemingly defiant stance, effectively rejecting the financial support a judge receives from interested parties as grounds for disqualification.[15] Other states have taken the Supreme Court's cue and adopted rules more in keeping with the Court's ruling in *Caperton*.[16] States that take the latter course can help to blunt the perceived influence of well-funded independent campaigns on judicial impartiality.

Lengthening Judicial Terms

Among the more serious concerns raised by critics of elected judiciaries is that judges, fearful of losing their tenure, alter their decision-making in the shadow of impending elections. The shorter a judge's term of office, the tighter the leash on the judge's independence, and in states with contested judicial elections, terms of office range from four to fourteen years.[17] For those who celebrate elections as a means to curb judicial independence run amok, this is, if anything, a reason to hold elections more frequently. On the other hand, insofar as election-year dependence is viewed as a troubling phenomenon, one option is to reduce the frequency of election-year dependence by lengthening terms of judicial office.

Making Appointed Judiciaries More Accountable

In jurisdictions that do not subject their judges to contested elections, there are incremental reforms that can aid in reassuring the public that appointed judges are accountable in other ways: publicizing existing accountability-promoting mechanisms, reinvigorating judicial disqualification procedures, and instituting rigorous judicial performance evaluations.

Publicizing Existing Accountability-Promoting Mechanisms

Court websites can identify, explain, and publicize the range of mechanisms in place to promote the judiciary's decisional, behavioral, and institutional accountability. When judges err, their decisions are subject to reversal on appeal, legislative override (when the decision is not a matter of constitutional interpretation), and constitutional amendment. When judges behave unethically, they are subject to disciplinary processes that can culminate in sanctions ranging from reprimands to removal. In cases of extreme misconduct, judges are subject to removal via impeachment or (in many states) legislative address. And by virtue of their control over appropriations, legislatures hold the judiciary accountable as an institution for their expenditures and operations.

Of the foregoing mechanisms for promoting accountability among judges not subject to contested elections, judicial discipline should be singled out for special mention. Every state judicial system has a disciplinary process in place, and those processes typically bring their applicable codes of judicial conduct to bear when investigating judicial conduct and imposing discipline. Unlike judicial elections in the modern era, codes of conduct do not regulate the decisions judges make, or hold judges answerable for rulings that the public deems unacceptable. But codes of conduct do regulate many of the behaviors that give rise to unacceptable rulings, and to that extent promote a highly relevant form of accountability.

For example, judges are subject to sanction for: Being incompetent or lazy;[18] performing the duties of judicial office with bias or prejudice;[19] being less than fair and impartial;[20] permitting social, political, financial, or other interests to influence their conduct;[21] and depriving parties of the "right to be heard according to law."[22] In addition, most codes of conduct direct judges to "uphold and apply the law," and add an explanatory comment that "each judge comes to the bench with a unique background and personal philosophy," but that "a judge must interpret and apply the law without regard to whether the judge approves or disapproves of the law in question."[23] Although discipline under this latter rule is used sparingly, because of its implications for judicial independence, it has been brought to bear when violations are chronic, egregious, or intentional.[24]

Disgruntled litigants often file frivolous disciplinary complaints in a misguided attempt to punish judges for issuing adverse rulings. Judicial systems may thus be reluctant to trumpet the availability of disciplinary processes to the general public for fear of opening the floodgates to a deluge of meritless accusations that impose an administrative burden on disciplinary authorities to process. Some may be concerned that the public will interpret the additional complaints that publicity generates as evidence that the judiciary is in disrepair. But in jurisdictions where the public lacks confidence in its appointed judiciary, publicizing a rigorous, accountability-enhancing disciplinary regime may be worth the price of additional staff to review and dismiss the resulting influx of groundless complaints. And disseminating information that quantifies and describes the frivolous complaints disciplinary authorities receive can help to neutralize the perception that such complaints are smoke that implies fire.

Reinvigorating Disqualification Procedure

The new politics of judicial elections are propelled by the view that elections empower voters to purge the courts of judges run amok, and that without periodic elections, judges would be free to act on their own biases to the detriment of the rule of law and the public good. Disqualification rules force judges off cases for real or reasonably perceived biases and conflicts of interest. Such rules do not apply to garden variety ideological "bias"—they do not force the disqualification of judges because they are registered Democrats, because they manifest a conservative judicial philosophy, or because their rulings tend to align with their putative ideological predilections. If the rules disqualified all judges who were subject to the influence of their backgrounds, judicial philosophies, or ideological leanings, those rules would likely disqualify everyone. But disqualification does remediate other, more targeted biases that have the potential to undermine the judiciary's legitimacy. Thus, disqualification rules protect the litigating public from judges who manifest bias (real or reasonably perceived) based on race, ethnicity, sexual orientation, close personal friendships, familial relationships, personal knowledge of the case, or financial entanglements.[25]

Although the substantive standards for disqualification are largely uniform across the states, procedural standards are not. And in many jurisdictions, disqualification procedures can fairly be criticized for being less than rigorous in ways that undermine the goals of holding judges accountable to substantive recusal standards and promoting public confidence in the courts.[26] Thus, for example, the prevailing norm is for judges whose disqualification is sought to grade their own homework and rule on whether they are too biased or conflicted to preside over the case. When it comes to justices on the state's high court, targeted justices often have the first and final word on whether they must withdraw from a case. The judge who disqualifies typically does so without explanation, while the judge who denies a motion to disqualify may or may not see fit to explain the decision. Disqualification disputes are between the movant and the judge, rather than between the parties; consequently, disqualification motions are often exempt from the rigors of the normal adversarial process. With rare exception, non-disqualification is subject to a highly deferential standard of review on appeal—it is not enough that the trial judge (who often presided over her own case) was in error: the error must be "clear" or constitute an "abuse of discretion." And on many state high courts, there is no procedure to replace a disqualified justice, which puts added pressure on the justice not to recuse lest the court be left short-handed.

Revising disqualification procedure to render it more rigorous is one way to reassure a skeptical public that appointed judges are accountable and will be removed from cases in which biases are exposed.[27] In the case of trial judges, disqualification requests may be assigned to a different judge; in the case of appellate judges, the task may be delegated to the entire court or a specially designated panel of judges. Disqualification procedure can be reinvigorated by following traditional motions practice, in which requests for disqualification are followed by responses from opposing parties, a hearing, and a ruling that includes reasons for the decision rendered. Jurisdictions that retain self-disqualification may employ a less deferential "de novo" standard of review that enables appellate courts to reverse non-disqualification when it concludes that disqualification was warranted. And procedures can be established to replace disqualified high court justices with retired justices or intermediate appellate court judges sitting by designation.

Instituting Rigorous Judicial Performance Evaluations

In many (if not most) states, bar organizations survey their membership in order to evaluate the performance of judges within their jurisdictions. Such evaluations may be helpful to lawyers practicing before the judges evaluated, but are neither comprehensive nor designed for public consumption. At least eight states, however, have instituted more elaborate judicial performance evaluation programs, for the benefit of voters in advance of retention elections.[28] These programs solicit and synthesize the views of lawyers, parties, jurors, and witnesses to the end of providing a more three-dimensional assessment of a judge's competence, impartiality, integrity, independence, diligence, and temperament.

States with contested elections have not employed comprehensive judicial performance evaluation processes for defensible reasons. Such processes evaluate incumbent judges. Subjecting incumbents but not their challengers to rigorous performance evaluations puts incumbents at an arguably unfair disadvantage or advantage relative to their unevaluated challengers, depending on whether their evaluations devastate or glow. It has been suggested that challengers might be evaluated too, in a manner akin to the American Bar Association's review of federal judicial nominees (who frequently have no prior judicial experience).[29] But having an election turn on an officially sanctioned body's apples-to-oranges comparison of incumbents and challengers generates an understandable measure of skepticism.

No similar problems arise, however, for judges who are subject to retention elections or who do not stand for election at all. With respect to the latter group, skeptics may doubt whether performance evaluations are likely to influence the conduct of judges who face no consequences at the ballot box if they fare poorly. That does not mean, however, that poor performance evaluations are consequence free. In extreme cases, reports that judges are abusive, incompetent, or lazy can lead to judicial conduct complaints and disciplinary proceedings. Moreover, for trained professionals who have aspired to and attained judicial office, negative reviews of their performance in office can motivate them to do better. For example, in the 1990s, the Civil Justice Reform Act required federal trial judges to issue periodic reports of delays on their dockets. Despite the fact that those judges were effectively appointed for life, the delays that judges reported diminished over time, leading researchers to infer that adverse publicity of excessive delays influenced judicial conduct for the better.[30] It is thus reasonable to hope that judges would respond constructively to the results of periodic performance evaluations, even if the judge's tenure does not hang in the balance.[31]

A New System of Selection

As deep interdisciplinarity narrows the divide between the law and politics camps, it becomes possible to think past incremental reform and contemplate new selection systems that transcend a binary choice and better accommodate the concerns of both sides. For example, one might revisit an idea I first suggested in 2003, in which supreme court and intermediate appellate court candidates prequalified by commission are chosen by the electorate in contested elections, for a single, lengthy term, or until a specified age. In so doing, this "qualified election" model offers the legitimacy-enhancing benefits of elective systems while preserving the independence-promoting benefits of appointive systems that forgo reselection processes.

Here is how a "qualified election" model might work: When a vacancy occurs, a screening commission of judges, lawyers, and non-lawyers would solicit applications from prospective judicial candidates. Like nominating commissions in many merit selection states, the commission would be charged with soliciting a diverse array of applicants. Unlike nominating commissions, which winnow the applicant pool to the best of the best, the screening commission's role would be limited to ensuring that all prospective candidates are capable and qualified—a role similar to that played by the American Bar Association in vetting federal judicial nominees.

Nominees pre-cleared by the screening commission would become eligible to run for office in a contested partisan or nonpartisan election. Campaigns would be subject to contribution limits and disclosure requirements, and candidates would be subject to code of judicial conduct restrictions, consistent with current practice in states that elect their judges. Judges who win election would then serve a single fifteen-year term, or until a specified age. If a judge retires, resigns, dies, or is removed before the end of her term, the governor would appoint a judge to fill the vacancy until an election can be held. The interim appointment would be chosen from a stable of former supreme or intermediate appellate court judges who choose to remain eligible for judicial service, but judges so appointed would be ineligible to run for election to fill the vacancy.

Judges selected via a qualified election model would be subject to disqualification if the campaign support they received or the campaign statements they made calls their impartiality into question in future cases that come before the judge's court. The same pool of former judges who would be available to fill vacancies on an interim basis would also be on call to replace disqualified judges.

The advantages of a qualified election model are several. First, it offers the legitimacy-enhancing benefits of contested elections. The data shows that in most instances, elections promote public confidence in the courts by enabling voters to participate in the selection of the judges who serve them.

Second, it provides a safety net to ensure that unqualified candidates are excluded from the pool. Studies show that while the quality of elected and appointed judges are comparable overall, elective systems have allowed more of the least qualified candidates into the mix. Screening commissions are well-suited to weed out the unqualified or unfit, but popular, candidate. A good example is former Alabama chief justice Roy Moore, who was elected, removed for misconduct, elected again, and removed a second time for subsequent misconduct. It is unlikely in the extreme that once removed, Moore would have survived screening commission review had he reapplied to run again after being removed.

Third, eliminating reselection processes will diminish judicial dependence on voters and campaign supporters. Once elected, judges will not be beholden to the electorate for their continuation in office, thereby obviating problems associated with judges altering their rulings to mollify the electorate as elections approach. The data also suggests that judges are less beholden to their campaign supporters when judges do not remain dependent on those supporters for their future reselection (for example, during the judge's final term in office, or after the judge has scored a landslide victory). By the same token, eliminating reselection processes in jurisdictions that currently provide for legislatures, governors, or commissions to reappoint incumbent judges after a term of years will eliminate judicial dependence on the reappointing authority.

Fourth, limiting judicial office to a single term of years or until a specified age seeks to end reselection, while creating an endpoint for judicial service after which the legitimizing benefits of judicial elections can be renewed with a new generation of candidates. When judges are elected, it is a virtual tautology to say that they are politically acceptable to the voters who elected them. Over time, however, judges' ideological orientations—and their political acceptability to voters—can change. On the U.S. Supreme Court, for example, there is a well-documented phenomenon of "ideological drift," where justices with limitless terms become more conservative or liberal over time.[32] To the extent that voters seek to elect judges whose ideological orientation is compatible with their own, ideological drift by the judges elected can undermine that objective over time. The problem is exacerbated if, at the same time, the electorate's ideological orientation drifts in the opposite direction from the judges.

Limited terms constrain ideological drift, but that constraint comes at a price: If we do not allow for reselection, then a limited term will remove capable, qualified, and experienced judges from office. The two options that the qualified elections model offers strike the balance in different places. A single fifteen-year term constrains the scope and duration of ideological drift at the expense of a term limit that may have negative ripple effects: Good judges can be forced off the bench prematurely, successful lawyers may be reluctant to seek judicial office if they must rebuild their practices after their terms expire, and judicial service may become the province of aging lawyers who time the expiration of their terms to coincide with retirement. Conversely, a term that ends when the judge reaches a specified age avoids the negative effects of a term of years, at the expense of extending the duration and extent of ideological drift (by the judge or the electorate).

Fifth, contribution limits, disclosure requirements, and disqualification regimes address perceived partiality problems that judicial campaigns create. Contribution limits ensure that judges will not receive direct financial support in amounts that create a reasonable perception of influence. Disqualification processes can ameliorate residual problems that arise when judicial candidates undermine their impartiality by expressly or impliedly committing to decide future cases in specified ways. And disqualification regimes, aided by disclosure requirements, can remediate perceptions of influence that arise when parties appearing before the judge have lent excessive financial support to independent campaigns on the judge's behalf.

Sixth, the qualified election model creates a bullpen of capable, qualified, and experienced part-time judges who serve two important purposes. First, they enable rigorous disqualification regimes to achieve their ends without leaving the court short-handed. Second, by being available to fill vacancies on an interim basis, this cohort of part-time judges can neutralize an incumbency advantage that would otherwise arise. In elective systems, it is common for judges to retire before the expiration of their terms, so that a like-minded governor might appoint the judge's successor until an election can be held. The net effect is to transform the appointee into an incumbent as she heads into her first election—a not inconsequential advantage that puts the governor's thumb on the scale of the electorate's choice.

As proposed, the elections envisioned by a qualified election model could be partisan or nonpartisan in character. Neither is ideal.

On the upside, partisan elections tend to be more competitive affairs, in which partisans and their allies spend more on their campaigns, piquing the interest and participation of voters who use the judge's party affiliation to inform their vote, all of which diminishes roll-off at the polls. On the downside, partisan elections send the message that judges are, well, partisans. By carrying the flag of the party that propelled them into office, partisan-elected judges look more like ordinary politicians than impartial arbiters of law who are subject to an ethical directive that they "not permit . . . political . . . . interests or relationships to influence the judge's judicial conduct or judgment."[33]

Nonpartisan elections, in contrast, are more compatible with the judicial role. Nonpartisan judges are not beholden to a political party for their nomination and are not identified as partisans in the voting public's mind. On the downside, nonpartisan elections are less able to generate voter interest and participation, which increases voter roll-off at the polls. Moreover, the data shows that nonpartisan elections remain quite partisan affairs behind the scenes—eliminating party labels from the ballot deprives voters of important informational cues as to the judge's ideological orientation without eliminating partisanship from the process. Given studies showing that judges are subject to the influence of their ideological predilections, nonpartisan elections seek to maintain the false pretense that judges are apolitical actors.

For purposes of this proposal, I remain agnostic on the question of whether partisan or nonpartisan races are preferable, but I lean toward the latter. The reality is that judges have ideological preferences that correlate with their party affiliations, which can influence some of the decisions they make. And the reality is that political parties have a stake in judicial decision-making that will motivate them to remain involved in judicial elections, whether their role is formal or not. But that does not mean that these realities need to be nurtured by openly embracing them as part of the selection process, when they are at odds with the impartial, independent judiciary we seek to promote. By way of analogy, the reality may be that we cannot stop teenagers from thinking and acting on their sexual impulses, but that does not mean we should therefore indulge those impulses by sending them to school with their pants off. The price we pay for discouraging partisanship and promoting a less politicized judiciary is a diminished level of voter engagement—and on balance, I can live with that. I characterize my preference for nonpartisan elections as a "leaning," because the new politics of judicial elections can render nonpartisan races so openly and pervasively partisan that little benefit is gained by refusing to call a fig a fig. Wisconsin is a good example, where judicial elections in an ostensibly nonpartisan system have devolved into partisan warfare so unrestrained that omitting partisan labels from the ballot may simply confuse voters.[34]

For reasons elaborated upon in the next section, "The Limits of Consensus," I do not present the qualified election method proposed here as universally optimal, for two reasons: First, because no one system is optimal for all states at all times; and second, because appointive systems remain a preferable default. On the latter point, it bears note that one of the most notorious examples of high-stakes judicial elections gone pear-shaped occurred in Illinois, which, like the qualified elections model, employs contested elections at the point of initial selection only. In 2004, the victor in a nine-million-dollar campaign observed at the time, "That's obscene for a judicial race. . . . How can anyone have faith in the system?"[35] That same justice nonetheless declined to disqualify himself later from a case in which a corporate defendant and its employees had made significant contributions to his election campaign while the appeal was pending, and the next year cast a critical vote in the defendant's favor.[36] The brunt of this imbroglio could have been lessened had Illinois imposed more meaningful contribution limits, disclosure processes, and disqualification rules, which are included in the qualified elections model that I propose. Clearly, however, the model is no panacea.

Rather, the qualified elections model may be best-suited for two scenarios. In the first, a state seeks to ameliorate the baleful effects of its contested elections, but is loath to adopt an appointive model with or without retention elections. In the second, the state is fed up with its appointive system, but would be open to an alternative that is less inimical to judicial independence than traditional contested elections and re-elections.

THE LIMITS OF CONSENSUS

As the foregoing section emphasized, deep interdisciplinarity enables us to approach consensus in a variety of ways. But consensus can never actually be achieved. Like being pregnant or dead, one cannot be a little bit appointed or mostly elected. Independence and accountability are so related that they have rightly been described as "different sides of the same coin."[37] But when it comes to judicial selection and whether to elect or appoint, it is not possible to devise a system in which both sides of that coin turn face up on the same toss.

States can make accommodations that narrow the divide between elective and appointive systems. The qualified election model I offer is one example. A merit selection system that couples commission-based appointment with retention elections is arguably another (although for reasons I discuss later, not really). Such accommodations cannot eliminate that divide altogether because at the end of the day, a state must choose to hold its judges accountable to the electorate or not. And that choice exposes an irresolvable conundrum at the core of American government: judicial independence from electoral accountability is both inimical and essential to democracy. In 1962, Alexander Bickel coined the term "countermajoritarian difficulty" to capture the irony of a representative democracy empowering unelected federal judges to thwart the will of electoral majorities via judicial review.[38] Thirty years later, Steven Croley used the term "majoritarian difficulty" to capture the irony of calling upon elected state judges, who are beholden to electoral majorities for their tenure, to protect the constitutional rights of electoral minorities.[39] The resulting conundrum is part of what David Pozen has described as "the irony of judicial elections."[40]

There are two ways to cope with the entrenched ironies of judicial selection. The first is to own and embrace them—to recognize their inevitability and consider the possibility that such ironies are not a flaw but a feature of a judicial selection menu that enables states to choose, and later reconsider, whichever system is optimal for their place and time. The second is to manage the conundrum these ironies create by means of a template that structures and sequences the selection choices that states should consider.

The ultimate failure to achieve consensus in the elections versus appointments debate is inevitable—and perhaps that is a good thing. The competing values underlying the choice between elective and appointive systems will remain in constructive and perpetual tension, despite best efforts to make both systems better and diminish the distance between them. Moreover, the unavoidably binary character of the election versus appointment choice, and the consequent inability to reach universal consensus, may be a virtue rather than a vice. It gives states the flexibility to accommodate changing times, changing circumstances, and changing legal cultures in different jurisdictions by keeping variations of two viable selection alternatives on the table. Which alternative is optimal will depend on which selection system's values take precedence in a given place at a given time.

There is an almost but not quite hidden empirical basis upon which to explain and justify the persistence of variation. Those who research election-related phenomena in multistate studies seek to draw general conclusions from the data they generate. That approach can bury the lede if the average result researchers report obscures dramatic variation between states or elections under study. Such variations are captured in standards of deviation, which are an essential part of any sound statistical analysis, and competent researchers report standards of deviation in their analyses. Because there is nothing especially sexy about results that are all over the place, however, the average of those results tends to receive top billing when studies are cited and discussed.

In the judicial elections arena, significant variations abound, and good scholars have called those variations to readers' attention. For example, after reporting on his "overall" analysis, Herbert Kritzer highlights wide state-to-state variations, leading him to conclude that "one must be cautious in making broad claims about whether, and if so, in what ways, contestation and competitiveness have changed in state supreme court elections."[41] Chris Bonneau reports evidence of a "quid pro quo" relationship between campaign contributors and judges in some states but not others, and notes too that "there is great variation among the states (and even within a state) in the costs associated with electing judges."[42] Larry Aspin reports that in retention elections there is "no consistent upward or downward trend in the affirmative vote," but adds that "the lack of a national trend may be the result of opposing trends at state level."[43] Malia Reddick found that elected judges were disciplined more frequently than merit-selected judges, but only in six of nine states under study, and took pains to add that "[c]aution should be exercised in relying solely on an aggregate analysis of disciplinary rates, rather than also examining individual states."[44]

These and other differences explain the persistence of variation in selection systems across the states, and the resistance to uniformity. Moreover, such variations belie sweeping assertions that when it comes to choosing the optimal selection system for any given state, one size necessarily fits all.

Appointive Systems as the Preferable Default

The inevitability and ultimate desirability of interstate variation, however, does not require that states resign themselves to channeling the 1960s mantra, "if it feels good do it," and lurch unguided from one selection system to another as the spirit moves them. Rather, I would argue that an appointive system is the preferable default; that an elective system becomes appropriate when essential to preserving or restoring the judiciary's legitimacy with the general public; and that a reversion back to an appointive model is warranted when the legitimacy benefits elections confer are offset by the corresponding costs they incur—including costs to the judiciary's legitimacy that arise when elections become too heated.

For appellate judiciaries, a commission-based appointive system unencumbered by reappointment processes,[45] in which judges serve a single, lengthy term or until a specified age, is a preferable default. There are three reasons to prefer this default, grounded in constitutional theory, institutional design, and judicial process.

First, as a matter of constitutional theory, a commission-based appointive system is most compatible with the appropriate role of the judiciary in a democratic republic that depends for its success on a system of checks and balances. The judicial power that all state constitutions delegate to their courts includes judicial review as the primary check on legislative and executive branch power. Judicial review calls upon judges to uphold the enduring will of the people, embodied in the text of state constitutions, by invalidating unconstitutional executive actions and legislative enactments that implement the will of more transitory majorities. Judges are better equipped to serve this "countermajoritarian" role if they are not put at risk of losing their jobs for doing their jobs.

There are two counterpunches to appointive systems, both of which rely on data demonstrating the extent to which judges are subject to ideological influences. One is that insofar as unelected judges are policymakers in robes who act on their ideological preferences rather than the law, the countermajoritarian judge is a cause for concern, not celebration. If nothing else, contested partisan elections furnish voters with a judge's party affiliation, which is a critical proxy for the policy predilections that voters can expect from their judge. For many path-dependent devotees of the politics narrative, this enables voters to align the judge's policy preferences with their own, which is reason enough for contested partisan elections to serve as the preferable default. I take issue with that conclusion. Without disputing that judges are subject to ideological influences at the margins, recent interdisciplinary research reveals that judges are nonetheless acculturated from their first days of law school to take law seriously, and data confirms that below the U.S. Supreme Court, law retains considerable influence over judicial decision-making. Because unelected judges tend to share the sentiments of their communities, their legal views will align with those of local majorities much of the time, but that does not render the countermajoritarian judge a myth. Insulating judges from the pressures of re-election enables them to take the infrequent step of upholding the law in the teeth of public outcry, when the judge recognizes that the law is at odds with popular preference.[46] Insofar as constitutional theory seeks to promote the rule of law, contested partisan elections are problematic because they nurture, rather than discourage, the primacy of partisan, ideological influence over the resolution of legal issues.

A related counterpoint is that because judges are subject to the influence of their policy perspectives, and because those perspectives are a product of the political cultures in which judges are immersed—a culture that brings pressure, political and otherwise, to conform—the countermajoritarian judge is a myth. That helps to explain why unelected federal judges implemented the will of white majorities during the Jim Crow era, by construing the post-Civil War Amendments to tolerate racial segregation under the rubric of "separate but equal." It is nevertheless true that independence from electoral accountability enables judges to rise above the majoritarian fray and uphold the law at critical moments in time—moments critical enough to justify an appointive system as the appropriate default. Hence, during the civil rights era, unelected federal judges served as a catalyst for change at a time when their elected state counterparts would lose their jobs to angry local voters had they done the same.

Second, as a matter of institutional design, an appointive system fosters unique perspectives on constitutional and other legal questions that provide a distinct counterpoint to the views of the other branches, which enriches the interbranch dialogue and better informs governmental decision-making.[47] Periodic elections motivate judges to avoid backlash by conforming their views to the will of popular majorities. Election proponents tout this as a virtue, but it is in significant respects more a vice. Judicial elections promote ideological homogenization, in which the same electoral majority spawns three branches of like-minded decision-makers. The judiciary's distinctive role is best preserved if it can interpret operative law and decide cases in a unique voice that is not auto-tuned by the same popular pressures that drive the decision-making of the elected branches of government.[48] An unelected judiciary thus encourages a diversity of perspective that is better-positioned to test and corroborate or contradict decisions that the majoritarian branches make. In state systems, where a court's constitutional interpretations are easier to override because their constitutions are easier to amend, the range of perspectives that appointed judges are liberated to share diversifies the dialogue to the benefit of the deliberative process.

Third, as a matter of sound judicial process, a commission-based appointive system better protects rights of the litigating public to a fair and impartial proceeding. Data showing that judges rule differently when elections are impending is of particular concern to litigants on the short end of that stick. Data suggesting that judges are influenced by the campaign support they receive should likewise trouble litigants who find themselves opposing parties who lent generous campaign support to the presiding judge. For litigants, the key to the legitimacy of the legal process lies in the perception that they received a fair hearing from an impartial judge[49]—a perception that is aided by a selection system that insulates judges from political pressure to contort their rulings to mollify voters and interest groups.

The qualified election model that I proposed earlier may reduce but cannot eliminate these problems. First, choosing judges in hotly contested elections casts them in the role of ordinary politicians, blurring the distinction between judges and other elected officials in the minds of litigating and general publics alike—a distinction critical to preserving the unique role that judges play in preserving the rule of law. In a related vein, forcing judicial candidates to compete in contested elections limits the candidate pool to judges who are willing to act the part of people-pleasing politicians in order to win popularity contests. Being a good politician is in tension with being a good judge, because judges are under an ethical directive not to be influenced by the public's preferences, to which the judge as a candidate was obliged to appeal. That may help to explain why there is some evidence that elected judges encounter ethical problems more frequently than their appointed counterparts. Third, well-financed, hotly contested elections can undermine the perceived fairness of the judicial process even if judges are not subject to reselection. When a future party lends financial support to a judicial candidate in amounts sufficient to help the candidate win the election, it can foster the perception of an illicit quid pro quo—or at least a debt of gratitude—regardless of whether the judge remains dependent on that party for support in a future election. As explained in chapter 4, rigorous disqualification rules are an ambulance at the base of the cliff that address perception problems after they arise: disqualification rules can render life-saving assistance to the judiciary's perceived integrity and impartiality, but cannot prevent disfiguring injury.

Studies show that with exceptions, elective systems enhance the general public's perception of the judiciary's legitimacy. The voting public exhibits greater confidence in judges whom it had a hand in selecting. The peril of an appointive system is that the judiciary can lose its legitimacy if the general public suspects that its judges are abusing their independence and going rogue, and feels helpless to stop it. That is far from inevitable. Public confidence in judiciaries of states that appoint their judges can be stable and strong. And it is no answer to quote survey data showing that the public regards elected judiciaries as more legitimate, if other problems associated with elected judiciaries offset the incremental gains to perceived legitimacy that elections supply. It is these other problems that justify a default in favor of appointive systems.

In states that favor commission-based appointment but insist on some form of electoral accountability, retention elections have long been the preferred option to minimize the impact of reselection on judicial independence and tenure. I would concur, and to that extent regard traditional merit selection systems with retention elections as a rough proxy for the default position I advocate, with one major caveat: To the extent that commission-based appointment with retention elections is the next best thing to commission-based appointment without retention elections, it is because retention elections, at their best, are pointless. They "work" only when they don't. Proponents favor retention elections because they threaten judicial tenure so rarely. But there is no data to support the inference that high retention rates are attributable to specific voter knowledge of and satisfaction with the judges they opt to retain. The better explanation is that retention rates correspond to the electorate's level of trust in political institutions generally.[50] That may help to explain why voter roll-off is so much higher in retention elections: many voters feel that they lack the information necessary to cast an informed ballot and drop off. For those who vote despite the paucity of available information, the most plausible inference is that voters who have confidence in the courts as institutions default to retain judges in the absence of information giving them reason to do otherwise.[51] And even when opposition surfaces, available evidence suggests that it rarely surfaces with sufficient energy and splash to affect outcomes.[52]

Conversely, on those "once in a blue moon" occasions when retention elections work as ostensibly intended by actually jeopardizing the tenure of a judge whose conduct in office is under scrutiny, they can pose a greater threat to judicial independence than contested elections. First, the judge is put at risk of being ambushed by an opposition campaign that attacks too late for the judge to mount a defense before the election is held, to the detriment of the incumbent (who is out of a job) and the voters (who were forced to make their choice after hearing only half of the story). Second, the electorate must consider the judge's shortcomings in a vacuum rather than in comparison to the shortcomings of other candidates, putting the incumbent at an additional disadvantage, and putting voters at risk of ousting a judge they dislike who will be replaced by another judge whom they will like even less. Third, aggressive, no-holds-barred campaigns in defense of retention are not part of the political culture in merit selection states: For incumbents who regard such politicking as injurious to judicial impartiality, independence, and integrity, and who decline to transform themselves into politicians, the rare, hotly contested retention election can leave them defenseless.

In the mid-twentieth century, marketing retention elections as the spoonful of sugar that helps the medicine of merit selection go down was an effective gambit for policymakers and their constituents who were loath to relinquish electoral accountability altogether. It is a less effective strategy today, as evidenced by the stall of the merit selection movement beginning in the 1980s. The specter of impending retention elections can influence judicial conduct, but with notable exceptions, retention elections are harmless because they are ineffective. To that extent, they are barely elections at all. That is why this book has situated merit selection systems (with or without retention elections) on the appointments side of the binary debate, and why the presence of retention elections does not operate as a significant departure from the default I advocate in favor of appointive systems. However, on those infrequent occasions when opposition campaigns in retention elections become meaningful—which recent increases in retention election spending suggests could become more common in the future—retention elections switch sides and join contested elections in the irreducibly binary choice that selection systems present. Thus, the retention election is not so much a moderate, hail fellow well met, middle of the road alternative, as a Jekyll and Hyde figure that is effete and impotent most of the time, except when it gets all hairy and awful.

Moving Off of the Default and Back

The merits of my proposed default position notwithstanding, the judiciary depends for its success on its continued legitimacy. In a representative democracy, all branches of government require the support and acquiescence of the governed. But that is particularly true of the judiciary, which lacks the executive branch's power to enforce court orders, and the legislative branch's power to appropriate revenue for court operations. Without legitimacy, the judiciary is helpless to thwart defiance of its rulings. Hence, there comes a tipping point, where the public ceases to trust its judges or those who appoint its judges, and where adding an element of electoral accountability can be necessary to preserve or restore legitimacy. At that tipping point, the default must yield to an elective system.

In states that have opted for elective systems, the question then becomes when a return to the default position is justified. Social science research suggests that in the new politics of judicial elections, a tipping point can occur in states with elective systems.[53] At that point, the perceived impact of elections on the litigating public and the rule of law (including the perception that justice is for sale in privately financed judicial campaigns) becomes adverse enough to outweigh the benefits of electoral accountability that justified a departure from the default position in the first place.

Underlying the concession that elective judiciaries can be justified under appropriate circumstances is a peculiar form of American exceptionalism. With the recent exception of Bolivia, the United States is the only nation on the planet to select a significant number of its judges in contested elections. For students of judicial systems in other countries, that renders the American experience an oddity, if not a punchline, given the inherent tension between judicial elections and judicial independence. The ubiquity of appointive systems around the globe contributes to my conclusion that they are the preferable default. But informed discussions of judicial selection in the United States do not occur in a vacuum; they occur in the context of a political culture in which elected judiciaries have been an entrenched part of the states' constitutional landscape for nearly two centuries. And in the modern era, those discussions occur in the context of state judicial systems that wield a form of judicial review more muscular than that exercised by their counterparts in most other countries, adding credibility to claims that elections can serve as an appropriate check on judicial power when necessary to preserve a given system's legitimacy with the general public.

JUDICIAL SELECTION AND TRIAL COURTS

Much of the scholarship and commentary on the relative merits of different selection systems across the states speaks categorically but focuses on appellate judiciaries—often without making that focus clear. The distinction is important, however, because differences between selection at the appellate and trial levels can affect the analysis in important ways.

In many respects, these differences render contested elections at the trial level more problematic. State high courts decide a small percentage of cases filed within the state—cases that are often hotly contested and fraught with policy implications that call upon the court to make new law. The bread and butter of trial courts, in contrast, consists of routine matters in which the law is clear and the policy implications of the court's legal rulings are limited. Moreover, pervasive intermediate appellate court review of trial court rulings keeps the excesses of trial courts in check. Contrast decisions of state supreme courts, which are subject to U.S. Supreme Court review only if their rulings touch upon issues arising under the U.S. Constitution or federal law, and then, only if the U.S. Supreme Court chooses a given case as one of the eighty it hears each year, of which only a third are appealed from state high courts (the remainder being appealed from lower federal courts). To the extent that contested judicial elections seek to align judicial policymaking with the public's preferences and discourage judicial policymaking gone rogue, the need for contested elections is diminished for trial judges, who make policy infrequently and are closely regulated by appellate courts when they do.

Trial judges may not make legal policy in the way appellate courts do, but they do exercise judgment and discretion in the context of the cases they hear. In those cases, trial judges have unique access to the facts and evidence presented in court that guide their discretion and judgment—access that voters lack. The specter of impending elections impinges on a trial judge's independence, as evidenced by studies showing that criminal defendants are likely to receive measurably longer terms of confinement if sentenced before an election when voters are looking over the judge's shoulder. While one can argue that this aligns sentencing practices with the electorate's policy preference for "getting tough" on crime, there are two reasons to second-guess that conclusion. First, the public lacks a judge's access to case-specific information that would inform the electorate's preferences if they knew what the judge knows, meaning that differences between judges and voters could have less to do with policy disagreements than information asymmetry. Second, judges sentence more harshly when elections approach even in liberal voting districts, where tough-on-crime campaigns hold no special appeal.[54] Researchers infer that judges do so as a precautionary measure, because judges are never at risk of losing their jobs for sentencing too harshly—the implication being that as elections approach in less conservative districts, risk-averse judges stiffen their sentences to avoid wildfires that a disgruntled minority of voters could ignite.[55]

Finally, trial court races are local, low-profile affairs. As such, they cannot generate the kind of voter interest and participation that arguably render hotly contested, well-financed statewide supreme court races information-rich, accountability-promoting events.[56] In states that select trial judges in partisan races, party affiliation may be the only information many voters have to work with. That has given rise to the unusual spectacle of trial judges of a given party being swept from office countywide, for reasons having nothing to do with their conduct in office.[57]

This latter point, however, cuts both ways. Low-profile races tend to be less threatening to incumbency—a national study found that 75 percent of trial court seats are uncontested.[58] While this calls into question the extent to which trial court elections hold judges accountable, it likewise suggests that such elections pose less of a threat to tenure and independence. Moreover, roll-off is not necessarily a bad thing to the extent that it limits the voting pool to those who are better able to make informed choices—although available research does not engender much optimism for this argument.[59]

Selection of judges for the trial courts needs to be studied separately and evaluated differently from the appellate bench. Because we do not know as much about the selection of trial judges, recommendations concerning preferred methods of selection must be more tentative. To date, the data do not justify a categorical departure from the default in favor of appointive systems, but local differences in political culture, demographics, and voter engagement counsel against sweeping generalizations.

Consider, for example, the issue of racial and gender diversity on the bench. Across the country, judges remain disproportionately white and male.[60] This is a problem for at least two reasons. First, the perceived legitimacy of the judiciary is significantly lower among African Americans— a phenomenon that has been linked to their underrepresentation on the bench.[61] Second, gender and race are among the life experiences that can inform a judge's discretion and judgment in difficult cases, particularly where issues relevant to race and gender are at stake; a diverse bench thus supplies a wider range of perspectives that enriches deliberation and improves decision-making.[62] Nationwide studies suggest that merit selection systems can do as well or better than contested elections at bringing minority, if not also female, candidates onto the bench.[63] But the data is made murky by significant local variations[64]: Much can depend on the racial composition of a given voting district, whether a voting district is resistant or receptive to minority or female candidates, whether a state's merit selection nominating commission is charged with or committed to creating a diverse candidate pool, and whether an appointing governor makes diversifying the bench a priority. Point being, this is just one illustration of local variations that can and should affect judicial selection choices in a given locale, even if one accepts that an appointive system is the preferable default, all else being equal.

CONCLUSION

The disciplinary divide between the law and politics camps that has led them to take unyielding positions in favor of appointive and elective systems respectively, is exaggerated by path dependence, assimilation bias, cognitive dissonance, and allegiance to different segments of the public. A more deeply interdisciplinary approach to judicial selection study and advocacy can narrow that divide, opening the door to incremental reforms and alternative systems of selection that accommodate both camps to varying degrees. But that divide cannot and perhaps should not be eliminated altogether. It cannot be eliminated because choosing to hold judges accountable to the electorate or not is ultimately a binary choice (with sub-variations), fraught with competing policy implications. That divide cannot be eliminated because one size does not fit all: Different states have different political cultures with different priorities, often justifying different selection systems at different points in their history. For reasons grounded in constitutional theory, institutional design, and judicial process, I have argued that appointive systems are the preferable default, or presumptive selection system of choice. But this is a soft and rebuttable presumption: appointive systems must yield to elective systems when the judiciary's legitimacy depends on supplying the people a greater measure of control over the judges who serve them.

THE FUTURE OF
JUDICIAL SELECTION

The debate over how best to pick judges in the United States has been endless, ever changing, and traditionally bound by a common thread. In the subtitle of his book, Jed Shugerman aptly describes the cycles of judicial selection reform he chronicles in terms of "pursuing judicial independence in America." When the countervailing impulse for judicial accountability and control has intruded upon judicial independence in ways perceived as problematic, reformers have jumped into the fray. Thus, widespread concern that King George and colonial governors exerted excessive control over the colonial judges they appointed catalyzed a move toward legislative appointment systems. Fears that state legislatures wielded excessive control over the judges they appointed spurred the partisan-election movement in the mid-nineteenth century. Concern that partisan-elected judges were beholden to the political parties that nominated them led to the nonpartisan election movement at the turn of the twentieth century. Worries that an uninformed electorate exerted too much control over the selection of nonpartisan judges, coupled with the suspicion that nominally nonpartisan systems did not end political party control but simply drove it underground, contributed to the launch of merit selection systems in the mid-twentieth century.

The Holy Grail in this epic quest has been a selection system in which judges are afforded independence from those who control their selection and tenure. One could spin the new politics critique of merit selection systems in a similar way: Merit selection systems arguably give excessive control over judicial selection to "elites," including lawyers, who are over-represented on nominating commissions, and governors who make the appointments.[1] But the primary objection to merit selection systems is not that commission-assisted appointment processes put judges under the thrall of lawyers, governors, or anyone else. The primary objection is that appointment processes, including merit selection, render judges too independent and too unaccountable. As Chris Bonneau and Melinda Gann Hall argue, the independence appointed judges enjoy is "the very feature[] that give[s] rise to their ability to decide cases without sanction based on their personal philosophies of law and public policy, which may or may not correspond with the rule of law...."[2]

The new politics of judicial elections, as described in chapter 3, add a recent twist to a centuries-old narrative. The new politics are new because the drivers and defenders of the new politics do not seek to promote an independent judiciary, but to constrain it. The core, nineteenth century justification for replacing appointive systems with popular elections—that it would protect judicial independence from encroachment by governors and legislatures—has been replaced with a new one: contested elections thwart rogue judges.[3] Against that backdrop, merit selection proponents are less "reformers," as they are often labeled by social scientists, than traditionalists. They rail against the new politics and the impulse to control judicial decision-making at the ballot box, and favor a system that better promotes an independent judiciary—the traditional justification for every new system of selection introduced since the eighteenth century.

For contemporary proponents, contested elections are legitimizing precisely because they constrain judicial independence and transfer to voters a measure of control over judges and the decisions they make. Well-financed, hotly contested judicial races in which a more engaged electorate ousts judges from office for rendering decisions at odds with the public's policy preferences embody democracy in action. In the modern era, then, those at the forefront of the new politics of judicial elections, who bankroll and defend competitive judicial campaigns, have, effectively, retitled the Shugerman story, "pursuing judicial dependence in America." To characterize the new politics in this way is not necessarily to condemn them. If judges are insufficiently different from other public officials to justify insulating them from the electoral accountability to which other public officials are subject, then pursuing a more dependent judiciary is a laudable objective. The crucial question is whether judges are different enough to justify a different system of selection.

Looking ahead, one can anticipate a period of calm relative to the recent past. Campaign spending shows signs of leveling off. That is not because the drivers of the new politics are losing steam. It is because they have prevailed. In the South, a period of intense, two-party competition began with upstart Republicans initiating a pitched battle to end a century of Democratic Party control over state supreme courts—a battle that the Republicans have won. Well-financed campaigns waged by the Chamber of Commerce and other business interests to repopulate state supreme courts with business-friendly judges—campaigns that bankrolled the new politics—have, for the most part, succeeded. And with victory, comes peace.

The ethos of the new politics, however, is likely to be more enduring. The merit selection movement was aided by what I have described elsewhere as the "rule of law paradigm."[4] That centuries-old paradigm postulates that independent judges will set extralegal influences aside and uphold the law. It underlies the law narrative described in chapter 5, which regards appointive systems (including merit selection) as independence promoting and hence more compatible with the rule of law. But the venerable rule of law paradigm is eroding. The vast majority of the public does not think that judges set their personal feelings or ideological preferences aside when deciding cases. And increasingly, the public finds that state of affairs unacceptable when its policy preferences deviate too markedly from the policies that judges putatively make in the decisions they render. This engenders skepticism of judicial independence and support for contested elections in the new politics of judicial selection that show no signs of going away.

To date, the judicial selection debate has, with exceptions, pitted two extremes against each other. On the one side, is the law narrative, which adheres to the rule of law paradigm, downplays extralegal influences on judicial decision-making, and regards appointive systems that insulate judges from electoral pressure as necessary to preserve judicial independence and the rule of law. On the other side is the politics narrative, which regards the role of law in judicial decision-making as malleable if not mythical, and conceptualizes judges as politicians in robes who, like other policymakers in a democratic republic, should be held accountable to their constituents in periodic elections. These competing narratives have contributed to a fractious and binary debate summarized in chapter 4.

For those who subscribe to the law narrative, judges uphold and apply rules of law like umpires call balls and strikes. Like umpires, judges cannot be expected to apply the rules of the game impartially if their jobs depend on keeping the fans happy. Hinging judicial tenure on the outcome of contested elections is thus anathema to independent and impartial administration of the law as evidenced by studies showing that judges rule differently to mollify their "constituents" as elections approach. Impact on judicial independence aside, contested elections are ill-advised because voters are incompetent to evaluate judicial candidates intelligently. Judges have specialized legal knowledge and training in law that voters are incompetent to assess. To make matters worse, voters are too apathetic to gather enough information about the candidates and issues to compensate for their incompetence, and so cast uniformed ballots or do not vote at all. Insofar as hotly contested, high-priced supreme court elections blitz the electorate with advertising, the information thereby imparted may have nothing to do with the candidate's qualifications, experience, diligence, or temperament. Rather, the money devoted to judicial campaigns may serve only to foster the perception, if not the reality, that those who bankroll the advertising are seeking to buy influence with the judge.

Proponents of elected judiciaries in contrast, conceptualize judges as policymakers in robes, who like other policymakers in a democratic republic, should be accountable in periodic elections to their constituents. If left to their own devices, judges will make policy that comports with their personal ideologies rather than the preferences of the people that judges ostensibly serve. To the extent that impending elections lead judges to vote differently out of concern for voter backlash, it is evidence of democracy in action. The democracy-enhancing benefits of contested judicial elections are further aided by contentious and well-financed, partisan campaigns, which increase voter knowledge and interest, and decrease roll-off. Moreover, whatever damage big money flowing into judicial races does to the judiciary's legitimacy (because of the perception that judges are beholden to their supporters) is typically offset by the legitimacy gains that electoral accountability supplies (because electoral accountability ensures that judges are acceptable to the people they serve).

As detailed in chapter 5, these dichotomous arguments are driven to opposite poles by pugnacious disputants who exaggerate their claims and ignore or mischaracterize opposing arguments and data. There are four possible explanations for this phenomenon:

—Path dependence and competing narratives: Those with legal training are acculturated to follow a well-trodden path that favors a law narrative, which begins by conceptualizing judges as umpires and leads to the conclusion that umpire-judges must be buffered from electoral accountability, to preserve the rule of law. Those with backgrounds in politics follow a different, equally well-worn path that begins with a politics narrative, which conceptualizes judges as politicians, and leads to the conclusion that politician-judges should be held accountable to the electorate, consistent with principles of representative democracy.

—Coping with cognitive dissonance: Cognitive psychology teaches us that when people receive new information that contradicts their existing beliefs, a common way to alleviate the resulting stress is to ignore or deny the new information. Thus, disputants cling to the judicial selection narrative they have embraced by disregarding or rejecting new information that undermines their arguments on its behalf.

—Motivated reasoning and assimilation bias: People are motivated to assimilate new information in ways compatible with their preexisting views. To the extent that new information in the judicial selection debate is ambiguous enough to tolerate competing interpretations, disputants will construe that information in ways consistent with their entrenched positions.

—Dueling publics: Devotees of elections and appointments both argue that the judiciary's legitimacy is promoted by their preferred method of selection, but often argue past each other. Proponents of elective systems tout the legitimacy-enhancing benefits of judicial elections for the voting public, while proponents of appointive systems argue that insulating judges from voter and special interest influence inspires confidence for the litigating public.

To no small extent, the schism between the election and appointment camps in the judicial selection debate is attributable to a disciplinary divide between law and politics. That schism pits those whose legal training and experience lead them to view independent judges as impartial guardians of law, against those whose training and experience in the rough and tumble of the political process lead them to view independent judges as unaccountable politicians. With exceptions, that has resulted in the law camp favoring appointive systems that promote judicial independence and the rule of law by insulating judges from electoral pressures, and the politics camp favoring elective systems that discourage rogue policymaking by holding judges accountable to the people they serve. These disciplinary ruts are deepened when disputants: hide from contradictory information as a means to avoid cognitive dissonance, assimilate ambiguous information in a manner consistent with their preexisting positions, and gravitate toward promoting the legitimacy of the judiciary for the benefit of whichever public is better accommodated by the disputants' preferred system of selection.

Chapter 6 argues that stridency can be lessened and the distance between the law and politics narratives diminished if academics and opinion leaders take a more deeply interdisciplinary approach to evaluating competing arguments in the judicial selection debate. Deep interdisciplinarity enables disputants to better identify exaggerated claims as such and to reconsider judicial selection alternatives in light of opposing data and claims. Such an approach reveals that neither the law nor the politics camps has gotten it right, and suggests the need for a new paradigm.

The long dominant rule of law paradigm is crumbling because its core premise—that independent judges follow the law and nothing else—is belied by data and rejected by those the paradigm seeks to guide. One can, however, reject the rigid rule of law paradigm and still accept the need for judicial independence. To say that more than law alone influences judicial decision-making is not to say that law is irrelevant. Judges are acculturated to take law seriously from their first days of law school. Studies support the conclusion that law matters in judicial decision-making, even if ideology and other extralegal factors can inform a judge's understanding of what the law requires—especially in difficult cases, when the law is indeterminate. Independence enables judges to uphold the law as they are acculturated to do, free from electoral intimidation to do otherwise. Independence liberates judges to afford litigants a full and fair hearing, unencumbered by pressure to reach a particular result by any means necessary. And independence creates a buffer that permits judges to set the public mood aside and dispense justice on the basis of case specific facts as applied to operative law—facts that judges are better situated than voters to know.

In an earlier work I argued for moving toward a new "legal culture paradigm," which proceeds from the premise that independent judges are predisposed to follow the law as they understand it to be written, but that legal indeterminacy requires judges to exercise judgment and discretion that can be influenced by extralegal factors, including their policy predilections. In acknowledging that judges are subject to ideological and other influences, the legal culture paradigm recognizes that judicial independence can be abused by judges who flout the judiciary's cultural norms, disregard the law, and impose their personal preferences. To deter such abuse, the legal culture paradigm appreciates a special need for judicial accountability.

The ultimate ambition of a legal culture paradigm is to render judges independent enough to follow the law, adhere to the established legal process, and administer justice, without being so independent as to enable them to disregard those objectives in pursuit of their personal agendas. The legal culture paradigm thus straddles the fence between the law and politics camps as I have described them here. It posits that judges are acculturated to take the law seriously, but that they are subject to ideological and other extralegal influences when exercising the judgment and discretion necessary to resolve legal disputes in which the law in relation to the facts is indeterminate. Viewed in that light, appointive systems can be defended as necessary to afford judges the independence they require to apply the law as they are acculturated to do. At the same time, elective systems can be defended as necessary to reassure the general public that independent judges can be deterred from succumbing to temptation and abusing their power by disregarding the law and imposing their personal policy preferences. In other words, the legal culture paradigm frames the arguments in the judicial selection debate without resolving them in favor of one selection system to the exclusion of the other.

To say that a final resolution is elusive, however, is not to say that we must throw our hands in the air. The comparative strengths that each system of selection brings to the table imply the presence of relative weaknesses that the rival system lacks. Hence, appointive systems can be criticized for rendering judges unaccountable to the people and free to impose their own biases, while elective systems can be criticized for rendering judges too dependent on majority whim. This state of affairs justifies an incremental reform agenda that renders judges in elective systems more independent and judges in appointive systems more accountable. And so, as chapter 6 argued, elective systems may better protect judicial independence and impartiality via campaign finance reform, disqualification rules requiring recusal for campaign conduct that engenders perceptions of bias and dependence, and longer terms of office that diminish the frequency of independence-threatening elections. At the same time, appointive systems can better promote public confidence in the accountability of the judiciary by: publicizing existing accountability-promoting mechanisms, most notably systems of judicial discipline; reinvigorating disqualification procedure to limit the opportunities for unelected judges to inflict their biases on litigants; and instituting rigorous judicial performance evaluations.

At the end of the day, however, incremental reform can shorten the divide between elective and appointive systems, but cannot eliminate it. Judges must either be subjected to contested elections or not. Retention elections, in which judges run against their records rather than opposing candidates may appear to steer a middle course but in practice, do not. The vast majority of the time, retention elections are rubber stamps that do not promote electoral accountability in any meaningful way. On those rare occasions in which opposition campaigns become meaningful affairs, retention elections threaten independence by rendering incumbents helpless to defend themselves in ways that contested elections do not.

The ultimately irreducible, either-or nature of the election versus appointment choice has never been resolved in favor of one over the other because neither system (nor any of their sub-variations) has established itself as universally optimal. Different states have different histories, different political cultures, and different problems with their courts that can be perceived in different ways at different times. Researchers have taken pains to emphasize the differences in experience with judicial elections that arise state-to -state and election-to-election. Those differences have rendered the judicial selection debate perpetual, and for good reason. Keeping different selection options on the table enables states to tailor selection systems to meet the particular needs of their respective jurisdictions at particular moments in time.

To say that no one system of selection is perfect or always optimal, however, is not to say that a state's choice between systems must be haphazard or unguided. Chapter 6 makes the case for a default in favor of appointive systems, for three reasons. First, appointive systems are more compatible with constitutional theory, which calls upon independent judges to keep the legislative and executive branches of government in check via (sometimes) countermajoritarian judicial review. Second, appointive systems are preferable as a matter of institutional design. They enable the judiciary to bring a unique perspective to its analysis of legal issues by virtue of the fact that it is not subject to the same majoritarian pressures that shape the thinking of the other departments of government. That enriches the inter-branch dialogue and improves deliberative democracy. Third, appointive systems are better suited to promote a sounder judicial process for the benefit of the litigating public by eliminating the influence of impending elections and campaign support on judicial decision-making.

Ultimately, a default in favor of appointive systems makes the most sense in light of the legal culture paradigm that I advocate. The starting point in that paradigm is with the defensible and documented premise that judges are acculturated to take law seriously. An appointive system proceeds from a similar premise—that judges who are independent from electoral pressure are predisposed to follow the law, and do not require voters breathing down their necks to do their jobs properly. Elections, in contrast, put judges under pressure to disregard the law whenever an outcome that the law requires is different from the outcome that the voters prefer.

That said, the legal culture paradigm does not suggest that the default in favor of appointive systems should be hard and fast. The new paradigm recognizes that judges are human, that they are subject to ideological and other influences that can get the best of them, and that more robust mechanisms for promoting judicial accountability may be necessary. For these reasons, there may be times when elective systems of judicial selection are needed to restore or preserve the general public's confidence in the legitimacy of a judiciary whose judges would otherwise be distrusted as unaccountable political actors promoting ideological (or other extralegal) agendas. At that tipping point, appointive systems must yield to elective.

Some readers are likely to quarrel with my conclusion that an appointive model is the better default, because they remain wedded to the politics narrative, because they do not buy into the legal culture paradigm, or because they do not think that a legal culture paradigm dictates a default in favor of appointive systems. Given the overarching point of chapter 6, that disagreement over the relative merits of elections and appointments can be diminished but not eliminated, I can live with the inevitability that some will deem contested elections a preferable default for all the reasons that chapter 4 offers in support of elective systems. But that inevitability does not contradict my more central point that whichever system is deemed a better default, it is nonetheless just a default. The centuries-old failure to reach consensus as to the optimal method of selection is both explained and justified in terms of a perpetual tension that will and should be resolved in favor of adopting different selection systems to meet the needs of changing times, circumstances, and priorities.

For states that are alert to the disadvantages of whichever system they have, but are loath to trade those drawbacks for different disadvantages that encumber the alternative, the "qualified election" model that I proposed in chapter 6 may be the best they can do. I do not make the case for a qualified election system being ideal (or preferable to the appointive system default that I recommend), but once you have determined that the food sources on your desert island are limited to lizards and seaweed, it is time to call off the search for ambrosia. The appeal of a qualified election approach lies in retaining the legitimacy-enhancing virtues of contested elections among qualified candidates, while rejecting the independence-threatening vices of reselection processes. In this way, a qualified election system seeks a middle ground that promotes general public confidence in the judiciary without sacrificing the litigating public's interest in a fair hearing. In jurisdictions where traditional contested elections and merit selection are regarded as unappealing choices akin to reptile slurry and algae surprise on the island menu, perhaps a qualified election system is iguana loin in kelp pesto: a welcome, if less than ideal alternative that may be the best under the circumstances.

Now is an important time to be thinking about the American judiciary, its judges, and how those judges should be selected. First, in the modern era, the judicial selection debate has pivoted away from its traditional focus on which system of selection is best suited to promote the rule of law by insulating judges from external interference with their impartial judgment. In its stead is a new focus on whether the rule of law is better promoted by elective systems that constrain—rather than promote—judicial independence, by deterring putatively rogue judges who disregard the law and impose their own idiosyncratic, ideological predilections. The outcome of this contemporary debate could redefine the role of American judges and courts for generations to come.

Second, it would be a mistake to think about state judicial selection independently of recent developments in American politics generally. In the United States, representative democracies with tripartite systems of government have long positioned their judiciaries as bulwarks against unconstitutional overreach by the legislative and executive branches of government. At the national level, that traditional role has been challenged by a new administration that regards as illegitimate judicial review adverse to its political agenda. As a traditionalist who has long defended the importance of a strong and independent judiciary, I confess to finding this development alarming. But that is beside a larger point to the extent that President Trump's impatience with an independent judiciary that is free to impose its "political" views is widely shared by those who propelled him into office. To the extent that significant segments of the public are becoming more skeptical of judicial systems operating independently of popular will, the debate over whether judges should be answerable to voters in contested elections acquires added urgency.

Finally, judicial selection reform has come and gone in waves. The last great reform movement—merit selection—stalled in the 1980s. The new politics of judicial elections that arose in the decades that followed was not a new selection reform movement, but a repurposing of existing selection processes for new(ish) ends, namely, to constrain at the ballot box the decision-making independence of the American judiciary. The new politics have, in effect, created a contentious lull, in which entrenched interests have doubled down on their binary positions in a perennial independence-versus-accountability debate over whether American judges should be elected or appointed.

History suggests that this current lull will precede a new reform movement to follow. One possibility is that a new movement could be prompted by a backlash against merit selection systems. States may tire of delegating selection to unelected "elites" on nominating commissions and return to a quasi-federal model (as some states have recently done) in which gubernatorial nomination is paired with legislative confirmation. Alternatively, disenchantment with merit selection may spark a new movement back to partisan election systems (as some leading political scientists recommend), if states accept the argument that judges are not different enough from other public officials to warrant insulating judges from the partisan electoral processes.

Conversely, the handful of jurisdictions that have moved from partisan to nonpartisan systems in recent decades could snowball and effectively eliminate partisan systems altogether, if such a move is bought and sold as a way to diminish the corrosive new politics of judicial elections in jurisdictions loath to end contested elections altogether. Alternativey, state courts could decide a new wave of hotly contested issues, prompting a resurgence of big money in judicial races and a concomitant concern about the legitimacy of courts under the thrall of special interests that is sufficient to reinvigorate the merit selection movement. Or generalized disenchantment with the existing menu of selection systems generally, and reselection processes in particular, could spark a movement toward something new, such as the qualified election model that I have proposed (without really proposing). In short, the current lull between reform movements affords an important opportunity to reflect on next steps.

The essential thrust of this book is to make peace with the prospect of approaching without achieving consensus. Disuniformity is both inevitable and desirable. It is inevitable as long as state and regional histories, political cultures, and current events, differ significantly enough to cultivate competing views as to whether judges can be counted on to uphold the law without voter supervision. It is desirable, because a menu of viable, alternative selection systems enables states to address the legitimacy problems that their courts encounter over time, without devolving into constitutional crises. There are good reasons to default in favor of appointive systems that keep the influence of interest group money at bay, and enable judges to apply the law, as they understand it to be written, without fear or favor. And there are circumstances in which that default should yield. Rather than fight the perpetual dynamism of diverse judicial selection alternatives in endless debates, perhaps the time has come to accept, and even celebrate that diversity.

NOTES

CHAPTER 1

1. 133 S. Ct. 2675 (2013).
2. *Hollingsworth v. Perry*, 133 S. Ct. 2652 (2013).
3. 135 S. Ct. 2584 (2015).
4. 135 S. Ct. 2584, 2608 (2015).
5. *Id.* at 2612 (Roberts, J., dissenting).
6. *Id.*
7. CHARLES GARDNER GEYH, WHEN COURTS AND CONGRESS COLLIDE: THE STRUGGLE FOR CONTROL OF AMERICA'S LEGAL SYSTEM (2008). In more recent work, I show how these norms have begun to erode—a cause for concern, relevant to the "new politics" of judicial elections at issue here. CHARLES GARDNER GEYH, COURTING PERIL: THE POLITICAL TRANSFORMATION OF THE AMERICAN JUDICIARY (2016).
8. Iowa Code §595.2(1) (2009).
9. *Varnum v. Brien*, 763, N.W. 2d 862, 875 (Ia. 2009).
10. *Id.* at 906.
11. TOM WITOWSKY & MARK HANSEN, EQUAL BEFORE THE LAW: HOW IOWA LED AMERICANS TO MARRIAGE EQUALITY 170 (2015).
12. Roy A. Schotland, *Iowa's 2010 Judicial Election: Appropriate Accountability or Rampant Passion?*, 46 CT. REV. 118, 123 (2011), available at http://scholarship.law.georgetown.edu/cgi/viewcontent.cgi?article=1680&context=facpub
13. *Id.*
14. The Eleventh Amendment overrode *Chisolm v. Georgia*, 2 U.S. 419 (1793) (holding that states lacked sovereign immunity from suit by citizens of other states); the Thirteenth and Fourteenth Amendments overrode *Dred Scott v. Sanford*, 60 U.S. 393 (1857) (holding that slaves were not citizens and that Congress was powerless to outlaw slavery); the Sixteenth Amendment overrode *Pollock v. Farmers' Loan & Trust Co.*, 158 U.S. 601 (1895) (holding that a federal income tax was unconstitutional); and the Nineteenth Amendment arguably overrode *Minor v. Happersett*, 88 U.S. 162 (1875) (holding that women had no constitutional right to vote).
15. 135 S. Ct. 475 (2014).

16. Federal courts, in contrast, do not make their own common law, but apply state common law when they exercise so-called diversity jurisdiction, which authorizes them to preside over cases governed by state law that arise between citizens of different or "diverse" states.
17. Gordon Tullock, *A Comment on Daniel Klein's "A Plea to Economists Who Favor Liberty,"* 27 EAST. ECON. J. 203, 2007, n.2 (2001).

CHAPTER 2

1. Jentleman's Case, 6 Co. Rep. 11a, 77 Eng. Rep. 269 (K.B.1606).
2. John Nichols, *Letter of Mr. Chamberlain to Dudley Carleton*, 2 THE PROGRESSES, PROCESSIONS, AND MAGNIFICENT FESTIVITIES OF KING JAMES FIRST 210 (1828).
3. *Id.*
4. J.R. TANNER, ENGLISH CONSTITUTIONAL CONFLICTS OF THE SEVENTEENTH CENTURY:1603–1689, at 36–37 (1947).
5. *Id.*
6. 4 W.S. HOLDSWORTH, A HISTORY OF ENGLISH LAW 173 (1924).
7. HENRY HALLAM, 1 THE CONSTITUTIONAL HISTORY OF ENGLAND, FROM ACCESSION OF HENRY VII TO THE DEATH OF GEORGE II 331 (1846).
8. SAMUEL GARIDNER, 2 A HISTORY OF ENGLAND FROM THE ACCESSION OF JAMES I TO THE DISGRACE OF CHIEF JUSTICE COKE 188 (1863).
9. HASTINGS LYON & HERMAN BLOCK, EDWARD COKE: ORACLE OF LAW 201 (1929).
10. Tanner, *supra* note 4, at 40.
11. CHARLES JAMES, CHIEF JUSTICE COKE: HIS FAMILY AND DESCENDANTS AT HOLKHAM 34 (1929).
12. Quoted and discussed in SCOTT DOUGLAS GERBER, A DISTINCT JUDICIAL POWER: THE ORIGINS OF AN INDEPENDENT JUDICIARY 1606–1787, at 48–49 (2011).
13. WILLIAM S. CARPENTER, JUDICIAL TENURE IN THE UNITED STATES 3 (1918).
14. EVAN HAYNES, THE SELECTION AND TENURE OF JUDGES IN THE UNITED STATES 101–35 (1945) (data drawn from table).
15. (R.I. 1786), private report reprinted in 1 THE BILL OF RIGHTS: A DOCUMENTARY HISTORY 417 (Bernard Schwartz ed., 1971).
16. For a fuller discussion of the circumstances surrounding this case, see WILLIAM S. CARPENTER, JUDICIAL TENURE IN THE UNITED STATES 16–19 (1918).
17. Brutus XVI, April 10, 1788.
18. Quoted in Barry Friedman, *The History of the Countermajoritarian Difficulty* (Part 1), 73 N.Y.U. L. REV. 333, 396 (1998).
19. *Id.* at 401.
20. Jed Handelsman Shugerman, *Economic Crisis and the Rise of Judicial Elections*, 123 HARV. L. REV. 1061, 1074–75 (2010).
21. FREDERICK ROBINSON, AN ORATION DELIVERED BEFORE THE TRADE UNIONS OF BOSTON 17 (1834).

22. Quoted in Kermit J. Hall, *The Judiciary on Trial: State Constitutional Reform and the Rise of an Elected Judiciary, 1846–60*, 45 THE HISTORIAN 337, 340–41 (1983).
23. Caleb Nelson, *A Reevaluation of Scholarly Explanations for the Rise of the Elective Judiciary in Antebellum America*, 37 AM. J. LEGAL HIST. 190 (1993).
24. Kermit L. Hall, *Progressive Reform and the Decline of Democratic Accountability: The Popular Election of State Supreme Court Judges, 1850–1920*, 1984 AM. BAR FOUND. RES. J. 345.
25. Jed Handelsman Shugerman, *Economic Crisis and the Rise of Judicial Elections*, 123 HARV. L. REV. 1061, 1076–92 (2010).
26. Andrew Hanssen, *Learning About Judicial Independence, Institutional Change in State Courts*, 33 J. LEGAL STUD. 431, 442 (2004).
27. 198 U.S. 45 (1905).
28. PETER G. FISH, THE POLITICS OF FEDERAL JUDICIAL ADMINISTRATION 18 (1973).
29. JAMES MANAHAN, RECALL OF JUDGES 9 (1912).
30. *Id.* at 12.
31. Quoted in WILLIAM G. ROSS, A MUTED FURY: POPULISTS, PROGRESSIVES AND LABOR UNIONS CONFRONT THE COURTS, 1890–1937, at 111 (1994).
32. *Id.* at 115 (quoting Utah Republican senator George Sutherland).
33. Special Message of the President of the United States, Returning Without Approval House Joint Resolution 14 at 4 (Aug. 15, 2011).
34. Richard Ruelas, *Judicial "Fib" Got Arizona Its Statehood*, ARIZONA REPUBLIC, Feb. 20, 2010.
35. Charles Boston, *Some Conservative Views upon the Judiciary and Judicial Recall*, 23 YALE L. J. 511 (1914).
36. Albert M. Kales, *Methods of Selecting and Retiring Judges*, BULLETIN VI, AMERICAN JUDICATURE SOC'Y 36 (1914).
37. Harold J. Laski, *The Technique of Judicial Appointment*, 24 MICH. L. REV. 529 (1926).
38. *Id.*
39. *The Eligible List of Judicial Candidates*, I 1 J. AM. JUD. SOC'Y 131, 131–32 (1928).
40. Discussed in Rachel Caufield, *What Makes Merit Selection Different?*, 15 ROGER WILLIAMS L. REV. 765, 768–69 (2010).
41. *The Press. Pants Afire*, TIME MAG., Jan. 23, 1939.
42. JED SHUGERMAN, THE PEOPLE'S COURTS: PURSUING JUDICIAL INDEPENDENCE IN AMERICA. 238 (2012).
43. *Id.*
44. *Id.* at 239.
45. James Bopp Jr., *The Perils of Merit Selection*, 46 IND. L. REV. 87 (2013); Seth Andersen, *Examining the Decline of Merit Selection in the States*, 67 ALB. L. REV. 793 (2004).
46. Beverly Gage, *How "Elites" Became One of the Nastiest Epithets in American Politics*, N.Y. TIMES MAG., Jan. 3, 2017; Magali Sarfatti Larson & Douglas Porpora, *The Resistible Rise of Sarah Palin: Continuity and Paradox in the American Right Wing*, 26 SOCIOLOGICAL FORUM 754 (2011).

CHAPTER 3

1. Stefanie Lindquist, *Judicial Activism and State Supreme Courts: Institutional Design and Judicial Behavior*, 28 STAN. L. & POL. REV. 61 (2017).
2. Roy Schotland, *A Plea for Reality*, 74 MO. L. REV. 507, 508 (2009).
3. Roy A. Schotland, *Comment*, 61 L. & CONTEMP. PROBS., 149, 150 (1998).
4. Anthony Champagne & Kyle Cheek, *The Cycle of Judicial Elections: Texas as a Case Study*, 29 FORDHAM URB. L.J. 907, 910–11 (2002).
5. *Id.* at 913–15
6. HERBERT KRITZER, JUSTICES ON THE BALLOT 118–19 (2015).
7. *Id.* at 120.
8. Cassandra Burke Robertson, *The Right to Appeal*, 91 N.C. L. REV. 1219, 1221–22 (2013).
9. COUNCIL OF CHIEF JUDGES OF THE STATE COURTS OF APPEAL, THE ROLE OF STATE INTERMEDIATE APPELLATE COURTS 2 (2012).
10. Gerald B. Cope Jr., *Discretionary Review of the Decisions of Intermediate Appellate Courts: A Comparison of Florida's System with Those of Other States and the Federal System*, 45 FLA. L. REV. 27 (1993); *Intermediate Appellate Courts*, BALLOTPEDIA, http://www.ballotpedia.org//Intermediate_appellate_courts.
11. PAUL CARRINGTON, DANIEL MEADOR & MAURICE ROSENBERG, JUSTICE ON APPEAL 4 (1976).
12. Margaret Meriwether Cordray & Richard Cordray, *The Supreme Court's Plenary Docket*, 58 WASH. & LEE L. REV. 737, 751 (2001); *See also* G. Alan Tarr, *State Judicial Selection and Judicial Independence*, App. D at 6–7, *in* AMERICAN BAR ASSOCIATION COMMISSION ON THE 21ST CENTURY JUDICIARY, JUSTICE IN JEOPARDY (2003).
13. William J. Brennan, Jr., *State Constitutions and the Protection of Individual Rights*, 90 HARV. L. REV. 489 (1977).
14. *City of Mesquite v. Aladdin's Castle, Inc.*, 455 U.S. 283, 293 (1982).
15. Shirley Abrahamson, *The Reincarnation of State Courts*, 36 Sw. L.J. 951 (1982).
16. William J. Brennan, *The Bill of Rights and the States: The Revival of State Constitutions as Guardians of Individual Rights* 61, N.Y.U. L. REV. 535, 548 (1986).
17. Abrahamson, *supra* note 15, at 962.
18. JOHN HAGAN, WHO ARE THE CRIMINALS? THE POLITICS OF CRIME POLICY FROM THE AGE OF ROOSEVELT TO THE AGE OF REAGAN 17 (2010).
19. M. SHAHIDULLAH SHAHID, CRIME POLICY IN AMERICA: LAWS, INSTITUTIONS, AND PROGRAMS 13–14 (2008).
20. Leo Wolinsky, *Governor's Support for Two Justices Tied to Death Penalty Votes*, L.A. TIMES, Mar. 14, 1986 at 3.
21. Stephen B. Bright & Patrick Keenan, *Judges and the Politics of Death: Deciding Between the Bill of Rights and the Next Election in Capital Cases*, 75 B.U. L. REV. 759, 763–64 (1995).
22. *Id.* at 761–62
23. Traciel V. Reid, *The Politicization of Retention Elections*, 83 JUDICATURE 68 (1999).
24. Anthony Champagne, *Television Ads in Judicial Campaigns*, 35 IND. L. REV. 669, 673 (2002).

25. Chris Bonneau, *The Dynamics of Campaign Spending in State Supreme Court Elections*, in RUNNING FOR JUDGE: THE RISING POLITICAL, FINANCIAL, AND LEGAL STAKES IN JUDICIAL ELECTIONS 59 (Matthew Streb ed., 2007).
26. JAMES SAMPLE ET AL., THE NEW POLITICS OF JUDICIAL ELECTIONS 2006, at 10 (2007).
27. SCOTT GREYTAK ET AL., BANKROLLING THE BENCH: THE NEW POLITICS OF JUDICIAL ELECTIONS 2013-14, at 49 (2015).
28. Alicia Bannon & Scott Greytak, *The Big Money Propping Up Harsh Sentences*, THE ATLANTIC, Nov.14, 2015, https://www.theatlantic.com/politics/archive/2015/11/the-big-money-propping-up-harsh-sentences/415362/
29. Tom Wicker, *In the Nation: A Naked Power Grab*, N.Y. TIMES, Sept. 14, 1986.
30. Michael L. Rustad & Thomas H. Koenig, *Taming the Tort Monster: The American Civil Justice System as a Battleground for Social Theory*, 68 BROOK. L. REV. 1, 42 (2002).
31. Mark E. Roszkowski & Robert A. Prentice, *Reconciling Comparative Negligence and Strict Liability: A Public Policy Analysis*, 33 ST. LOUIS U. L.J. 19, 25–30 (1988).
32. Michael L. Rustad & Thomas H. Koenig, *Taming the Tort Monster: The American Civil Justice System as a Battleground for Social Theory*, 68 BROOK. L. REV. 1, 5 (2002).
33. Victor E. Schwarz & Marke A. Behrens, *Punitive Damages Reform: State Legislatures Can and Should Meet the Challenge Issued by the Supreme Court of the United States in Haslip*, 42 AM U. L. REV. 1365, 1369–70 (1993).
34. John C. Coffee, Jr., *Class Wars: The Dilemma of the Mass Tort Class Action*, 95 COLUM. L. REV. 1343 (1995); See also Alvin B. Rubin, *Mass Torts and Litigation Disasters*, 20 GA. L. REV. 429 (1986).
35. Robert A. Prentice & Mark E. Roszkowski, *"Tort Reform" and the Liability "Revolution": Defending Strict Liability in Tort for Defective Products*, 27 GONZ. L. REV. 251 (1992).
36. Rachel M. Janutis, *The Struggle over Tort Reform and the Overlooked Legacy of the Progressives*, 39 AKRON L. REV. 943, 944–45 (2006).
37. For a discussion of the 1988 Texas campaign, *see* Anthony Champagne, *Tort Reform and Judicial Selection*, 38 LOY. L.A. L. REV. 1483, 1483–84 (2005).
38. *Id.* at 1499–506.
39. For a more detailed discussion of these developments, see CHARLES GARDNER GEYH, COURTING PERIL: THE POLITICAL TRANSFORMATION OF THE AMERICAN JUDICIARY, ch. 2 (2016).
40. CHARLES GARDNER GEYH, WHEN COURTS & CONGRESS COLLIDE: THE STRUGGLE FOR CONTROL OF AMERICA'S JUDICIAL SYSTEM 196–222 (2006).
41. Charles Gardner Geyh, *Preserving Public Confidence in the Courts in an Age of Individual Rights and Public Skepticism*, in BENCH-PRESS: THE COLLISION OF THE COURTS, POLITICS AND THE MEDIA 18 (Keith Bybee ed., 2007).
42. Paul Carrington, *Politics and Civil Procedure Rulemaking: Reflections on Experience*, 60 DUKE L.J. 597 (2010).
43. 2011 Year-End Report on the Federal Judiciary 4 (2011), https://www.supremecourt.gov/publicinfo/year-end/2011year-endreport.pdf.

44. Charles Gardner Geyh, Courting Peril: The Political Transformation of the American Judiciary 80–85 (2016).
45. Julie Hirschfield Davis, *Supreme Court Nominee Calls Trump's Attacks on the Judiciary "Demoralizing,"* N.Y. Times, Feb. 8, 2017.
46. Herbert Kritzer, *Contestation and Competitiveness in State Supreme Court Elections, 1946–2015*, in Judicial Elections in the 21st Century 33, 51 (Chris W. Bonneau & Melinda Gann Hall eds., 2017).
47. For online editions of all "New Politics of Judicial Elections" reports, *see* http://www.brennancenter.org/analysis/new-politics-judicial-elections-all-reports.
48. James Sample et al., The New Politics of Judicial Elections 2000–2009, at 5 (2010).
49. Adam Skaggs et al., The New Politics of Judicial Elections 2009–2010, at 5 (2011).
50. *Id.*; Scott Greytak et al., Bankrolling the Bench: The New Politics of Judicial Elections 2013–14, at 9 (2015).
51. Alicia Bannon et al., The New Politics of Judicial Elections 2011–12, at 6 (2013).
52. Chris Bonneau, *A Survey of Empirical Evidence Concerning Judicial Elections*, Federalist Society State Courts White Paper, Feb. 12, 2012, https://fedsoc.org/commentary/publications/a-survey-of-empirical-evidence-concerning-judicial-elections ("The body of evidence, taken together, suggests that if a state changes its method of selection from partisan to nonpartisan elections, this will result in lower levels of contestation . . . ").
53. The same is not true for incumbent spending. That is presumably because incumbency confers advantages that increased spending cannot do as much to improve upon.
54. Scott Greytak et al., Executive Summary, The New Politics of Judicial Elections: 2013–14 Report—Bankrolling the Bench (2015).
55. Larry T. Aspin, *Judicial Retention Elections*, in Judicial Elections in the 21st Century 93, 95, 132 (Chris W. Bonneau & Melinda Gann Hall eds., 2017).
56. Paul Blumenthal, *This Dark Money Group Is Spending Big on Judicial Elections, and No One Knows Why*, Huffington Post, Nov. 3, 2016, http://www.huffingtonpost.com/entry/dark-money-judicial-races-center-for-individual-freedom_us_581b5234e4b0c43e6c1e740d.
57. Alicia Bannon et al., The New Politics of Judicial Elections 2011–12, at 5 (2013).
58. Scott Greytak et al., Bankrolling the Bench: The New Politics of Judicial Elections 2013–14, at 2 (2015).
59. Chris W. Bonneau, *Fundraising and Spending in State Supreme Court Elections*, in Judicial Elections in the 21st Century 79, 88–89 (Chris W. Bonneau & Melinda Gann Hall eds., 2017).
60. Melinda Gann Hall, Attacking Judges: How Campaign Advertising Influences State Supreme Court Elections 74 (2015).
61. *Id.*; Herbert M. Kritzer, Justices on the Ballot 165 (2015).
62. Hall, *supra* note 60, at 74, 77, 90.

63. *Id.* at 76.
64. *Id.* at 75.
65. *Republican Party of Minnesota v. White*, 536 U.S. 765 (2002).
66. *Caperton v. A. T. Massey Coal Co.*, 556 U.S. 868 (2009).
67. *Citizens United v. Fed. Election Comm'n*, 558 U.S. 310 (2010).
68. *Williams-Yulee v. Florida State Bar*, 135 S. Ct. 1656, 1662 (2015).

CHAPTER 4

1. *See* chapter 2, for a description of these five systems and how they evolved in relation to each other, and chapter 3, Tables 3-1 and 3-2 for a summary of which states employ what selection systems.
2. American Bar Association Division for Public Education, *How Courts Work*, last visited Sep. 13, 2018, http://www.americanbar.org/groups/public_education/resources/law_related_education_network/how_courts_work/judge_role.html.
3. Chief Justice Roberts, Statement at Nomination Process (Sept. 12, 2005) (transcript available at http://www.uscourts.gov/educational-resources/educational-activities/chief-justice-roberts-statement-nomination-process).
4. *Justice Stevens Criticizes Election of Judges*, WASH. POST, Aug. 4, 1996, at A14.
5. Gregory A. Huber & Sanford C. Gordon, *Accountability and Coercion: Is Justice Blind When It Runs for Office?* 48 AM. J. POL. SCI. 247 (2004).
6. *Id.* at 248.
7. Richard Caldarone, Brandice Canes-Wrone, & Tom S. Clark, *Partisan Labels and Democratic Accountability: An Analysis of State Supreme Court Abortion Decisions*, 71 J. POL. 560 (2009).
8. Sanford C. Gordon & Gregory A. Huber, *The Effect of Electoral Competitiveness on Incumbent Behavior*, 2 Q.J. POL. SCI. 107 (2007).
9. Carol Savchak & A.J. Barghothi, *The Influence of Appointment and Retention Constituencies: Testing Strategies of Judicial Decisionmaking*, 7 ST. POL. & POL'Y Q. 394 (2007).
10. *Republican Party of Minn. v. White*, 536 U.S. 765, 804 (2002) (Ginsburg, J. dissenting).
11. *Id.*
12. MODEL CODE OF JUDICIAL CONDUCT, Rule 2.4 (2007). The directive not to be swayed by public clamor first appeared in the 1924 Canons of Judicial Ethics. CANONS OF JUDICIAL ETHICS Canon 14 (1924), http://www.americanbar.org/content/dam/aba/migrated/cpr/pic/1924_canons.authcheckdam.pdf.
13. ABA COMMISSION ON THE 21ST CENTURY JUDICIARY, Formal Op. 2 (2003).
14. For a discussion of the antagonism directed at lower federal court judges in the southern states during the civil rights era, *see* JACK BASS, UNLIKELY HEROES (1981).
15. Terri Peretti, *Does Judicial Independence Exist? The Lessons of Social Science Research*, *in* JUDICIAL INDEPENDENCE AND THE CROSSROADS: AN INTERDISCIPLINARY APPROACH 103, 111 (Stephen Burbank & Barry Friedman eds., 2002).

16. John M. Scheb II & William Lyons, *The Myth of Legality and Public Evaluation of the Supreme Court*, 81 Soc. Sci. Q. 928 (2000).
17. JEFFREY A. SEGAL & HAROLD J. SPAETH, THE SUPREME COURT AND THE ATTITUDINAL MODEL 17 (1993).
18. CHRIS BONNEAU & MELINDA GANN HALL, IN DEFENSE OF JUDICIAL ELECTIONS 14 (2009).
19. *Id.* at 15.
20. Dmitry Bam, *Voter Ignorance and Judicial Elections*, 102 KY. L. J. 553, 566–68 (2013).
21. For a timeline of the events described here, *see A Roy Moore Timeline: From Ten Commandments to Senate Candidate*, AL.COM (last updated Dec. 12, 2017, 1:42 PM), http://www.al.com/news/birmingham/index.ssf/2016/05/a_roy_moore_timeline_from_ten.html#0.
22. RICHARD A. WATSON & RONDAL G. DOWNING, THE POLITICS OF THE BENCH AND THE BAR 283 (1969) (fewer merit-selected judges rank in lowest quality quartile than elected judges); Malia Reddick, *Judging the Quality of Judicial Selection Methods: Merit Selection, Elections, and Judicial Discipline* (2010), https://papers.ssrn.com/sol3/papers.cfm?abstract_id=2731018 (merit-selected judges disciplined less frequently in six of nine jurisdictions studied).
23. Laurence Baum, *Judicial Elections and Judicial Independence: The Voter's Perspective*, 64 OH. ST. L.J. 213 (2003) (discussing data from unpublished paper by Melinda Gann Hall).
24. Roscoe Pound, *The Causes of Popular Dissatisfaction with the Administration of Justice*, 40 AM. L. REV. 729 (1906).
25. James Podgers, *O'Connor on Judicial Elections: "They're Awful. I Hate them,"* ABA J. (May 9, 2009), http://www.abajournal.com/news/article/oconnor_chemerinsky_sound_warnings_at_aba_conference_about_the_dangers_of_s/.
26. *Republican Party of Minn. v. White*, 536 U.S. 765 (2002).
27. Joanna Shepherd, *Money, Politics, and Impartial Justice*, 58 DUKE L J. 623, 669 (2009).
28. Stephen J. Ware, *Money, Politics and Judicial Decisions: A Case Study of Arbitration Law in Alabama*, 30 CAP. U. L. REV. 583 (2002); Eric Waltenburg & Charles Lopeman, *Tort Decisions and Campaign Dollars*, 28 SE. POL. REV. 241 (2000); Matias Iaryczower & Matthew Shum, *Money in Judicial Politics: Individual Contributions and Collective Decisions* (2012), available at http://papers.ssrn.com/sol3/papers.cfm?abstract_id=1998895; Daman M. Cann, *Justice for Sale? Campaign Contributions and Judicial Decisionmaking*, 7 ST. POL. & POL'Y Q. 281 (2007); Vernon V. Palmer, *An Empirical Assessment of the Risk of Actual Bias in Decisions Involving Campaign Contributors* (2010), available at http://papers.ssrn.com/sol3/papers.cfm?abstract_id=1721665; Chris M. Bonneau & Damon M. Cann, *The Effect of Campaign Contributions on Judicial Decisionmaking* (2009), available at http://papers.ssrn.com/sol3/papers.cfm?abstract_id=1337668; Amon McLeod, *Bidding for Justice: A Case Study About the Effect of Campaign Contributions on Judicial Decision-Making*, 85 U. DET. MERCY L. REV. 385 (2008); Adam Liptak & Janet Roberts, *Tilting the*

Scales?: The Ohio Experience; Campaign Cash Mirrors a High Court Ruling, N.Y. TIMES, Oct. 1, 2006; Madhavi McCall, *The Politics of Judicial Elections: The Influence of Campaign Contributions on the Voting Patterns of Texas Supreme Court Justices, 1994–1997*, 31 POL. & POL'Y 314 (2003); Mondhavi McCall & Michael McCall, *Campaign Contributions, Judicial Decisions, and the Texas Supreme Court*, 90 JUDICATURE 214 (2007). A Nevada study found no correlation, and studies in Wisconsin reached mixed results.

29. Stephen J. Ware, *Money, Politics and Judicial Decisions: A Case Study of Arbitration Law in Alabama*, 30 CAP. U. L. REV. 583, 584 (2002).
30. Daman M. Cann, *Justice for Sale? Campaign Contributions and Judicial Decisionmaking*, 7 ST. POL. & POL'Y Q. 281 (2007).
31. Chris M. Bonneau & Damon M. Cann, *The Effect of Campaign Contributions on Judicial Decisionmaking* (2009), available at http://papers.ssrn.com/sol3/papers.cfm?abstract_id=1337668.
32. JOANNA SHEPARD, JUSTICE AT RISK: AN EMPIRICAL ANALYSIS OF CAMPAIGN CONTRIBUTIONS AND JUDICIAL DECISIONS 1 (2013).
33. Justice Sandra Day O'Connor, *Introduction* to THE NEW POLITICS OF JUDICIAL ELECTIONS 2000–2009 (2010).
34. *Tort Reformers Score Victories in Midwest Judicial Races*, INS. J. (Nov. 22, 2004), http://www.insurancejournal.com/magazines/features/2004/11/22/49934.htm.
35. Charles Gardner Geyh, *Why Judicial Elections Stink*, 64 OH. ST. L.J. 47 (2003).
36. JAMES GIBSON, ELECTING JUDGES: THE SURPRISING EFFECTS OF CAMPAIGNING ON JUDICIAL LEGITIMACY 105–28 (2012).
37. JAMES L. GIBSON & GREGORY A. CALDEIRA, CITIZENS, COURTS, AND CONFIRMATIONS: POSITIVITY THEORY AND THE JUDGMENTS OF THE AMERICAN PEOPLE (2009).
38. Mark Jonathan McKenzie & Ryan Rebe, *Trial Court Campaign Messaging in a Post-White Environment*, in JUDICIAL ELECTIONS IN THE 21ST CENTURY 158, 169–70 (Chris W. Bonneau & Melinda Gann Hall eds., 2016).
39. *Id.* at 170.
40. This is essentially a one-sentence summary of Bonneau and Hall's argument in defense of judicial elections—an argument they support with extensive reference to the social science literature, much of which they have authored.
41. BONNEAU & HALL, *supra* note 18 at 98.
42. *See generally,* CHRIS W. BONNEAU & DAMON M. CANN, VOTERS'S VERDICTS: CITIZENS, CAMPAIGNS, AND INSTITUTIONS IN STATE SUPREME COURT ELECTIONS (2015).
43. Jazmine Ulloa, *As Brock Turner Is Released, Politicians Demand Ouster of Judge in Stanford Rape Case*, L.A. TIMES (Sept. 2, 2016), http://www.latimes.com/politics/la-pol-ca-aaron-persky-recall-brock-turner-release-20160902-snap-story.html.
44. Matt Ferner, *Judge Handcuffs Defense Attorney in Court to Teach Her "a Lesson" for Speaking Out*, HUFFINGTON POST (May 27, 2016), http://www.huffingtonpost.com/entry/judge-handcuffs-defense-attorney_us_5748744ee4b0dacf7ad4bea3.

45. Matt Ferner, *Las Vegas Judge Who Humiliated Defense Attorney Loses Election in a Landslide*, HUFFINGTON POST (Dec. 19, 2016), http://www.huffingtonpost.com/entry/conrad-hafen-judge-loses_us_57618da5e4b09c926cfdd61f.
46. Henry R. Glick & Craig F. Emmert, *Selection Systems and Judicial Characteristics: The Recruitment of State Supreme Court Judges*, 70 JUDICATURE 228 (1987).
47. GREG GOELZHAUSER, CHOOSING STATE SUPREME COURT JUSTICES: MERIT SELECTION AND THE CONSEQUENCES OF INSTITUTIONAL REFORM 110 (2016).
48. Stephen J. Choi, Mitu Gulati & Eric Posner, *Professionals or Politicians: The Uncertain Case for an Elected Rather than Appointed Judiciary*, 26 J.L. ECON. & ORG. 290 (2010).
49. BONNEAU & HALL, *supra* note 18 at 137.
50. RICHARD A. WATSON & RONDAL G. DOWNING, THE POLITICS OF BENCH AND BAR 107–11 (1969).
51. ALLAN ASHMAN & JAMES J. ALFINI, THE KEY TO JUDICIAL MERIT SELECTION: THE NOMINATING PROCESS 75 (1974).
52. JOANNE MARTIN, MERIT SELECTION COMMISSIONS: WHAT DO THEY DO? HOW EFFECTIVE ARE THEY? 20–22 (1993).
53. Brian T. Fitzpatrick, *The Politics of Merit Selection*, 74 MO. L. REV. 675 (2009).
54. BONNEAU & HALL, *supra* note 18, at 26–28.
55. *Id.* at 80–81.
56. ABA Comm'n on Pub. Fin. of Judicial Campaigns, Formal Op. 30 (2002).
57. The general, and all but universally adopted disqualification standard, calls upon judges to disqualify themselves when their impartiality "might reasonably be questioned." MODEL CODE OF JUDICIAL CONDUCT, Rule 2.11(A) (2007).
58. Tony Mauro, *New Recusal Controversy in West Virginia High Court*, THE BLT (Sept. 24, 2010), http://legaltimes.typepad.com/blt/2010/09/new-recusal-controversy-in-west-virginia-high-court.html.
59. MODEL CODE OF JUDICIAL CONDUCT, Rule 2.11(A)(5) (2007).
60. *Caperton v. A T. Massey Coal Co.*, 556 U.S. 868 (2009).
61. MODEL CODE OF JUDICIAL CONDUCT, Rule 2.11(A) (2007).
62. *See, e.g.*, GA. CODE OF JUDICIAL CONDUCT, r. 3.9(B) (2014) (subjecting judges to disqualification for campaign contributions or support under specified circumstances, with commentary creating a rebuttable presumption against disqualification for contributions below the statutory contribution limit).

CHAPTER 5

1. Pew Research Center, *Negative Views of Supreme Court at Record High, Driven by Republican Dissatisfaction* (July 29, 2015), http://www.people-press.org/2015/07/29/negative-views-of-supreme-court-at-record-high-driven-by-republican-dissatisfaction/ ("Seven-in-ten Americans (70%) say that in deciding cases, the justices of the Supreme Court 'are often influenced by their own political views.' ").
2. Theodore W. Ruger, Pauline T. Kim, Andrew D. Martin & Kevin M. Quinn, *The Supreme Court Forecasting Project: Legal and Political Science Approaches to Predicting Supreme Court Decisionmaking*, 104 COLUM. L. REV. 1150, 1152 (2004).

3. Quoted in Lawrence Baum, *Law and Policy: More and Less than a Dichotomy*, in WHAT'S LAW GOT TO DO WITH IT?: WHAT JUDGES DO, WHY THEY DO IT, AND WHAT'S AT STAKE 71, 85 (Charles Gardner Geyh ed., 2011).
4. CHRIS W. BONNEAU & MELINDA GANN HALL, IN DEFENSE OF JUDICIAL ELECTIONS 15 (2009) ("We think it far better for justices to draw upon public perceptions . . . when resolving difficult disputes[.] In fact, strategic contingencies... should bring justices into line with the rule of law rather than negate it.").
5. CHRIS W. BONNEAU & MELINDA GANN HALL, IN DEFENSE OF JUDICIAL ELECTIONS 14–15 (2009) (relying on U.S. Supreme Court studies to support the conclusion that unelected state supreme court justices "engage in the unfettered pursuit of their own personal preferences").
6. LEE EPSTEIN, WILLIAM M. LANDES & RICHARD A. POSNER, THE BEHAVIOR OF FEDERAL JUDGES: A THEORETICAL AND EMPIRICAL STUDY OF RATIONAL CHOICE 9 (2013); FRANK B. CROSS, DECISION MAKING IN THE U.S. COURTS OF APPEALS 51, 228 (2007).
7. Sara C. Benesh & Wendy L. Martinek, *Context and Compliance: A Comparison of State Supreme Courts and the Circuits*, 93 MARQ. L. REV. 795, 815 (2009).
8. Stefanie A. Lindquist, *Stare Decisis as Reciprocity Norm*, in WHAT'S LAW GOT TO DO WITH IT?: WHAT JUDGES DO, WHY THEY DO IT, AND WHAT'S AT STAKE 173, 184–85 (Charles Gardner Geyh ed., 2011). Lindquist found that supreme courts selected via nonpartisan elections and merit selection fell between these extremes.
9. Sara C. Benesh & Wendy L. Martinek, *Context and Compliance: A Comparison of State Supreme Courts and the Circuits*, 93 MARQ. L. REV. 795, 815–16 (2009).
10. Roy A. Schotland, *Iowa's 2010 Judicial Election: Appropriate Accountability or Rampant Passion?*, 46 CT. REV. 118, 123 (2011).
11. Richard P. Caldarone, Brandice Canes-Wrone, & Tom S. Clark, *Partisan Labels and Democratic Accountability: An Analysis of State Supreme Court Abortion Decisions*, 71 J. POL. 560, 571 (2009).
12. James L. Gibson & Gregory A. Caldeira, *Knowing the Supreme Court? A Reconsideration of Public Ignorance of the High Court*, 71 J. POL. 429, 431–33 (2009).
13. *Id.* at 432.
14. *Id.* at 433 (the researchers phrased the judicial review question in terms of whether the Court had the "last say" on the Constitution).
15. *Id.* at 433, 439.
16. CHRIS W. BONNEAU & MELINDA GANN HALL, IN DEFENSE OF JUDICIAL ELECTIONS 98, 133 (2009).
17. James L. Gibson & Gregory A. Caldeira, *Knowing the Supreme Court? A Reconsideration of Public Ignorance of the High Court*, 71 J. POL. 429, 433 (2009).
18. James L. Gibson, *Judging the Politics of Judging: Are Politicians in Robes Inevitably Illegitimate?*, in WHAT'S LAW GOT TO DO WITH IT: WHAT JUDGES DO, WHY THEY DO IT, AND WHAT'S AT STAKE 281, 293 (Charles Gardner Geyh ed., 2011).
19. This explanation is consonant with the impetus for the merit selection movement, which was premised in part on the concern that name recognition, rather than qualifications, influenced voter decision-making in contested judicial elections.

20. When candidates with prior judicial experience identify themselves as "judge," it can invite the false inference that they are incumbents—an issue that has given rise to ethical issues. CHARLES GARDNER GEYH, JAMES J. ALFINI, STEVEN LUBET & JEFFREY L. SHAMAN, JUDICIAL CONDUCT AND ETHICS § 11.09(2) (5th ed. 2013).
21. CHRIS W. BONNEAU & MELINDA GANN HALL, IN DEFENSE OF JUDICIAL ELECTIONS 98 (2009).
22. Matthew J. Streb & Brian Frederick, *When Money Cannot Encourage Participation: Campaign Spending and Rolloff in Low Visibility Judicial Elections*, 33 POL. BEHAV. 665 (2011).
23. Herbert M. Krtizer, *Roll-Off in State Court Elections: The Impact of the Straight-Ticket Voting Option*, 4 J.L. & CTS. 409, 410 (2016).
24. Chris W. Bonneau & Eric Loepp, *Getting Things Straight: The Effects of Ballot Design and Electoral Structure on Voter Participation*, 34 ELECTORAL STUD. 119, 125 (2014), http://www.pitt.edu/~cwb7/assets/papers/ElecStud%2014%20article.pdf.
25. JAMES L. GIBSON, ELECTING JUDGES: THE SURPRISING EFFECTS OF CAMPAIGNING ON JUDICIAL LEGITIMACY 107 (2012).
26. James L. Gibson, *Challenges to the Impartiality of State Supreme Courts: Legitimacy Theory and "New Style" Judicial Campaigns*, 102 AM. POL. SCI. REV. 59, 69 (2008).
27. Benjamin Woodson, *The Two Opposing Effects of Judicial Elections on Legitimacy Perceptions*, 17 ST. POL. & POL'Y Q. 24, 24 (2016).
28. James L. Gibson, *Challenges to the Impartiality of State Supreme Courts: Legitimacy Theory and "New Style" Judicial Campaigns*, 102 AM. POL. SCI. REV. 59(2008).
29. I do not mean to imply that this finding is unimportant, because it reflects a view at odds with traditional conceptions of the courts as countermajoritarian institutions.
30. Penny J. White, *Judicial Independence in the Aftermath of* Republican Party of Minnesota v. White, *in* POUND CIVIL JUSTICE INSTITUTE, THE LEAST DANGEROUS BUT MOST VULNERABLE BRANCH: JUDICIAL INDEPENDENCE AND THE RIGHTS OF CITIZENS: REPORT OF THE 2007 FORUM FOR STATE APPELLATE COURT JUDGES 5, 8 (2007), http://www.poundinstitute.org/sites/default/files/docs/2007PoundForumReport.pdf ("[T]oday's efforts to undermine the independence of state courts, spearheaded by special interest groups and catapulted by the Supreme Court's decision in *Republican Party of Minnesota v. White*, are much more likely to succeed . . . State court judges, few of whom hold their positions for life, are being enticed by special-interest groups with large coffers and constituencies to compromise their independence in order to maintain their positions.").
31. Chris W. Bonneau, Melinda Gann Hall & Matthew J. Streb, *White Noise: The Unrealized Effects of* Republican Party of Minnesota v. White *on Judicial Elections*, 32 JUST. SYS. J. 247, 266 (2011) ("[P]redictions about the destructive effects of *Republican Party of Minnesota v. White* have been overestimated. This intriguing conclusion should help to allay the fears of those concerned with the politics of judicial elections and also should counter any claims that *White* has radically altered the judicial campaigns game. For the other side of the aisle, it would appear that some of the most fundamental assumptions driving the movement against competitive elections lack empirical support.").

32. Greg Goelzhauser, Choosing State Supreme Court Justices: Merit Selection and the Consequences of Institutional Reform 110 (2016).
33. Chris W. Bonneau & Melinda Gann Hall, In Defense of Judicial Elections 137 (2009).
34. Richard A. Watson & Rondal G. Downing, The Politics of Bench and Bar 283 (1969) (fewer merit selected judges rank in lowest quality quartile than elected judges).
35. Model Code of Judicial Conduct, Rule 2.4(A) (2007).
36. *Id.* Rule 2.10(A).
37. *Id.* Rule 2.10(B).
38. Malia Reddick, *Judging the Quality of Judicial Selection Methods: Merit Selection, Elections, and Judicial Discipline* 6 (2010), https://papers.ssrn.com/sol3/papers.cfm?abstract_id=2731018 (merit selected judges disciplined less frequently in six of nine jurisdictions studied).
39. James Gibson, Electing Judges: The Surprising Effects of Campaigning on Judicial Legitimacy 139 (2012).
40. Chris W. Bonneau & Melinda Gann Hall, In Defense of Judicial Elections 136–37 (2009). (Authors acknowledge that "[c]ertainly, we can take issue with the various indicators of quality used to date in the empirical research on recruitment" (as I do here), but evidently they do not, given their ultimate conclusion that "the available empirical evidence suggests ... the best judges may, in fact, be the product of democratic politics.")
41. Stephen J. Choi, G. Mitu Gulati & Eric A. Posner, *Professionals or Politicians: The Uncertain Empirical Case for an Elected Rather than Appointed Judiciary*, 26 J.L. Econ. & Org. 290, 290 (2010). The authors also found that the opinions of appointed judges were cited more frequently, which led them to conclude that appointed judges were more skilled. *Id.* at 316 ("Overall, and particularly compared with Election Partisan judges, the models are consistent with the view that Appointed judges write the best opinions."). Insofar as the cases cited in judicial opinions are selected by clerks who graduated from law school the year before, relying on those selections as a proxy for the "skill" of the opinion-writers whose cases clerks cite seems a dubious extrapolation. A safer conclusion may be that such findings reflect a tendency to cite courts and opinion-writers perceived as more prestigious, which may or may not be a reflection of skill. David Klein & Darby Morrisroe, *The Prestige and Influence of Individual Judges on the U.S. Courts of Appeals*, 28 J. Legal Stud. 371, 391 (1999).
42. Stephen J. Choi, G. Mitu Gulati & Eric A. Posner, *Professionals or Politicians: The Uncertain Empirical Case for an Elected Rather than Appointed Judiciary*, 26 J.L. Econ. & Org. 290, 296 (2010).
43. *Id.*
44. *Id.* at 297.
45. Allan Ashman & James J. Alfini, The Key to Judicial Merit Selection: The Nominating Process 75 (1974).
46. Chris W. Bonneau & Melinda Gann Hall, In Defense of Judicial Elections 137–38 (2009).

47. *Id.*
48. Allan Ashman & James J. Alfini, The Key to Judicial Merit Selection: The Nominating Process 75 (1974) (2 percent reported "always"; 10 percent reported "frequently").
49. *Id.*
50. Brian T. Fitzpatrick, *The Politics of Merit Selection*, 74 Mo. L. Rev. 675, 699 (2009).
51. *Id.* at 691.
52. *Id.* at 675–76.
53. The author acknowledges this possibility, which is beside his larger point that contested partisan elections can offset the bar's liberal bias and preserve a partisan balance more in line with the public that judges serve. My point, for purposes here, however, is limited to the observation that this study does not tell us much about the ideological bias of nominating commissions, or whether such commissions favor liberal applicants in the vetting process.
54. *Id.* at 684 (state high court non-retention rates at 1 percent); B. Michael Dann & Randall M. Hansen, *Judicial Retention Elections*, 34 Loy. L.A. L. Rev. 1429, 1430 (2001) (trial court non-retention rates at 1 percent).
55. Elisha C. Savchak & A.J. Barghothi, *The Influence of Appointment and Retention Constituencies: Testing Strategies of Judicial Decisionmaking*, 7 St. Pol. & Pol'y Q. 394, 404 (2007).
56. *Id.* at 408.
57. *Caperton v. A.T. Massey Coal Co.*, 556 U.S. 868 (2009).
58. Morgan L.W. Hazelton, Jacob M. Montgomery & Brendan Nyhan, *Does Public Financing Affect Judicial Behavior? Evidence from the North Carolina Supreme Court*, 44 Am. Pol. Res. 587, 587 (2016). It bears emphasis, however, that the sample size of this study was small, and that the introduction of public financing coincided with the state's move from a partisan to a nonpartisan selection system.
59. Paul Blumenthal, *This Dark Money Group is Spending Big on Judicial Races, and No One Knows Why*, Huffington Post (Nov. 3, 2016), http://www.huffingtonpost.com/entry/dark-money-judicial-races-center-for-individual-freedom_us_581b5234e4b0c43e6c1e740d.
60. Charles Gardner Geyh, Myles Lynk, Robert S. Peck & Toni Clark, *The State of Recusal Reform*, 18 N.Y.U. J. Legis. & Pub. Pol. 515, 530 (2015).
61. *See, e.g.,* Cara Lombardo, *Wisconsin Supreme Court Rejects Campaign Donor Recusal Rules*, U.S. News & World Rep. (Apr. 20, 2017), https://www.usnews.com/news/best-states/wisconsin/articles/2017-04-20/wisconsin-supreme-court-to-consider-campaign-donation-rule.
62. James L. Gibson & Gregory A. Caldeira, *Campaign Support, Conflicts of Interest, and Judicial Impartiality: Can Recusals Rescue the Legitimacy of Courts?*, 74 J. Pol. 18, 18 (2012).
63. William H. Sewell, *Three Temporalities: Toward an Eventful Sociology*, in The Historic Turn in the Human Sciences 245, 262–63 (Terrence J. MacDonald ed., 1996).

64. Eileen Braman & J. Mitchell Pickerill, *Path Dependence in Studies of Legal Decision-Making*, in WHAT'S LAW GOT TO DO WITH IT?: WHAT JUDGES DO, WHY THEY DO IT, AND WHAT'S AT STAKE 114, 115 (Charles Gardner Geyh ed., 2011).
65. JEFFREY A. SEGAL & HAROLD J. SPAETH, THE SUPREME COURT AND THE ATTITUDINAL MODEL 65 (1993).
66. *Id.* at 69–73
67. LEE EPSTEIN, WILLIAM M. LANDES & RICHARD A. POSNER, THE BEHAVIOR OF FEDERAL JUDGES: A THEORETICAL AND EMPIRICAL STUDY OF RATIONAL CHOICE 154 (2013).
68. C.K. ROWLAND & ROBERT A. CARP, POLITICS & JUDGMENT IN FEDERAL DISTRICT COURTS 158 (1996).
69. EILEEN BRAMAN, LAW, POLITICS, AND PERCEPTION: HOW POLICY PREFERENCES INFLUENCE LEGAL REASONING 13–41 (2009).
70. Robert J. MacCoun, *Biases in the Interpretation and Use of Research Results*, 49 ANN. REV. PSYCHOL. 259, 281 (1998).
71. Brian T. Fitzpatrick, *The Politics of Merit Selection*, 74 MO. L. REV. 675, 703 (2009).
72. *See, e.g.,* Robert Hume, *Legitimacy, Yes: But at What Cost?*, 96 JUDICATURE 209 (2013) (reviewing JAMES L. GIBSON, ELECTING JUDGES: THE SURPRISING EFFECTS OF CAMPAIGNING ON JUDICIAL LEGITIMACY (2012)).
73. LEON FESTINGER, A THEORY OF COGNITIVE DISSONANCE (1957).
74. JAMES GIBSON, ELECTING JUDGES: THE SURPRISING EFFECTS OF CAMPAIGNING ON JUDICIAL LEGITIMACY 107 (2012) (finding that judicial elections produce a net gain for legitimacy); Benjamin Woodson, *The Two Opposing Effects of Judicial Elections on Legitimacy Perceptions*, 17 ST. POL. & POL'Y. Q. 24, 24 (2016) (finding that judicial elections can undermine legitimacy in extreme cases).
75. Tom R. Tyler, *The Role of Perceived Injustice in Defendants' Evaluations of Their Courtroom Experience*, 18 L. & SOC. REV. 51, 69–70 (1984); TOM R. TYLER, ROBERT J. BOECKMANN, HEATHER J. SMITH & YUEN J. HUO, SOCIAL JUSTICE IN A DIVERSE SOCIETY 82–83 (1997).

CHAPTER 6

1. For a discussion of the emergence of this interdisciplinary collaboration, *see* CHARLES GARDNER GEYH, COURTING PERIL: THE POLITICAL TRANSFORMATION OF THE AMERICAN JUDICIARY 51–60 (2016).
2. Frank Cross, *Political Science and the New Legal Realism: A Case of Unfortunate Interdisciplinary Ignorance*, 92 NW. U. L. REV. 251, 251–53 (1997).
3. Barry Friedman, *Taking Law Seriously*, 4 PERSP. ON POL. 261 (2006).
4. WHAT'S LAW GOT TO DO WITH IT?: WHAT JUDGES DO, WHY THEY DO IT, AND WHAT'S AT STAKE 1–4 (Charles Gardner Geyh ed., 2011).
5. JAMES GIBSON, ELECTING JUDGES: THE SURPRISING EFFECTS OF CAMPAIGNING ON JUDICIAL LEGITIMACY 107 (2012) (finding that judicial elections produce a net gain for legitimacy); Benjamin Woodson, *The Two Opposing Effects of Judicial Elections on Legitimacy Perceptions*, 17 ST. POL. & POL'Y Q. 24, 26 (2016) (finding that judicial elections enhance legitimacy most of the time).

6. CHARLES GARDNER GEYH, COURTING PERIL: THE POLITICAL TRANSFORMATION OF THE AMERICAN JUDICIARY 51–60 (2016).
7. For a state by state summary of contribution limits in judicial campaigns, *see* National Center for State Courts, *Judicial Campaigns and Elections*, last visited Sep. 13, 2018, http://www.judicialselection.us/judicial_selection/campaigns_and_elections/campaign_financing.cfm?state.
8. Illinois, for example, imposes contribution limits as high as $125,000. *See supra* note 6.
9. James J. Sample, *Democracy at the Corner of First and Fourteenth: Judicial Campaign Spending and Equality*, 66 N.Y.U. ANN. SURV. AM. L. 727, 782 (2011).
10. James L. Gibson & Gregory A. Caldeira, *Campaign Support, Conflicts of Interest, and Judicial Impartiality: Can Recusals Rescue the Legitimacy of Courts?* 74 J. POL. 18, 18 (2012).
11. *Id.*
12. MODEL CODE OF JUDICIAL CONDUCT, Rule 2.11 (2007).
13. *Caperton v. A.H. Massey Coal Co.*, 556 U.S. 868, 889 (2009).
14. Charles Gardner Geyh, Myles Lynk, Robert S. Peck & Toni Clark, *The State of Recusal Reform*, 18 N.Y.U. J. LEGIS. & PUB. POL. 515, 520 (2015).
15. Brennan Center for Justice, *Judicial Recusal Reform Two Years After Caperton* (June 2, 2011), https://www.brennancenter.org/analysis/judicial-recusal-reform-%E2%80%93-two-years-after-caperton/.
16. *Id.*
17. USLegal, *State-by-State Summary of Judicial Selection*, last visited Sept. 13, 2018, https://courts.uslegal.com/selection-of-judges/state-by-state-summary-of-judicial-selection/.
18. MODEL CODE OF JUDICIAL CONDUCT, Rule 2.5 (2007).
19. *Id.* Rule. 2.3.
20. *Id.* Rule. 2.2.
21. *Id.* Rule 2.4.
22. *Id.* Rule 2.6.
23. *Id.* Rule 2.2, cmt. 2.
24. CHARLES GARDNER GEYH, JAMES J. ALFINI, STEVEN LUBET & JEFFREY L. SHAMAN, JUDICIAL CONDUCT AND ETHICS § 2.02 (5th ed. 2013).
25. *Id.* § 4.
26. Amanda Frost, *Keeping Up Appearances: A Process-Oriented Approach to Judicial Recusal*, 53 U. KAN. L. REV. 531, 551–53 (2005); Steven Lubet, *It Takes a Court*, 60 SYRACUSE L. REV. 221, 226 (2010).
27. Charles Gardner Geyh, *Why Judicial Disqualification Matters. Again.*, 30 REV. LITIG. 671, 719 (2011).
28. David C. Brody, *The Use of Judicial Performance Evaluation to Enhance Judicial Accountability, Judicial Independence, and Public Trust*, 86 DENV. U. L. REV. 115, 118 (2008).
29. Dmitry Bam, *Voter Ignorance and Judicial Elections*, 102 KY. L.J. 553, 588–91 (2013).

30. Charles Gardner Geyh, *Adverse Publicity as a Means of Reducing Judicial Decision-Making Delay: Periodic Disclosure of Pending Motions, Bench Trials and Cases Under the Civil Justice Reform Act*, 41 CLEV. ST. L. REV. 511, 513 (1993); R. Lawrence Dessem, *Judicial Reporting Under the Civil Justice Reform Act: Look, Mom, No Cases!*, 54 U. PITT. L. REV. 687, 714–16 (1993).
31. In jurisdictions with appointed judiciaries subject to reappointment processes, this is not a concern; to the contrary, the threat to independence of judges subject to reappointment may be greater than for judges subject to contested re-election. Stefanie A. Lindquist, *Judicial Activism in State Supreme Courts: Institutional Design and Judicial Behavior*, 28 STAN. L. & POL'Y. REV. 61, 61 (2017).
32. Lee Epstein, Andrew D. Martin, Kevin M. Quinn & Jeffrey A. Segal, *Ideological Drift Among Supreme Court Justices: Who, When, and How Important?*, 101 Nw. U. L. REV. 1483, 1504 (2007) (finding drift among twenty-two of twenty-six justices, with twelve becoming more liberal, seven more conservative, and three drifting "in more exotic ways"); Andrew D. Martin & Kevin M. Quinn, *Assessing Preference Change on the U.S. Supreme Court*, 23 J.L. ECON. & ORG. 365, 365 (2007) (finding drift among fourteen of sixteen justices who served on the Court for more than ten years).
33. MODEL CODE OF JUDICIAL CONDUCT, Rule. 2.4 (2007).
34. For a summary of the Wisconsin elections experience, *see* CHARLES GARDNER GEYH, COURTING PERIL: THE POLITICAL TRANSFORMATION OF THE AMERICAN JUDICIARY 85–86 (2016).
35. Debra Cassens Weiss, *O'Connor Decries Political Pressure on Judges*, A.B.A. J. (Feb. 25, 2008), http://www.abajournal.com/news/article/oconnor_decries_political_pressures_on_judges_in_parade_article.
36. Deborah Goldberg, James Sample & David E. Pozen, *The Best Defense: Why Elected Courts Should Lead Recusal Reform*, 46 WASHBURN L.J. 503, 509–11 (2007); *Avery v. State Farm Mut. Auto. Ins. Co.*, 835 N.E.2d 801 (Ill. 2005). The author served as an expert witness for plaintiffs in a subsequent civil action against the corporation involved.
37. Stephen B. Burbank, *The Architecture of Judicial Independence*, 72 S. CAL. L. REV. 315, 339 (1999).
38. ALEXANDER M. BICKEL, THE LEAST DANGEROUS BRANCH: THE SUPREME COURT AT THE BAR OF POLITICS (1962).
39. Steven P. Croley, *The Majoritarian Difficulty: Elective Judiciaries and the Rule of Law*, 62 U. CHI. L. REV. 689, 694 (1995).
40. David E. Pozen, *The Irony of Judicial Elections*, 108 COLUM. L. REV. 265, 278–92 (2008).
41. Herbert M. Kritzer, *Contestation and Competitiveness in State Supreme Court Elections 1946–2015*, *in* JUDICIAL ELECTIONS IN THE 21ST CENTURY 33, 50–51 (Chris W. Bonneau & Melinda Gann Hall eds., 2016).
42. Chris W. Bonneau, *Fundraising and Spending in State Supreme Court Elections*, *in* JUDICIAL ELECTIONS IN THE 21ST CENTURY 79, 79–80 (Chris W. Bonneau & Melinda Gann Hall eds., 2016).

43. Larry T. Aspin, *Judicial Retention Elections*, in JUDICIAL ELECTIONS IN THE 21ST CENTURY 93, 95 (Chris W. Bonneau & Melinda Gann Hall eds., 2016).
44. Malia Reddick, *Judging the Quality of Judicial Selection Methods: Merit Selection, Elections, and Judicial Discipline* 6 (2010), https://papers.ssrn.com/sol3/papers.cfm?abstract_id=2731018.
45. One study has found that reappointment processes discourage the exercise of judicial review by courts in appointive systems, relative to their elected counterparts. Stefanie A. Lindquist, *Judicial Activism in State Supreme Courts: Institutional Design and Judicial Behavior*, 28 STAN. L. & POL'Y. REV. 61, 80 (2017).
46. CHARLES GARDNER GEYH, COURTING PERIL: THE POLITICAL TRANSFORMATION OF THE AMERICAN JUDICIARY 51–60 (2016).
47. *See generally* David E. Pozen, *The Irony of Judicial Elections*, 108 COLUM. L. REV. 265, 278–82 (2008).
48. David Pozen, *Are Judicial Elections Democracy-Enhancing?*, in WHAT'S LAW GOT TO DO WITH IT?: WHAT JUDGES DO, WHY THEY DO IT, AND WHAT'S AT STAKE 248, 272 (Charles Gardner Geyh ed., 2011) ("A system that ties judges too tightly to public opinion ... can usurp the achievements of future generations by foreclosing judicial innovations that might have helped generate, consolidate, and legitimize new understandings of the law.").
49. Tom R. Tyler, *The Role of Perceived Injustice in Defendants' Evaluations of Their Courtroom Experience*, 18 L. & SOC. REV. 51, 69–70 (1984); TOM R. TYLER, ROBERT J. BOECKMANN, HEATHER J. SMITH & YUEN J. HUO, SOCIAL JUSTICE IN A DIVERSE SOCIETY 82–83 (1997).
50. Larry T. Aspin & William K. Hall, *Political Trust and Judicial Retention Elections*, 9 L. & POL'Y. 451, 451 (1987).
51. Perhaps the most one can say for specific voter knowledge in retention elections is that some voters appear to be aware of incumbents' party affiliations and act on that knowledge. That leads a small (but statistically significant) number of Republicans to vote against the retention of Democratic incumbents and a smaller (but still statistically significant) number of Democrats to vote against the retention of Republican incumbents—but virtually never in numbers sufficient to derail retention. CHRIS W. BONNEAU & DAMON M. CANN, VOTERS' VERDICTS: CITIZENS, CAMPAIGNS, AND INSTITUTIONS IN STATE SUPREME COURT ELECTIONS 96–98 (2015).
52. Brian T. Fitzpatrick, *The Politics of Merit Selection*, 74 MO. L. REV. 675, 684 (2009) (state high court non-retention rates at 1 percent); Michael Dann & Randall M. Hansen, *Judicial Retention Elections*, 34 LOY. L.A. L. REV. 1429, 1430 (2001) (trial court non-retention rates at 1 percent).
53. Benjamin Woodson, *The Two Opposing Effects of Judicial Elections on Legitimacy Perceptions*, 17 ST. POL. & POL'Y. Q. 24, 40–42 (2016).
54. Gregory A. Huber & Sanford C. Gordon, *Accountability and Coercion: Is Justice Blind When It Runs for Office?*, 48 AM. J. POL. SCI. 247, 258–62 (2004).
55. *Id.* at 261–62.
56. Lawrence Baum, *Judicial Elections and Judicial Independence: The Voter's Perspective*, 64 OHIO ST. L.J. 13, 20 (2003) (noting that "rolloff is even higher in contests for

lower-level judgeships," citing data showing that it in retention elections national roll-off increased from 28 percent in high court elections to 34.5 percent in trial courts); Matthew J. Streb & Brian Frederick, *When Money Cannot Encourage Participation: Campaign Spending and Rolloff in Low Visibility Judicial Elections*, 33 POL. BEHAV. 665, 666 (2011) (finding that increases in campaign spending does not correlate to increased voter participation in lower court elections).

57. In Houston, for example, voters swept all Republican county judges on the ballot from office in the 2016 election—a result attributed to Donald Trump's candidacy for president, which motivated Harris County Democrats to turn out and elect Democratic candidates across the ballot. Andrew Schneider, *Explaining the Democrats' Near Sweep of Harris County*, HOUSTON PUBLIC MEDIA (Nov. 10, 2016), https://www.houstonpublicmedia.org/articles/news/2016/11/10/176953/explaining-the-democrats-near-sweep-of-harris-county/

58. Michael J. Nelson, *Uncontested and Unaccountable? Rates of Contestation in Trial Court Elections*, 94 JUDICATURE 208, 208–09 (2011), http://jedi.wustl.edu/files/general-jurisdiction-trial-courts/other/Nelson_2011.pdf.

59. Lawrence Baum, *Judicial Elections and Judicial Independence: The Voter's Perspective*, 64 OHIO ST. L.J. 13, 20 (2003) ("[T]he subset of voters who participate in a judicial contest may include a great many who possess little information about the candidates in that contest . . . surveys in Ohio Supreme Court contests have found that substantial proportions of the people who vote in those contests do not *recognize* the candidates' names, and many of those who do recognize those names have insufficient information to rate the candidates.").

60. ALICIA BANNON, RETHINKING JUDICIAL SELECTION IN STATE COURTS 14 (2016), https://www.brennancenter.org/sites/default/files/publications/Rethinking_Judicial_Selection_State_Courts.pdf.

61. DAVID B. ROTTMAN, RANDALL M. HANSEN, NICOLE MOTT & LYNN GRIMES, PERCEPTIONS OF THE COURTS IN YOUR COMMUNITY: THE INFLUENCE OF EXPERIENCE, RACE, AND ETHNICITY (2003), http://cdm16501.contentdm.oclc.org/cdm/ref/collection/ctcomm/id/22 (reporting on diminished confidence in courts among African Americans); KATE BERRY, BUILDING A DIVERSE BENCH: A GUIDE FOR JUDICIAL NOMINATING COMMISSIONERS 4–5 (2016), https://www.brennancenter.org/sites/default/files/publications/Building_Diverse_Bench.pdf (reporting data on lack of gender and racial diversity on the bench, and linking lack of diversity to diminished confidence).

62. Victor D. Quintanilla, *Beyond Common Sense: A Social Psychological Study of Iqbal's Effect on Claims of Race Discrimination*, 17 MICH. J. RACE & L. 1, 39 (2011) (showing that white judges dismissed racial discrimination cases more frequently than black judges). This phenomenon is easiest to appreciate in the context of appellate court decision-making, where a multiplicity of perspectives (including gender and race) can enhance the deliberative process horizontally among the judges who comprise a given appellate court. But it can also be relevant vertically—diverse trial and appellate courts can each inform the perspectives of the other.

63. GREG GOELZHAUSER, CHOOSING STATE SUPREME COURT JUSTICES: MERIT SELECTION AND THE CONSEQUENCES OF INSTITUTIONAL REFORM 110–11

(2016); Malia Reddick, Michael J. Nelson & Rachel Paine Caufield, *Racial and Gender Diversity on State Courts: An AJS Study*, 48 JUDGES J. 28, 32 (2009).
64. ALICIA BANNON, RETHINKING JUDICIAL SELECTION IN STATE COURTS 24 (2016), https://www.brennancenter.org/sites/default/files/publications/Rethinking_Judicial_Selection_State_Courts.pdf.

CHAPTER 7

1. *See, e.g.*, Brian T. Fitzpatrick, *The Politics of Merit Selection*, 74 MO. L. REV. 675 (2009).
2. CHRIS W. BONNEAU & MELINDA GANN HALL, IN DEFENSE OF JUDICIAL ELECTIONS 138 (2009).
3. As discussed in chapter 2, the partisan election movement did not take flight during the Jacksonian era, when calls to hold judges accountable to the people were common. Rather, the movement was launched a decade later, as a means to end cronyism by severing gubernatorial control over judicial selection, and enabling judges to keep legislatures in check by ending legislative control over judicial selection and retention.
4. CHARLES GARDNER GEYH, COURTING PERIL: THE POLITICAL TRANSFORMATION OF THE AMERICAN JUDICIARY (2016).

INDEX

Abrahamson, Shirley 57
advertising, campaign 10, 19, 59–60, 70–71, 108, 162–63
apathy. *See* voter apathy
assimilation bias—impact on the selection debate 119–21, 122, 126, 127–28, 164

Bacon, Frances 26
Baker, David 6
Bickel, Alexander 145–46
Bird, Rose 57, 59, 60, 84–85
Bonneau, Chris 83, 84, 93–94, 105, 106, 121, 160
Bork, Robert 63
Boston, Charles 37–38
Brennan, William 56–57
Brown, Jerry 59

Cady, Mark 4–5
campaign advertising. *See* advertising, campaign
campaign finance
 contribution limits 130–31, 133, 140, 142, 144–45
 direct contributions 10, 67, 90, 95–96, 108
 independent expenditures 19, 69, 70–71, 73, 74, 89–90
 influence on decision-making 10–11, 73, 89–90, 95–96, 108, 115, 130, 133–34
 public financing 95–96, 114–15, 132
 reform (*see* reform proposals)
 speech, freedom of (*see* speech, freedom of)
Carter, Jimmy 52–53, 58, 62–63
Clements, Bill 53
Clinton, Bill 50, 62–63
Coase, Ronald 23
cognitive dissonance—impact on the selection debate 121, 126–27, 163–64
Coke, Sir Edward 25–27
Commission assisted appointment. *See* merit selection
contestation rates and competitiveness of elections 53, 66, 68, 91, 92, 94–95, 143, 147
crime, as issue in judicial races 58–60, 79–80, 156
Croley, Steven 145–46
Culver, Chet 5

Deukmejian, George 59
disclosure of campaign contributions and expenditures 69–70, 96, 115–16, 131, 142

discretionary supreme court review and
politicization 54–55
disqualification, judicial 64–65, 96–97,
116–17, 132, 136, 142–43
constitutional implications 73, 74,
97, 134
diversity and judicial selection 157
Douglas, James 40

elections, Judicial
new politics of 44
causes 51
consequences 66
partisan elections 44, 46–47, 68, 71,
80, 89–90, 91, 92, 101–3, 106–7,
110–11, 123, 143–44, 156, 163
history of (*see* history of
judicial selection)
non-partisan elections 46–47, 68,
71, 79–80, 89–90, 92, 103,
107, 143–44
history of (*see* history of
judicial selection)
qualified election model 21, 139,
151, 169
recall elections 93
history of (*see* history of
judicial selection)
retention elections 5–7, 46–47,
57, 59, 68, 79–80, 94–95, 107,
113–14, 152–53
history of (*see* history of
judicial selection)
expertise in judicial decision-making.
See judicial decision-making

First Amendment. *See* speech,
freedom of

George III, King 27–28, 159–60
Gibson, James 91

Ginsburg, Ruth Bader 80–81
gubernatorial appointment 44, 47
history of (*see* history of judicial
selection)

Hafen, Conrad 93
Hall, Melinda Gann 70–71, 83, 84,
93–94, 105, 106, 160
Hill, John 53
history of judicial selection
colonial courts 27–28
English courts 25–27
gubernatorial
appointment 25–28, 39–40
legislative appointment 28–30
merit selection and retention
elections 37–41
Nonpartisan elections 34, 38
Partisan elections 31–33, 42
recall elections 35–37
Humphrey, Hubert 52–53

ignorance. *See* voter ignorance
interdisciplinary study of judicial
selection 127
interest groups and judicial races 55, 60,
89–90, 115, 131, 132
intermediate appellate courts, impact
on new politics of judicial
elections 54

Jackson, Andrew 31–33, 37
James I, King 26
Johnson, Lyndon 52–53
judicial accountability and
independence. *See* judicial
independence and accountability
judicial conduct and discipline 65–66,
73, 86–87, 110–11, 135–36
judicial decision-making
expertise, role of 30, 85

influence of campaign support
    (*see* campaign finance)
influence of ideology 63–64, 79–80,
    82–83, 84–85, 100–2, 113,
    119–20, 141–42, 143–44,
    148–49, 161–62, 165–66
influence of impending elections
    79–80, 84, 101–2
judicial elections. *See* elections, judicial
judicial independence and accountability
    as focus of selection debate
    16–17, 47, 77, 83–84, 113–14,
    126, 130
judicial performance evaluations 138
judicial qualifications-impact of selection
    systems on 110
judicial selection—methods of
    across the states 44–47
    importance of 12–15
judicial terms of office, lengthening 134,
    139–40, 145–47, 159–60

Kales, Albert 38–39
Kennedy, Anthony 2, 13
Kritzer, Herbert 53, 147

Lanphier, David 59–60
Laski, Harold 39
legal culture paradigm 165–66, 168–69
legislative appointment. *See* history of
    judicial selection
legitimacy of courts
    campaign finance and 89–90, 102,
        108, 122, 123–24
    elections and 32, 84, 89, 91, 108–9,
        141, 151–52, 154
    voting and litigating publics
        compared 122–23, 127
Lincoln, Abraham 117–18
litigation campaigns—impact on state
    court politicization 55–57

Manahan, James 35–39
McGraw, Warren 59–60
media 63–64, 65–66
merit selection 5–7, 47–50, 53, 86–89,
    93–94, 110–1, 112–14, 152
    history of (*see* history of
        judicial selection)
    retention elections (*see* elections,
        judicial-Retention)
Missouri plan. *See* merit selection
Moore, Roy 86–87, 141
Mosby, John Singleton 52
motivated reasoning—impact on judicial
    selection debate 119–21, 122,
    126, 164

Nixon, Richard 52–53, 56, 58, 62–63
nominating commissions. *See* merit
    selection
non-partisan Elections. *See* elections,
    judicial

Obama, Barack 14
O'Connor, Sandra Day 89, 90,
    123–24

Padberg, Eugene 40–41
Palin, Sarah 43
partisan elections. *See* elections, judicial
path dependence—impact on
    judicial selection debate
    117–19, 121, 127–29
Pendergast, Thomas 40
Persky, Aaron 64
Phillips, Tom 53
politicization of courts 62–66
Pound, Roscoe 37–38, 88–89
Pozen, David 145–46
public confidence in courts.
    See legitimacy of courts
public financing. *See* campaign finance

qualified election proposal 139–46, 151, 169, 171

Reagan, Ronald 52–53, 58
recall elections. *See* elections, judicial
recusal. *See* disqualification, judicial
Reddick, Malia 147
Rehnquist, William 104–5
retention elections. *See* elections, judicial
Roberts, John 2–3, 65–66, 79, 100–1
Robinson, Fredrick 31–32
roll-off in judicial elections. *See* voter apathy
Roosevelt, Franklin 58, 62–63
rule of law paradigm 22, 161–62, 165

same sex marriage
 in Iowa Supreme Court 4–7
 in U.S. Supreme Court 1–3
Shugerman, Jed 25, 41, 43, 159–61
Southern states, impact on new politics of judicial elections 52–53
speech, freedom of, and judicial campaigns 72–74
Stark, Lloyd 40
Stevens, John Paul 56–57, 79

Streit, Michael 6
Sutherland, George 36

Taft, William Howard 36
Ternus, Marsha 6–7
Thurmond, Strom 52–53
tort reform, as issue in judicial races 60–62, 71
trial courts—appellate court races compared 155–57
Truman, Harry 52–53
Trump, Donald 43, 63–64, 66, 170

umpires—judges compared 79, 85, 97–98, 100–1, 162–63

voter apathy 87–88, 92, 94–95, 106–7, 143, 156–57
voter ignorance 85–87, 104–6

Wallace, George 52–53
Warren, Earl 39–40, 55–56, 62–63
White, Penny 59–60

Yates, Robert ("Brutus") 30

www.ingramcontent.com/pod-product-compliance
Ingram Content Group UK Ltd.
Pitfield, Milton Keynes, MK11 3LW, UK
UKHW022153230426
12049UKWH00003BA/81